MW01289217

Making the Difference:

Differentiation in International Schools

William Powell and Ochan Kusuma-Powell

TABLE OF CONTENTS

ACKNOWLEDGMENTS

The writing, printing, and distribution of this manual were made possible thanks to a grant from the Overseas Schools Advisory Council (OSAC). All activities connected with this project were administered and supported by the Office of Overseas Schools, the Association of International Schools in Africa and the East Asia Regional Council of Overseas Schools.

The following OSAC members* and other U.S. corporations and foundations contributed funds for this project:

Abbott Laboratories

*AOL

Atwood Oceanics, Inc.

*Caterpillar Foundation

*Citigroup Foundation

*ConocoPhillips

Deloitte & Touche

*EADS North America Defense

*E.I. duPont de Nemours and Co.

*ExxonMobil Corporation

Fluor Corporation

Hunt Consolidated, Inc.

*ING Financial Advisers

Maersk

*MasterCard International

McDonalds

*Microsoft

Lockheed Martin Foundation

*Pfizer

*PricewaterhouseCoopers

*Procter & Gamble Company

The Boeing Company

TRW Automotive

General Motors Foundation

There were many people who contributed to this book – knowingly and unknowingly. The single largest group has been the students that it has been our privilege over the years to teach. We can only hope that they have learned half as much from us as we have learned from them.

We are most grateful to the individuals who took time away from their busy teaching schedules and administrative duties to contribute important chapters to this book: Patsy Richardson, former Coordinating Librarian at the International School of Kuala Lumpur (ISKL); Susan Napoliello, former Elementary Principal at ISKL; and David Suarez, Middle School Math teacher at Jakarta International School.

We are also grateful for the inspiration and support of the late Frances Hoffman, former Coordinating Librarian at the International School of Kuala Lumpur, whose laughter and insight continue to guide us still.

We would also like to extend our gratitude to the individuals that read portions of the manuscript in draft and made valuable comments and criticisms. These included Dr. Nancy Robinson, Professor Emerita of Psychiatry and Behavioral Science from the University of Washington; Dr. Phyllis Aldrich, Coordinator for Gifted Education, Saratoga Board of Cooperative Educational Services; Karen Moreau, Coordinator of Professional Development at Taipei American School; Kristen Pelletier, Coordinator of Special Needs Education, International School of Brussels; Rob Mullen, former School Psychologist, International School of Kuala Lumpur; and Rose White, Curriculum Coordinator at Kaohsiung American School.

We are grateful to the Association for Supervision and Curriculum Development for permission to reprint "Using Observation to Improve Instruction" (Chapter Sixteen) which originally appeared in the February 2005 issue of *Educational Leadership* and to the Council of International Schools for permission to reprint "Knowing Ourselves: the Student Perspective" (Chapter Four) and "Differentiating for Girls and Boys" (Chapter Ten) both of which originally appeared as articles in *International Schools Journal.*

We owe a debt of gratitude to the Executive Directors of the regional associations of international schools who have been enthusiastic and active supporters of our work: Miffie Greer, formerly at the Association of International Schools in Africa (AISA); the late Bob Sills and his wife Linda at the East Asia Regional Council of Overseas Schools (EARCOS) and subsequently Dick Krajczar, David Chojnacki at the Near East South Asia Regional Council of Overseas Schools (NESA), and Paul Poore at the Association of American Schools in South America (AASSA).

We also extend our sincere thanks for the continued support of the Office of Overseas Schools at the U.S. Department of State, especially to Connie Buford, David Cramer, Keith Miller; and to Joe Carney, who saw us through the early part of this project.

There have been many, many individuals who have contributed ideas and moral support. From ISKL, these include: Esther Moo, Gary Blanton, Susan Napoliello, Michael and Diana O'Leary, Michael O'Shannassy, Marie-France Blais, Hisae Ubl, Grant Millard, Alex Smith, and Bill's long-standing Cognitive Coaching partner, Naomi Aleman. From elsewhere around the world, we are grateful to Areta Williams, Head of the Overseas School of Colombo in Sri Lanka; John Roberts, Superintendent of the International School of Kenya; Kevin Bartlett, Director of the International School of Brussels, and Colette Belzil and Anne Brennan, also from ISB; Walter Plotkin, Director of Copenhagen International School; Mark Jenkins, Coordinator of Professional Development at Jakarta International School; Michael Fox, Coordinator of Professional Development at Taipei American School; Matthew Parr; Nancy Holodak, Nick and Rhona Bowley; and Jon Nordemeyer from Shanghai American School.

Finally, we want to express a debt of enormous gratitude to the finest teacher we know, our friend and mentor, Bob Garmston, to whom this book is dedicated.

William Powell and Ochan Kusuma-Powell

Kuala Lumpur, Malaysia

June, 2013

To Bob Garmston
friend, guide and mentor par excellence

1 INTRODUCTION

Sixteen year old YuRa stands in front of the class next to a beautifully designed miniature theater that she has built out of cardboard. It is clear that YuRa has spent many, many hours working on this project. The scenery is intricately painted. The furniture is perfectly to scale. The actors and actresses are meticulously dressed in flowing robes. A North American or European English teacher would be forgiven for not recognizing the famous scene immediately. YuRa has re-constructed the scene from *Hamlet* when Polonius is stabbed to death in Queen Gertrude's chamber as it might have appeared in Korea in the 16th century. The queen's bed has been replaced by an *e-bool*. Wall-hung tapestry has been placed by an oriental screen on which are displayed brush paintings of long legged birds and bamboo forests. The actors and actresses are wearing *han-bok*. Instead of a sword, Hamlet wields a *jang-gum*.

Despite the fact that YuRa is an ESL student who is still receiving specific English language support, she has just completed an oral presentation to the class on how the Shakespearean tragedy might have appeared in Korea. She also prepared a written explanation of how she would stage *Hamlet* in a Korean context.

YuRa's English teacher helped her to design this creatively differentiated performance assessment. Both teacher and student acknowledge the effectiveness of the project. "I knew YuRa was proud of her Korean cultural heritage and I thought linking our literature study to something in which she had expertise would not only increase her understanding of the play but also provide a boost for both her motivation and her self-esteem. YuRa is also quite a talented artist. I knew that she likes to build things. The total project – the model building, the oral presentation and the essay – demonstrated that she had really made a personal connection to the play."

YuRa's comments were equally enthusiastic. "Before the project, *Hamlet* was just some reading for school. I had no feeling for it. Just a lot of acts and scenes, a lot of entrances and exits that had to be read for homework. But when I thought about the play in Korea, it joined together into full meaning. I could understand Hamlet's problems. I mean, I could understand the whole of it."

* * *

From Katmandu to Kuala Lumpur, from Bamako to Buenos Aires, international school teachers are exploring how they can maximize the effectiveness of their teaching by the use of differentiated instruction. In grade level teams, subject area departments, in workshops, graduate level courses and at professional conferences, teachers are re-thinking and re-defining their work with students. In so doing, they are also re-framing their values and professional identities as educators.

When we present teacher training workshops, we are often confronted with questions such as "What exactly is differentiated instruction?" "Does it mean twenty-five different lesson plans?" "What does it look like in a real classroom?" These are excellent questions because they cut through the mystique that -- like the bramble forest that came to surround Sleeping Beauty's castle – quickly grows around educational jargon.

In its essence, differentiation is responding to the learning needs of all students. It is recognizing, expecting and appreciating student learning differences. It is understanding these differences and incorporating them into our instructional planning. There is nothing "new" or "faddish" about differentiation. In one form or another it has been with us since the first cave-dwelling Magdalenian mother recognized the differing talents of her brood of children. What is *new* is our concerted and systematic effort to identify and utilize these differences to maximize the learning of children.

When we think of a differentiated classroom, three powerful adjectives come to mind. A differentiated classroom is a place where teaching and learning are **flexible**, **purposeful** and **respectful.**

Differentiation doesn't mean a separate lesson plan for every student. It does, however, presume that there is enough flexibility of instruction, activities and assessment that a diverse group of learners will find a good fit most of the time (Tomlinson & Allan, 2000). The differentiating teacher is a keen and empathetic observer and listener. She is constantly monitoring the activity and interaction of the students. She is constantly assessing the learning of her students. She knows that nothing in her classroom is so rigid that it cannot be adapted to facilitate greater learning. Instructional strategies, time, materials, content, the grouping of students and the means of assessment are all **flexible.** The teacher is the architect of that flexibility.

Everything in the learning environment of the differentiated classroom is **purposeful.** The teacher has identified precise learning goals and has determined clear success indicators. She knows her students as learners and her planning is thoughtful and rigorous. She knows why the students are grouped the way they are, why the furniture is arranged the way it is, why Johnny needs to move after ten minutes of seat work and why Zahara benefits from "think aloud" activities. The teacher has assumed the role of designer – purposefully designing and orchestrating the multitude of classroom variables to achieve the maximum learning of all students.

Perhaps most importantly, the differentiated classroom is **respectful.** The origin of the word "respect" is the Latin *respectus* which is a combination of *re* meaning "again" or "back" and *specere,* meaning "to look". Thus *respect* means literally "to look again" -- to consider something sufficiently worthy that we would dignify it with our attention for a second or third time. A respectful classroom dignifies the differences that students bring with them to the learning experience. While students have different readiness levels and different interests, respectful pedagogy means that every child is presented with tasks, activities and challenges that are equally interesting and engaging, and each student is provided equal opportunity for the development of conceptual understanding.

The crucial need for differentiated instruction in international schools has been brought home to us by two very real changes that our schools have undergone in the past three decades: demographic and perceptual shifts.

Demographic Shifts
Many international school were founded in the decade or two following World War II as national schools in overseas locations. Typically these schools, using the medium of English, taught either an American or British curriculum to mostly expatriate children. These students were, for the most part, dependents of the diplomatic, aid development or the international business community. In the early stages of their development, these international schools reflected the high expectations of their parent community by being almost exclusively college preparatory. While the student population may have been ethnically and racially diverse, the learners were perceived, for the most part, as educationally homogenous. Whether the students were from Ghana or Guatemala, they were expected to have a reasonable command of English and to be university entrance material. Some of these early international schools had English as a Second Language (ESL) programs at the elementary level. Others flatly refused entrance to less than fluent English speakers. Most had English language admissions tests in the Middle School and High School. Very few of these schools had any specific support for children with learning disabilities. Often parents were confronted with the attitude that they were lucky to find an English speaking school at all and if they wanted such specialist programs (e.g. Learning Disabilities, Resource Room, Gifted and Talented etc.), they should have stayed in their home country. A number of these early international schools were modeled after the most exclusive private schools in the US and UK and myopically equated an inflexible curriculum and unresponsive instruction with high

7

academic expectations. Flexibility was seen as compromising standards. The child was expected to adapt to the classroom, not the other way around.

In the past three decades, international schools have seen a number of significant demographic shifts. Probably the most obvious is the increasing mobility of non-English speaking parents and their children. Whether the children come from the host country, neighboring nations or from the other side of the globe, most international schools have seen a dramatic increase in their intake of students who have limited acquisition of English. Most international schools have adapted by developing extensive ESL, ESOL, or ELL support for these students.

We have also seen a growing number of parents traveling overseas with children with diagnosed learning disabilities. Changes in public statutes, such as US Public Law 94-142, guaranteeing an education to LD children in the least restrictive environment, have tacitly encouraged parents to expect, and in some cases *demand*, special education support in international school schools. For the vast majority of international schools, the days of simply refusing admission to children who learn differently are long gone.

Because many international schools combine the attributes of both private and public schools, a number of our overseas schools have become political and emotional crucibles for these changes. For example, when there is only one international school in an overseas location the pressure to practice inclusive "public school" admissions is intense. When a child is denied admission, the family often has no choice but to leave the country with the concomitant negative effects on parental employment and the education of siblings. This "inclusive" pressure is often *perceived* to be in direct contrast with the equally intense demands for academic rigor that comprise the expectations of "private" school parents. This tension has resulted in more than a few conflicts, several of which have actually reached the level of hearing by Boards of Directors or even litigation in the law courts.

Over the last thirty years, these powerful demographic shifts have caused international educators to re-think our mission and our methodology.

Perceptual Shifts
At the same time as the demographics of international schools have been changing, our perceptions of our students have also been undergoing a profound shift. Over the last decade and a half, an enormous amount of

research has been published that has profound implications for teaching and learning. We have seen an explosion in knowledge in the fields of neuroscience, cognitive psychology, evolutionary biology, leadership theory, group dynamics, curriculum design and learning theory. New research has appeared so rapidly that we classroom-practitioners have been struggling to assimilate it, let alone apply it. This barrage of information is re-shaping our view of education, our perception of the learner and even our identity as teachers. We are rethinking the conditions under which children learn most efficiently, how the curriculum should be structured and the role the teacher should play in the classroom. We are becoming acutely aware of the remarkable learning diversity that each classroom presents. Even in schools that practice selective admissions, the myth of the homogenous classroom is being exploded.

Increasingly educators are coming to understand and appreciate the considerable learning differences that children bring to the complex business of constructing and retaining knowledge. Teachers are becoming aware that our own preferred learning style may have translated itself into our preferred teaching style. It is natural, but erroneous, to think that everyone learns "just like I do." The truth is, in many cases the teacher's preferred style may not be the preferred learning style of most students. For example, Bill prefers long stints of unbroken concentration when he is writing. Ochan, on the other hand, writes in short intermittent bursts separated by phone calls, household tasks or other seemingly unrelated activities. Both manage to get to the end of the chapter but their respective journeys are quite different.

To illustrate how important sensory preference is to the process of learning, try this small experiment. Stand in front of your class, place your hand on your forehead and instruct the students to touch their chins. Some of the class will respond by touching their foreheads. While all of the students will have "heard" your instruction to touch their chins, for some of them (perhaps a majority) the visual data (the sight of you touching your forehead) has over-ridden the verbal. For many people the preference for visual processing of information is dominant over auditory. Sousa (2001) suggests that the percentages of sensory preference in the general population break down as follows: visual 46%; kinesthetic-tactile 35% and auditory 19%. We really do take different paths to similar learning goals.

Our knowledge of learning styles and intelligence preferences is growing as is our skill in analyzing the content of the curriculum. Our appreciation of how different environmental conditions (time of day, temperature, lighting etc.) affect the learning of different students is deepening. These are important dimensions in the growth of our knowledge base about student learning and differentiated instruction. Increasingly, educators are becoming aware of the specific components that make up individual students' unique learning profiles and are able to use this information to match learning preferences to instructional strategies.

Differentiation: Not Simply a Larger Toolbox of Strategies

When we surveyed international school teachers in Africa and Asia in 2003 (Kusuma-Powell, 2003) many respondents commented that if only they had more strategies in their instructional repertoire, they would be able to differentiate instruction within their classrooms. While there is no question that a broad repertoire of instructional strategies is an essential component of effective differentiation, a bigger toolbox is not enough in and of itself. Teachers are understandably attracted to practical training workshops that provide engaging instructional strategies which can be used "on Monday morning". However, teacher training workshops that present such instructional strategies in isolation from learning theory do little to enhance the learning of children. In fact, they may actually be promoting the notion that teaching is little more than "platform chicanery" (Skinner, 1976). Teaching is not just a bag of "tricks".

In fact, the overly simplistic belief that the acquisition of new instructional strategies is all one needs for differentiation can actually stand as an obstacle in the professional development of teachers. The acquisition of a new teaching strategy – however novel and potentially engaging -- in the absence of a deep knowledge of one's students as learners and an advanced knowledge of the curriculum is, more often than not, a recipe for wasted instructional time. The new strategy becomes another component in a solely activity-based classroom, which may be both engaging and entertaining, but lacks thoughtful design and specific learning outcomes. As Tomlinson & Allan (2000) correctly point out "no instructional strategy can compensate for a teacher who lacks proficiency in his content area, is unclear about learning goals, plans an unfocused activity or does not possess the leadership or management skills to orchestrate effective classroom functioning." (p.11)

We have seen time and time again that there is a direct positive correlation between the depth and quality of thought that the teacher puts into planning instruction and the depth and quality of student thought that results from the lesson. Any attempt to simplify or reduce the intellectual rigor of instructional planning short changes the education of children.

A Personal Paradigm Shift

The power and effectiveness of differentiated instruction is only realized when a teacher addresses the subject at the level of personal values. In her article "Deciding to Teach Them All", Carol Ann Tomlinson (2003) writes about this personal paradigm shift when an individual teacher embraces the challenge of teaching *all*, not some or even most, but *all*, of the students in her class. Too often in the past, teachers have assumed a tacit license to dismiss or disregard the learning of a few students in each class. Too often have teachers assumed that colleagues and administrators will understand and accept that in every class there are a few unreachable children – students who are too lazy, too emotionally disturbed, too ESL, too LD, too inattentive, too lacking in intelligence or self-control.

Tomlinson suggests to us that when we take the decision to teach each individual child, our perceptual framework undergoes a profound shift. We shift from looking at labels (ADHD, LD, ED etc) to searching for interests and needs. We shift from focusing upon a student's deficits -- what he or she cannot do -- to an examination of a child's strengths. We move away from the question "how do I remediate this child?" to "what do I do to ensure that each student works at the highest level of thought and production?" The shift may appear subtle, but it is, in fact, profound. The personal breakthrough in becoming a differentiating teacher comes not when we build a larger toolbox of strategies but when we redefine ourselves as educators and take the courageous decision to "teach them all".

Seven Principles that Support "Teaching Them All"

During our work to support international schools on their journey towards developing differentiation, we have sought to identify underlying principles that form a foundation for this work. We have identified seven principles which we believe reside at the core of differentiated instruction.

1. **All children can, do and will learn (not always what and when we would like):** Bill once attended an educational conference in Portland, Maine where he met a young principal who gave him a pencil with his school district's motto printed on it: *All students can learn.* The verb "can" bothered us. It suggested that while all students have the potential to learn, some may *not.* Had the pencil read "All children can succeed in school", we might have been more comfortable with it. But to suggest that learning may or may not occur is contrary to everything we know about the human brain. It's rather like saying "All children can breathe" or "All rivers can flow down hill." The only function that the human brain can engage in is learning. It is incapable of performing any other function.

Having said that, we have no guarantee that students will learn what we want, when we want it. Some students may be learning how to disguise their incomprehension with a mask of supposed attentiveness. There is some evidence to suggest that a significant proportion of girls may have managed to conceal learning disabilities in this fashion. It may be that our students are learning how to preserve their self-esteem in the face of repeated school failure by developing less than constructive behaviors. When a high school student learns to peddle drugs or to use violence to enhance self-image, he is learning.

So the question is not how to make children learn -- the notion that education is something that happens to you like having a cavity filled in the dentist's office -- but rather, the challenge for the differentiating teacher is how to guide the naturally occurring learning progress so that the child's curiosity, wonder and energy are focused into constructive and positive endeavors.

From our study of biology, we know that our internal organs are not created with attitudes. The brain is not a lazy or obdurate organ. Intellectual apathy is a highly unnatural state, probably symptomatic of some other condition; and, in children and young adults, it is most probably a learned response.

Two other important pieces of the learning puzzle have emerged in the last three decades. We now understand that intelligence is plural, not singular and that it is dynamic not static. Howard Gardner and Robert Sternberg, among others, have theorized that human intelligence is composed of a number of dimensions. Gardner (1993) has proposed that each of us has at least seven distinct types of intelligences. Sternberg's (1985) model suggests that we have three intelligence preferences (analytic, problem solving, and creative). Every one of us has the innate capacity for all of these intelligences or intelligence preferences to varying degrees. Our innate intelligence pattern is one of a number of features that make us unique. However, what is more important for educators to bear in mind is that each and every one of these intelligences is malleable. We can use it and develop it. Or we can ignore it and it will atrophy. Gone are the days when we thought of an IQ score as a monolithic and permanent measure of a child's intelligence.

As teachers we are coming to understand that it is not only important to teach to a child's strength, but that by teaching in a variety of ways we provide greater access to the curriculum and deepen students' understanding and retention of concepts.

2. **Diversity enriches:** For international schoolteachers the statement "diversity enriches" is probably like preaching to the choir. A school wouldn't be an "international" school if it didn't value the rich cultural, ethnic and linguistic variety that our students bring with them to the schoolhouse. However, we are not using the word diversity to refer to cultural, racial or ethnic differences. We are putting forward the principle that recognizing and responding to *learning* diversity enriches education for all children.

While all people, irrespective of their cultural or linguistic background, share common feelings and needs (and international schools need to help us understand and respect these commonalities), individual students do differ significantly as learners. These differences matter in the classroom, and schools need to help us to understand, respect and utilize these differences. We have previously mentioned the important role that differing learning styles and intelligence preferences can play. We will return to these learning differences later in this book. For now, suffice it to say that teachers who are responsive to an array of learning styles and preferences meet the educational needs of more children than teachers who either teach exclusively to their own best learning style ("one size fits all and *I am that size*") or teach the way they were taught when they were in school ("it worked for me and *look where I am now.*").

In his observation of third grade classrooms, Professor Elliot Eisner (1998) became aware that when a teacher focused on meeting the specific learning needs of a particular child often many other children benefited. "Thus, a teacher who teaches one child is often teaching the entire class. In this sense, individualized instruction is seldom individualized (p.193)."

We believe that effective heterogeneous classrooms are the glue that holds vibrant school communities together. Meeting diverse needs truly improves education for all.

3. **Children learn most enthusiastically and most efficiently when they are encouraged to use their strengths:** This may sound like we are stating the obvious, but you might be surprised at the large number of teachers who are still laser-focused upon student learning deficits. In a great many classrooms, the order of the day is still the

remediation of deficits at all costs. What the child *cannot* do occupies the spotlight in center stage. The absent knowledge or the skill that cannot yet be performed is the teacher's primary focus. It soon becomes the parents' preoccupation and the child lives with this deficit hanging, like the sword of Damocles, over her head until one of four things happen: the child gives up, the teacher gives up, the child is passed on to a different teacher, or the child manages to master the required knowledge or skill (while simultaneously developing an intense dislike for anything associated with school). Dwelling on student deficits and ignoring their strengths also causes us to under-estimate the capacity of children as learners. We know the tremendous power that teacher expectation can have upon student learning. Arguably, there is no more potent force in the classroom. The researchers have shown us the power of the Pygmalion effect (Rosenthal & Jacobsen, 1992). Focusing on student strengths allows us to operationalize the old adage: *When in doubt, teach up*.

By utilizing students strengths in the classroom, teachers provide more opportunities for students to succeed and thus to internalize what David McClelland (1988) referred to as "achievement motivation." This is the enthusiasm and energy that comes from striving after personal accomplishment whether in the classroom or the concert hall or on the sport field. It is competition against oneself for maximum growth and progress.

We classroom teachers have much to learn from quality athletic coaches about teaching to student strengths and achievement motivation. While Bill was employed as High School Principal at Jakarta International School, he attended a swim meet in Perth, Australia. The Jakarta team was swimming against a large local school district. Jakarta was not doing very well. By mid-afternoon, the JIS Aqua Dragons were many points behind the local team. It was then time for the 100-metre butterfly event. Jakarta's best butterfly swimmer came in fifth place in a race of six swimmers. When he hit the touch pad at the end of the pool, he paused momentarily to check his time and then leapt out of the water with a cry of jubilation. Although he had come in second to last, he had beaten his own best personal time for the 100-metre butterfly. This was achievement motivation.

Encouraging children to use their strengths is superficially simple, but holds some surprising complexities. Let us illustrate this with the story of George that appeared in ASCD's March 2002 *Education Update*.

George was a formidable challenge in Dana Flowers' third grade classroom. "He never volunteered for anything," she said. "His handwriting was awful, he had a crummy attitude, and he never showed any signs of wanting to participate. I was really worried about him."

These behaviors changed dramatically when, after one particular unit, Flowers offered her students a choice. As an alternative to a traditional pencil and paper test, the children could choose different ways of showing that they had understood the content of the unit. To Flowers' surprise, George chose to do a musical routine. "Here he had hardly spoken a single word all year, and now he wanted to get up in front of the entire class and sing a song."

But this is exactly what George did, and it was so well received that he sang it not once, but twice. "He sang an entire song about water…He covered every concept that we were looking for – evaporation, condensation, you name it—and just sang his little heart out. He really was 'Joe Cool!'"

Since then, Flowers reports, George's hand is regularly in the air and "he has continued to blossom, sharing what he learns through further songs."

Clearly differentiated instruction made a difference for George. By providing students with the opportunity to show what they have learned using their individual talents and strengths, Flowers not only permitted George to show deep conceptual understanding of the water cycle, but also to emerge as an increasingly self-confident and self-directed learner who was keen to participate in other units.

Teaching to students' strengths makes learning success transferable.

4. **Effective teachers can teach all children:** The traditional and customary approach to teaching children who learn differently has been what we refer to as the "medical model". In this model, the learning difference was perceived as an abnormality or condition that needed to be "cured". Accordingly the student was diagnosed and an Individual Education Plan (IEP) was drawn up. The IEP often contained a prescribed number of hours per week in some specialized setting outside the regular classroom, such as a Resource Room, where the child received special assistance from a special education specialist. Many times this special assistance bore little resemblance to the regular curriculum. The theory was that once the child had overcome his learning difference, he could be returned to the mainstream classroom as a full and successful participant.

The "medical model" has shown time and time again that it doesn't work effectively (Kusuma-Powell & Powell, 2000). Learning differences are not temporary aberrations that can be "cured" in isolation from the regular classroom. However, the practice has been widespread and has had the undesirable by-product of disempowering many mainstream teachers. By removing children who learn differently from their classrooms, we have given many regular classroom teachers two unfortunate messages: 1) "You don't have the requisite skills or special knowledge to teacher this special population", and 2) "The education of these children isn't your responsibility." We are now struggling to overcome both of these perceptual legacies.

Effective teachers can have a profound influence on student learning. Good teaching is, after all, good teaching and all students benefit from it. No amount of clever and gimmicky strategies, charisma or popularity can compensate for a teacher who lacks content area knowledge or learning theory. William Sanders and his team of researchers write: "Effective teachers appear to be effective with students of all achievement levels, regardless of the level of heterogeneity in their classrooms. If the teacher is ineffective, students under the teacher's tutelage will show inadequate progress academically regardless of how similar or different they are regarding their academic achievement." (in Marzano, 2001, p.63).

5. **The teacher is the most important architect of a child's learning environment:** In our work in schools, we can often become confused between what is *central* to student learning and what is in fact *peripheral*. World class facilities are nice. An excellent curriculum is important. Clear policies have a great deal to recommend them and an ample supply of resources makes our professional work much easier. However, there can be no question that the most important asset in a school is the teaching faculty.

We know that learning takes place in a social context (Vygotsky, 1986) and that the teacher is the prime architect of the social context of the classroom – either by design or by default. The relationship between teacher and child is an essential feature of the learning environment.

In the 1960's and 70's a number of researchers including James Coleman (1966) and Christopher Jencks (1972) presented findings, which suggested that socio-economic factors had a more significant influence on student achievement than schools. Since the socio-economic backgrounds of students (economic status, ethnicity, parental expectations etc.) are not something over which educators generally have control, these research reports made for fairly pessimistic reading. However, the next decade and a half saw a plethora of additional research that confirmed what most parents know intuitively: even if the school is ineffective, good teachers can make a powerful difference in the learning of children from all socio-economic backgrounds (Brophy & Good, 1986).

Lou Danielson, the US Undersecretary of State for Education in 2002, opened the OMNI Summer Conference at Johns Hopkins University with the provocative words: "In education, if it's not best practice, its malpractice." Danielson went on to stress how critical it is for teachers to use pedagogy that has its effectiveness confirmed by research. Too much of what we attempt to justify as best practice has its basis in unexamined common practice and idiosyncratic belief systems. Separate studies New York City, Dallas, Boston and Tennessee underscore the importance of teachers as the prime architects of children's learning. The Tennessee study demonstrates that elementary children who were assigned to ineffectual teachers three years in a row scored fifty percentile points lower on achievement tests than those assigned to the most effective teachers over the same period of time (Hammond & Ball, 1997). Some educational leaders are speculating that two years in a row of ineffective teaching at the elementary level may result in a child experiencing irreparable educational damage.

6. **Strategies that define and comprise good teaching are applicable to all children:** All learners require respectful, powerful and engaging schoolwork to develop their individual capacities so that they become fulfilled and productive members of society. This is as true for six years olds as it is for sixty-year olds. It is as true in learning science as it is learning mathematics. It is true for the highly capable learner, the student with a learning difference and for the child learning English as a second language.
While some pedagogical approaches will be more effective with particular learners, stimulating and engaging teaching is effective for all students.

At the conclusion of teacher workshops on differentiation, it is not uncommon for a participant to approach either Bill or Ochan and say something to this effect: "But all this is just good teaching." Of course, effective differentiation is good teaching. Actually, to be more precise, differentiation makes good teaching more accessible to a larger student population. As Carol Ann Tomlinson (2000) has written, "Excellent differentiated classrooms are excellent first and differentiated second (p.17)."

Our real issue with the response "But all this is just good teaching" is with the word "just", which implies that good teaching is common place, easily achieved and not really worthy of much discussion at a professional development workshop. How absurd the word "just" would appear in other similar contexts: "That's just skillfully performed surgery" or "That's just an eloquent and persuasive piece of writing." Good teaching is complex and challenging work!

While there is no formula or recipe for good teaching, there are certain principles that we know about teaching and learning that have wide application across age groups, gender, and cultural differences. For example, we know that a high degree of stress causes the brain to down shift and makes higher level or creative thinking impossible. We also know that most children finding whole to part learning more accessible than instruction that moves from part to whole. In other words, children find it very useful to have the big picture before they start analyzing the pieces. Since the time of John Dewey, we have known that students learn more and learn more efficiently when they are active participants in their learning – as opposed to passive recipients.

Good teaching really is good teaching; however, it's anything but simple and easy.

7. **A professional partnership is exponentially more effective (and more satisfying) than the sum of its parts:** Several years ago a popular keynote speaker at educational conferences would draw laughs from a nervous audience by commenting that while teaching wasn't the world's oldest profession, it was arguably the second most private.

    The jokes aside, his point about a long tradition of teacher isolation must be taken seriously. For most of the last century, teachers were expected to plan on their own, teach in isolation and assess student learning without any support or assistance from colleagues. This isolation has been a hallmark of our profession and has served as one of the greatest impediments to teacher professional growth and student learning.

    Thankfully, for most schools team work and collaboration are the order of the day and the benefits of this collegiality are nowhere more evident than in the area of developing differentiated classrooms.

As we have become increasingly aware of the differences that children and young adults bring to our classrooms – differences that we as teachers need to respond to in our planning and our delivery of instruction -- we have also become aware of the increasing challenge that truly effective teaching poses. This is not a profession for those who blanch in the face of complexity or those unaccustomed to the demands of intellectual rigor or those who are uncomfortable with ambiguity. Teaching is hard cognitive labor and teachers have every right to expect support in their work. The most effective support comes from professional colleagues through common planning, co-teaching and collaborative assessment of student work. We would argue that one of the most important messages that any teacher can receive about differentiation is that *no teacher needs to go it alone.*

Expertise Doesn't Have a Past Tense

Occasionally we are asked "When can we be finished with differentiation?" The implication is that either differentiation is an educational fad that will fade out of existence when the next flavor of the months comes along (very unlikely) or that differentiation is something that can be accomplished like learning to drive a car and then never thought of again. Both the former and the latter suggest a very simplistic understanding of the differentiated classroom.

Differentiation is a journey towards mastery. Just as the master craftsman constantly works to improve her skills and talents, so the teacher constantly works to develop her instructional craft. Given the plethora of research that is becoming available to classroom practitioners on a daily basis, it is a truism to say that expertise does not have a past tense.

An administrative colleague of ours is fond of saying that there is no status quo for schools; they are either improving or they are deteriorating. We would say the same for the teaching profession.

2 FOUR KEYS TO DIFFERENTIATION

Watching the European Spring unfold in the French Pyrenees offers a splendid metaphor for the differentiated classroom. Spring in these parts isn't a well-rehearsed or synchronized event. On the contrary, the mountain flora seems to operate on a multitude of different readiness schedules. Spring in these foothills, often like the development of children in the differentiated classroom, is an erratic, unpredictable, at times messy, but stunningly beautiful event.

From our kitchen window, we have a panoramic view of the Massat Valley. Middle March heralds the harbingers of spring: the sudden carpet of saffron-yellow primroses and purple and blue crocuses. Egg-yoke daffodils and bridal-veil-white snowberries appear by the side of the track that leads to our farmhouse. Moments, or perhaps days later, they are joined by carmine poppies, Spanish bluebells, and buttercups. The Japanese quince bush in the front lawn suddenly bursts into scarlet blossom and is soon followed by the white-frosted cherry and peach trees. A little later come the deep purple lilacs and amethyst cascade of wisteria

Each of the flowering shrubs and trees has its own schedule. Each wild flower waits for the appropriate combination of sunshine, warmth and moisture. How dissimilar is this to the children in our classrooms – each waiting for that unique combination of intellectual stimulation, self-confidence, interest and personal connection that will provide maximum access to the curriculum? If no two flowers are identical, if no two snowflakes are really the same, why in the world would we act as if children are cut out of the same mold?

Matt
Both the Middle School Counselor and the Learning Specialist are concerned about Matt. He has had several psycho-educational evaluations and, despite

his parent's persistent denials, his learning disability is well documented. He is reading three grade levels below his age group. His handwriting is almost illegible. In a one-to-one situation, Matt can exhibit surprising flashes of insight and his critical thinking skills can be astute and penetrating. However, in the seventh grade classroom he is silent and withdrawn.

During the last semester, the concern of the Counselor and Learning Specialist has increased because Matt has become the target of teasing. A group of children in the seventh grade have taken to calling Matt "Retard". This name-calling has extended to graffiti appearing on both Matt's locker and his loose-leaf binder. Unfortunately, Matt's thick prescription glasses and his poor hand-eye coordination add to the impression of general awkwardness.

On one occasion the Learning Specialist observed Matt in the cafeteria carrying his tray to a table already occupied by a group of his classmates. When he arrived at the table, his classmates stared at him incredulously. Their body language spoke louder than their unspoken words: *Do you really think you're going to sit with us?* Realizing that he had forgotten a fork and spoon, Matt placed his tray on the table and returned to the serving line. When he returned to the table, all of his classmates had disappeared, as had his tray of food.

In recent weeks, the Counselor and Learning Specialist have noticed a significant change in both Matt and his interaction with peers. A month ago, Matt auditioned for the Middle School play. Once on stage, the thick glasses and the awkward gait disappeared. Matt stepped into character and literally "blew away" the director and the rest of the would-be cast. "Holy Smokes! Matt's a natural. Who would have guessed that he had such acting talent! He is a completely different child on stage!"

Actually, Matt's success in the audition is making him a completely different child off-stage too. His teachers look at him differently. Their expectations have risen. They have a new and expanded vision of his potential. His success has been unmasked. His peers have stopped calling him "Retard" and he is participating more in class discussions. His grades remain fairly dismal, but he and his teachers have a plan for improvement. Most importantly, Matt has stopped having to eat his lunch in solitude.

Rupa

Rupa is a very bright young lady, or she used to be last year in the fourth grade. Her previous school report card indicates a straight "A" record for achievement in academics. However, her work in her new international school has been barely average. Homework has often been late or incomplete. If she knows how to do something, the assignment will come in errorless, but if she is unsure of herself, the homework will be left in her locker, lost on the school bus or eaten by the dog. Rupa will participate in class but only when she is called upon directly by the teacher. She appears to lack self-confidence and often doesn't seem to understand the teacher's expectations.

Her parents are distraught by the decline in Rupa's school achievement. They have visited her teachers almost every other day and are in the process of hiring a private tutor for math. Television and computer privileges have been suspended indefinitely. Her father has repeated numerous times that Rupa will have to go to India for university where the competition for admission is very intense. "With these grades, she just won't make it. And she doesn't speak Hindi!"

Rupa's father owns and runs a successful furniture company in Kenya and has now opened a branch in South East Asia, where the family has moved. Rupa's previous schooling has been in a local Roman Catholic convent school in the suburbs of Nairobi. While the medium of instruction was English, the language of the playground was a patois of English, Gujarati and Kiswahili. The emphasis in her previous school was on rote memory at which Rupa excelled.

Rupa is ethnically Indian, but has never lived in India. She was born in Africa, but doesn't feel any sense of being Kenyan or African. Her family is Hindu, but she knows more about the *Catechism* than she does the *Vedas*. Her father and mother pay lip service to traditional Indian culture when it serves their purposes, but the intrusion of Western values and commercialism is all too real in their lives. Ten-year-old Rupa remembers being a success last year and grieves for her past life.

Frank

At the conclusion of Frank's valedictory speech the entire audience was on its feet applauding. Everyone knew that Frank had defied all odds and had won a four-year scholarship to study pre-med. at Yale. The thunderous applause echoed throughout the commencement hall capturing the enormous pride the school community took in his accomplishment.

Frank had overcome some major obstacles. He was a host country scholarship student. His parents were both schoolteachers in a rural African school who in no way could have afforded big city, international school fees.

Another obstacle was not so obvious and had formed the centerpiece of Frank's valedictory speech. He had spoken about the culture shock he had experienced when he had first come to this international school. He had described the difference between studying in a traditional government school and the intellectual demands of the IB diploma program. "For the first three or four months I was at this school, I didn't say a word in class. I was in a state of total confusion and shock. It was as though I'd landed on a different planet. I didn't understand what the teachers wanted. I was used to a school in which there were right and wrong answers. You were rewarded for right answers and punished for wrong answers. But here, the teachers wanted you to think. They expected you to have ideas. They were interested in your opinions. You were evaluated not on a basis of right and wrong, but on the basis of how well thought out your answers were. If you have never been in a traditional government school, you have no idea of the magnitude of this change! You have no idea how terrifying it is to appear before a teacher who expects you to think. Now, I recognize it as the greatest gift that anyone can ever receive!"

May Ling

Thirteen year old May Ling is visibly nervous during the admissions interview. She answers questions softly with single words or short phrases. For most of the time, she scrutinizes her shoes and her hand is kept firmly in front of her mouth. She is easily flustered and, at least once, appears on the verge of tears.

Although she has been in an English medium school in Macao for the past five years, the ESL placement test indicates that she is at Level One (Beginner Level). The language of May Ling's home is mixed. Her Chinese mother speaks to her in Cantonese; her Danish father speaks to her in English.

When May Ling is not so nervous, her social English is deceptively competent. Socially, she would appear to be a fluent English speaker. However, her written language in both English and Chinese reveals that she is struggling with abstract expression in both languages. The fact is that May Ling doesn't have a strongly developed mother tongue. She is not just wrestling with the acquisition of English; she is wrestling with the *acquisition of language*.

As these four brief vignettes illustrate, international school students bring with them the most extraordinary diversity of talents and expectations,

> In medical practice, highly specific knowledge of the individual needs of a patient is indispensable when selecting the best treatment. This holds true in all 'helping professions'—especially in education.
>
> --*Mel Levine,* Celebrating Diverse Minds

learning preferences and obstacles, cultural backgrounds, linguistic competencies, personal interests and family histories. However, the trouble with truth is that it is has an unfortunate tendency to become an easily dismissible platitude. How often have we heard a colleague bring a discussion of learning different child to a premature close with the expression: "But all our children are unique!?"

Differentiation requires us to go beneath the platitudes and re-discover how remarkably different our students really are. In his charming essay "What a Professor Learned in the Third Grade", Elliot Eisner (1998) reflects on his three-month visit to two third grade classrooms. He writes:

> *Consider, for example, the idea that all children are different. To professors of education, that notion is about as prosaic as can be, but seeing the ways in which a group of eight-year-olds can differ in size, temperament, maturity, interests, energy level, and personal style is quite another matter. Their presence makes plain the vacuity of the concept of "the average eight-year-old"...Teachers cannot deal with abstractions or averages when they teach. Their knowledge of individuals is crucial in enabling them to make appropriate assignments, to provide comfort and support, to impose sanctions, to define limits to behavior, to remind individual students of obligations, to encourage participation and to foster attitudes of cooperation (p.190).*

In our classroom work over the last thirty years, we have identified what we consider to be the Four Keys that serve as a foundation for differentiated instruction. These four keys or dimensions of differentiation do not stand alone but are intricately interwoven into the fabric of teaching and student learning.

Four Keys to Differentiation

Knowing your students (and yourself as teacher)

Knowing your curriculum

Developing a repertoire of strategies

Starting simple, moving slowly, and keeping our work social

Key One: Knowing Your Students (and yourself as a teacher)

Again, it is easy to dismiss "knowing your students" as either a vacuous platitude or a statement of the obvious. However, if we ask: 'What knowledge about our students do we need in order to customize their learning?' we begin the process of uncovering a critical dimension of effective differentiation.

By "knowing our students" we mean more than mere social or administrative information. It is a given that teachers would know their students' names, ages, something about friendship circles, and something about their family backgrounds. But to maximize learning we need to dig deeper than this superficial information. We need to come to know the child as a learner in the specific areas of **readiness, interests** and **learning profile.**

Readiness disposición, preparación, estar listo

We use the term "readiness" as opposed to "ability" because readiness suggests to us that it is malleable (that it will change and can be influenced by skilled instruction) and that it will vary considerably depending on circumstance, topic or subject and developmental stage. Ability, on the other hand, suggests innate talents over which neither the child nor teacher has much influence.

The concept of readiness is slippery because grammatically it is a *noun* but in real life it acts as a *verb*. We often think of readiness as in the phrase "reading readiness" as a condition that is achieved as a prerequisite for the next level of challenge or achievement. However, readiness is actually a dynamic process over which the teacher has considerable influence. It is not enough for us to be able to identify or even foster "readiness", we must also be able to anticipate it and mediate it upwards. Perhaps we should not think of *readiness* but of *readying*. Vygotsky (1986) writes that "the only good kind of instruction is that which marches ahead of development and leads it; it must be aimed not so much at the ripe as at the *ripening* functions (*emphasis ours*)...instruction must be oriented towards the future, not the past." (p.188-189)[1].

As teachers, we make decisions and judgments daily about the readiness level of our students. Should we teach *Julius Caesar* in Grade Eight? What understandings need to be in place prior to introducing the concept of division? At what age or grade should we expect students to be able to

---

[1] Please see the sidebar on the Zone of Proximal Development.

produce a five or six paragraph essay? These are questions of group readiness. If we are to differentiate instruction, we need to think of readiness in *both* group and individual terms.

Mihalyi Csikszentmihalyi (1991), the author of *Flow: The Psychology of Optimal Experience* perceives readiness as the necessary condition for human learning and enjoyment. Readiness, for Csikszentmihalyi, is connected to the demands of the challenge that confronts us. Learning and enjoyment occur at the confluence of challenge and ability, when the opportunities for action are equal to the individual's capacity. For those who don't have the right skills, an activity is not challenging: it is simply meaningless. "Playing tennis, for instance, is not enjoyable if two opponents are mismatched. The less skilful player will feel anxious and the better player will feel bored. The same is true of every other activity: the piece of music that is too simple relative to one's listening skills, will be boring, while music that is too complex will be frustrating." According to Csikszentmilalyi, "enjoyment appears at the boundary between boredom and anxiety, when the challenges are just balanced with a person's capacity to act (p.50)."

We would suggest that this is the exact location of the differentiated classroom – on the frontier between challenges that are too difficult and therefore frustrating and challenges that are too easy and therefore boring. Only when a child works at a level of difficulty that is both challenging and attainable for that individual does learning take place. Therefore it stands to reason that if readiness levels in a class differ, so must the levels of challenge provided for students. (Tomlinson, 2003; Jensen, 1998; National Research Council, 1999; Sousa, 2001, Vygotsky,1978, 1986; Wolfe,2001).

Zone of Proximal Development

In his classic work *Thought and Language* (1986), the Russian cognitive psychologist Lev Vygotsky coined the expression "the Zone of Proximal Development." The phrase has come into common parlance in many schools and is often used as a synonym for a child's intellectual readiness for a given task or for the understanding of an abstract concept. The Zone of Proximal Development is a way of looking at readiness, but it is a very specific kind of readiness and it may be useful to look back at what exactly Vygotsky meant by it.

Vygotsky contrasts the usefulness of measuring a child's level of mental development based solely on his or her independent practice as opposed to his or her performance when thinking is mediated by adult intervention. The discrepancy between what the child can accomplish independently and what the child can achieve with skillful adult intervention is what Vygotsky called the Zone of Proximal Development.

"Having found the mental age of two children (level of independent functioning) *was, let us say, eight, we gave them harder problems that they could manage on their own and provided some slight assistance: the first step in a solution, a leading question, or some other form of help. We discovered that one child could, in cooperation, solve problems designed for twelve-year olds, while the other could not go beyond problems intended for nine-year-olds. The discrepancy between a child's actual mental age and the level he reaches in solving problems with assistance indicates the zone of his proximal development...Experience has shown that the child with the larger zone of proximal development will do much better in school (p.187)."*

Lev Vygotsky, *Thought and Language*

Learning readiness can be thought of as the knowledge, understanding and skills an individual brings to a new learning situation. However, we also need to appreciate that readiness is profoundly influenced by prior learning, self-esteem, one's sense of efficacy, social status within the class or group, life experience, dispositions and attitudes and habits of mind. Readiness is no less complex than any one of the children entrusted to our care.

Interests

There are two types of student interests that form useful information for the teacher planning a differentiated classroom. First, there are pre-existing student interests. These are those subjects, topics and pursuits about which an individual student has an existing curiosity or passion. They are areas in which the student readily pursues new knowledge and the acquisition of new skills without external motivation. These are areas of the curriculum (including extra-curricular activities and athletics) or outside interests in which the students readily invests time and energy. Relevance to the student is obvious and engagement is immediate.

Secondly, there are areas of potential interest. These are topics, activities or pursuits that the student may not have yet discovered or may not have been exposed to. Potential interests are as powerful as pre-existing interests but their relevance needs to be mediated.

Effective teachers pay attention to both types of student interest. When we are able to link the classroom curriculum to student interest we are able to tap into internalized achievement motivation – where goals are personal, motivation comes from within and achievement is deeply meaningful. Mediating connections between classroom learning and student interests is one of most powerful strategies that teachers can employ towards the goal of creating enthusiastic life-long learners.

Learning Profile

Knowing your students as learners means knowing how they learn best. It means knowing their strengths and talents as well as their deficits. It means knowing their preferred learning modalities (visual, auditory, tactual or kinesthetic) and having an understanding of their intelligence preferences.

Knowing the learning profile of a student means having some idea of how culture and gender may influence the acquisition of new knowledge and skills. In an international school that may have fifty or sixty different nationalities represented in the student population, making connections between cultures and their influence on learning can be challenging and complex.

Understanding learning profiles includes knowing under what environmental conditions a given student works best. Does Frank do his best thinking in the morning or afternoon? Is Rupa's concentration affected by temperature (does she become distracted when the classroom is too warm or too cold?) When Matt is struggling to read, does he do better in a hard straight-backed chair or when he is lounging on a soft pillow on the floor?

Finally, having insight into a student's learning profile also means having an understanding of her attitudes and dispositions, her temperament, her self-esteem in relation to school work and the social status accorded her by her peer group (Cohen 1998). We know that emotion and cognition are inextricably bound together. Attitudes and dispositions are exterior manifestations of internal emotions. These emotions can have powerful effects on learning and success in school. For example, how does May Ling's introverted personality affect her acquisition of language? Or how has Rupa's low frustration threshold affected her willingness to take intellectual risks?

Linked closely with "knowing your student" is "knowing yourself as a teacher". Time and time again, educational research tells us that learning takes place in a social context (Vygotsky, 1986) and that the teacher/student relationship can be crucial to student achievement. The most effective teachers also those teachers who have self-consciously cultivated their own emotional intelligence (Goleman 1995), particularly in the areas of self-awareness and regulation, social awareness and relationship management.

Key Two: Knowing Your Curriculum

A number of years ago, a large international school in South East Asia identified two schoolwide annual goals: the first was to develop a standards and benchmarks framework for its curriculum and the second was to promote differentiated instruction in every classroom in the school.

It was not long before a teacher raised her hand at a faculty meeting and asked if these two goals weren't diametrically opposed. "Don't they contradict each other?" she asked. "For example, defining standards and benchmarks requires us to identify what knowledge and skills we expect the average fifth grader to have. We are standardizing the curriculum and our expectations of children. Differentiation, on the other hand, demands that we look at each child as a unique learner. How on earth can we do both at the same time?"

We were grateful for this question because it opened up a lively and insightful conversation about the relationship between settings standards and catering for diverse learning needs. It also reflects the fact that the standards based movement in education and initiative in differentiation grew up separately with little reference to each other until Tomlinson & McTighe (2006) married them in their seminal book *Integrating differentiated instruction and Understanding by design.*

On one level, the questioning teacher had a point. Setting standards and benchmarks for student achievement may *seem* contradictory to the efforts we make to differentiate instruction. However, there may be another way of looking at the situation. Rather than begin from the position that they are mutually exclusive, let's assume that they may be mutually inclusive. Let's ask what would happen to one without the presence of the other.

We know, all too well, what happens when the individual learner gets forgotten or disregarded or dismissed in the bureaucratic and often political move towards the standardization of student achievement. In the absence of differentiation (concern for responding to different students learning needs), standards often translate themselves into a narrow focus on objective accountability, especially high stakes testing. In some instances, these supposedly objective tests of student achievement have asserted a tyrannical hold over not just assessment but also classroom instruction.

On the other hand, imagine what would become of the differentiated classroom without clearly defined learning standards and benchmarks of student achievement. We would see either the individualized programmed learning of the 1960's (25 different programs for 25 different students with virtually no cooperative learning or direct instruction from the teacher) or muddled and disorganized instruction lacking in clear learning outcomes and objectives. Benchmarks of student achievement provide clear attainment targets for teachers. Differentiation provides a multitude of paths to reach those targets.

We would contend that standards and benchmarks and differentiation are complementary as opposed to contradictory. It is through the development of shared standards and benchmarks of student achievement that teachers truly come to know their curriculum.

By "knowing the curriculum" we do not mean simply subject area mastery (although this is a crucial part of the knowledge we are referring to). We are referring to that in-depth knowledge of the curriculum that allows the teacher to identify the primary concepts and to distinguish between enduring understandings (Wiggins & McTighe, 1998) and the peripheral information that may be interesting to know but is not essential to conceptual understanding.

Key Three: Developing a Repertoire of Strategies
In the introduction to this book, we go to some lengths to stress that differentiation is not simply a larger toolbox of instructional strategies. The words "not simply" are important. It would be a gross over-simplification to reduce differentiation in such a way. However, there can be no denying that a broad, research-based repertoire of instructional strategies is a vital component in the differentiated classroom.

Engaging instructional strategies do not in and of themselves ensure high quality student learning. We have all witnessed the activity-driven classroom, where the teacher has prepared highly engaging and entertaining activities for the students with little thought given to the actual learning objectives or outcomes. The children have a wonderful time. The teacher is enviably popular. But little learning is accomplished.

Effective instructional strategies triangulate the three critical features of the classroom: the learning outcomes, the curriculum content, and the students themselves. Effective strategies embody learning theory and principles and are often generic enough to be transferable to many different subjects and age levels.

We would urge teachers to name the strategies they are using and tell their students why they are using it. When we provide students with the rationale for a classroom activity, we uncover and share learning theory and in doing so we assist students in developing self-knowledge about themselves as learners – a critical dimension in fostering metacognition and self-directed learning.

Key Four: Keeping it Simple and Social

Differentiation is subject to two common causes of premature mortality: over-worked teachers being overwhelmed or over-worked teachers being under-whelmed.

It is very easy to see how the challenges and demands of differentiating a complex curriculum can be overwhelming. First there is the challenge of knowing twenty five diverse learners (and that's if you are an Elementary teacher with one class. The task of knowing your students becomes even more complex when you are a high school English teacher who may teach a hundred or more students during the course of a typical week.) And then the task really becomes daunting when we try to match the learning needs of specific children with a profound understanding of the curriculum -- the primary concepts and the essential questions. The stressed-out, over-worked teacher is already shaking her head in dismay and we haven't yet got to designing learning activities and performance assessments with children's strengths and learning styles in mind. It is easy to see how the challenge of differentiated instruction can be over-whelming.

However, in our experience the under-whelmed teacher can pose an equally difficult challenge. Here is the teacher who has grasped a simplistic understanding of differentiation and then dismisses it because: *I'm doing all that already*. It is not uncommon for a teacher to identify one or two aspects of the differentiated classroom (a value she shares or a strategy that she is familiar with) and conclude that she doesn't need to do anything further in this area.

In reality, differentiation is a long, complex and challenging journey and it is the highly experienced, master teacher who recognizes that developing one's craftsmanship is never fully complete. There are, however, three important ways that teachers can avoid the dangers of being either over or under-whelmed.

First of all, **start simple**. This means setting realistic and reasonable objectives for one's self. A teacher doesn't become a master craftsman overnight. Select one of the keys to differentiation and then identify one or two specific strategies that you are going to focus on and practice. For example, if your objective for the next eight weeks is to gain greater insight into your students as learners, you might decide to practice a clinical observation strategy and engage in some collaborative analysis of student work. Setting manageable goals for one's self requires a degree of self knowledge and a modicum of humility.

Once you have a reasonable and realistic differentiation goal, **move slowly** but surely in the direction of mastery. Researchers who study change in schools and other organizations have identified what they call the "implementation dip". This is when individual performance deteriorates as a result of the implementation of a new strategy or program. Because the curriculum, methodology, strategy etc. is new to the teacher it is virtually inevitable that she will be less efficient with it initially than she was with her old "tried and true" methods. It is not uncommon for teachers to become discouraged and disillusioned during the implementation dip. They become impatient and dissatisfied with themselves professionally and then transfer those feelings of inadequacy onto the new curriculum, methodology or strategy. *"The new curriculum just isn't working. The students aren't producing the way they used to…"*

When we are able to perceive the big picture, we understand that we need to move beyond the implementation dip before we are able to get an accurate assessment of whether the change we have initiated is actually beneficial to student learning.

Finally, and perhaps most importantly, it is vital that we have supportive traveling companions on our journey towards differentiation. In other words, we need to **keep it social** – we need our professional colleagues. We need collaboration.

However, high quality professional relationships are made, not born and we have, for the most part, provided teachers with very little explicit training in how to work collaboratively. As a matter of some urgency, schools need to support teachers as they develop their collaborative skills. Administrators need to help teachers address issues such as:

- What behaviors foster shared goals, greater trust and interdependence?
- What can I do to promote shared accountability?
- How can I support the deep thinking of my colleagues?
- How do I handle conflict in the group?
- How are high functioning teams developed and maintained?

As we stated earlier, differentiation is complex and challenging work. The good news is that no teacher needs to "go it alone". Our teaching colleagues are probably the most powerful professional resource available to us. And, for the most part, this is a resource that is just waiting to be tapped. It is the skills of collaboration that unleash the energy and power of this vital resource.

A Framework for Differentiation

We have used a technique called "Segmentation" as a graphic organizer for the critical dimensions of differentiation. As Figure #1 illustrates, we have created four quadrants by placing a continuum of "Knowing Your Student" on the vertical axis and a continuum of "Knowing Your Curriculum" on the horizontal axis. At the far left there is limited knowledge of the curriculum and at the far right there is advanced knowledge of the curriculum. The same type of continuum is present on the vertical axis stretching from complex knowledge of students (and self) at the top of the figure to limited knowledge at the bottom of the figure.

The danger of any such graphic organizer is that it creates generalizations. While few real teachers fit neatly into the quadrants of Figure #1, we believe the visual structure is useful in illustrating the relationships between the Four Keys to Differentiation.

The lower left hand quadrant is the home of the Beginning Teacher. Because the novice lacks the expertise that is bred of experience, his knowledge of both the curriculum and students will, by definition, be limited. While the young teacher may be wonderfully enthusiastic and energetic, it is likely that his collaborative skills have not yet had a chance to mature in a professional environment and that he has not yet had the opportunity to develop a broad repertoire of instructional strategies.

The upper left hand quadrant reflects the Relationship-Oriented teacher. This is the teacher who has developed a deep knowledge of her students and

33

herself as a teacher, but who lacks an advanced knowledge of the curriculum. This is the teacher who creates a warm and trusting classroom climate. This teacher has excellent interpersonal skills and a high degree of emotional intelligence. She is a skillful, reflective listener and is in tune with both the spoken and unspoken emotional needs of her students. She is often popular with both the children and their parents. She cares deeply for the youngsters in her class and both students and parents come to know and appreciate this. The children in her classroom feel a strong sense of belonging. They identify with their membership in the class and there is extensive empathy.

But, we are compelled to ask, where in this wonderful class climate is the curriculum? How much planned learning is actually going on? With only a beginning knowledge of the curriculum, this teacher is unable to forge meaningfully appropriate learning objectives. The lesson outcomes are fuzzy and ill-defined. The learning activities may be entertaining and engaging for the students, but the connection between these activities and the lesson's purpose is tenuous at best. Teacher questioning tends to be spontaneous and haphazard, rather than planned. It is often simplistic and superficial. This is the teacher who easily drifts off the subject (perhaps because there isn't a clearly defined "subject") into personal anecdotes and stories and complex cognitive processes (e.g. analysis, comparison, evaluation, etc.) may not be taught explicitly.

The lower right hand quadrant of Figure 1 is the dwelling place of the Subject-Oriented teacher. This is the teacher with an advanced knowledge of the curriculum, but limited knowledge of students. This is the traditional content area expert – the teacher who "really knows (and often loves) her stuff". This teacher knows what her students need to know and be able to do in order to perform well on public examinations. The subject-oriented teacher tends to each subjects as opposed to students, but many times has the reputation of being one of the "best" and most demanding teachers in the school (often this is because she is assigned the highest achieving students). She is an expert in physics or mathematics or literature. This teacher is highly effective with older, brighter, self-motivated students. She tends to do extremely well in teaching students in the IB Diploma, Advanced Placement or "A" level programs which have selective admissions. Her students achieve outstanding examination results and are admitted to the most prestigious universities.

However, one should not make the mistake of assigning the subject-oriented teacher to a Middle School class or a class with students who learn differently or with variable motivation. The challenges that these students present are more often than not beyond the expertise and patience of the subject-oriented teacher. Developing student motivation, mediating relevance, or responding to individual learning needs may not be perceived as part of her teaching responsibility. She tends to teach in the manner in which she learns best (perhaps in the manner in which she herself was taught) and is quick to mentally discard students who do not share her own preferred learning style, or who do not produce clearly recognizable (read "traditional") products of high achievement. Because this teacher has very limited knowledge of her students as learners, she also has a very limited repertoire of instructional strategies. She tends to rely on lecture and seminar discussion, pencil and paper tests and quizzes and research papers.

The upper right hand quadrant we have labeled the Differentiating Teacher. Because this person combines complex knowledge of students and self with advanced knowledge of the curriculum, she is able to frame clear and meaningful learning goals and match her methodology to student readiness, interests and learning profiles. She has a wide repertoire of instructional strategies that provides her with both flexibility and self-confidence within the classroom. Because she has an advanced knowledge of the curriculum, she is able to devote a considerable portion of her in-class attention to clinical observation of her students and in doing so, she is able to identify and work in their Zones of Proximal Development (ZPD). This is the teacher who actively mediates the upward movement of the ZPD. Not only does she have a large "toolbox" of instructional strategies, she has a deep conceptual understanding of the learning theory that is embedded in this pedagogy and is thus able to mix and match her knowledge of her students' learning needs with her advanced knowledge of the curriculum.

Because this teacher actively mediates both relevance of learning and potential student interests, she is tapping into intrinsic motivation and setting an expectation for an internal locus of control and responsibility.

Again, these four quadrants form simplistic and over-generalized portraits. It is unlikely that any real teacher would fit neatly into any such pigeon-hole. However, as an organizer of teaching and learning principles, the framework illustrates the interdependent relationships between teacher knowledge and teacher effectiveness.

Relationship Between Teacher Knowledge & Teacher Effectiveness

Advanced Knowledge
of Student & of Self

Relationship Orientation
Trusting classroom climate
Extensive empathy
Excellent interpersonal skills

The Differentiating Teacher
Works within the child's ZPD
Mediates upward movement of ZPD/
student independence
Internal focus of control &
responsibility

Beginning
Knowledge of
Curriculum

Advanced
Knowledge of
Curriculum

Beginning Teacher

Subject Area Mastery/ Task Orientation
Content area expert
Tends to teach subjects as opposed to
students
Very effective with highly motivated,
bright students

Development of
Pedagogy &
Strategies

Limited Knowledge
of Student & of
Self

3 WHO ARE WE TEACHING?

Knowing Our Students as Learners

Several years ago a Dutch friend shared with us a story of his schooldays. It is a story of a young man's remarkable resilience, but also a story that underscores how important it is for teachers to come to know their students as learners.

Arthur was born in the Dutch East Indies, what is now Indonesia, and had just seen his 13th birthday when the Japanese invaded. For the duration of the war, Arthur, his parents and siblings were interned in a Japanese concentration camp in West Java. While Arthur and his family survived the ordeal, life in the camp was hard and brutal. There was chronic hunger; periodic out-breaks of deadly diseases; the cruelty of the guards and an ever-present atmosphere of fear and anxiety. As a young boy, Arthur was not insulated from the realities and horrors of a world at war.

Four years later, following the fall of Japan and the return of the Dutch to Indonesia, Arthur and his family together with thousands of other camp survivors were repatriated to the Netherlands where Arthur was promptly enrolled in a government school.

Given the amount of schooling that he had missed, Arthur was placed in a class with children three years younger than himself. The school authorities and the teacher perceived Arthur through the lens of his deficits. They only saw what he was lacking in basic academic skills. They only perceived what he couldn't do or what he was struggling with. There was no question that Arthur's basic skills in writing, reading and math were considerably behind his peers. But the school made no provision for the intellectual and emotional learning that Arthur had been engaged in during his time in the camps.

Arthur, who is now a retired oil engineer in his late seventies, recalls himself as an alienated and confused adolescent. "Because I was behind in my reading, the teacher treated me as she would a much younger child. She gave me the same books as the other younger students. No one seemed to understand or appreciate my experience. The other children? They were interested in movies and shopping and clothes. All of which I didn't know anything about. They were kind and friendly. I just couldn't understand them. There was nothing I could relate to. I felt as though I had been dropped into another planet." As a result, school simply didn't work for Arthur.

Unfortunately Arthur is not a historical anomaly. He has many more recent counterparts in our international schools. Bill recalls that in the mid 1980's a Ugandan diplomat stationed in Tanzania brought his thirteen year old daughter for an admissions interview at the international school in Dar es Salaam.

Christine-Apollo presented as an extremely shy and withdrawn girl. She appeared physically much younger than her chronological age. Her gaze was downcast and she steadfastly refused to make eye contact. Her facial expression was blank and her eyes, when she did raise them from the floor, were vacant. Having said that, she often moved suddenly, casting her gaze around the office, like a small animal on the outlook for predators. She was dressed in an ill-fitting, well-worn school uniform from a Ugandan government school – clearly a hand-me-down. The father explained that Christine-Apollo didn't speak English and that her schooling had been "interrupted".

As Bill probed deeper, a more complete picture began to emerge. Christine-Apollo not only didn't speak English, she also didn't speak Kiswahili. She communicated only in her tribal language. She was the daughter of the diplomat's third wife and had been brought up in a bush village in Northern Uganda. For the past four years, Christine-Apollo had been a nomadic refugee in her own country – moving from village to village hiding from the horrors and ravages of the civil war that raged during the years following the fall of Idi Admin.

As Christine-Apollo rose to leave Bill's office, she tripped and fell to her knees. Both Bill and her father jumped to help. Christine-Apollo was clearly mortified. Her father apologized.

"She is not usually so clumsy. It's one of the few times she has worn shoes."

The childhood experiences of Arthur and Christine-Apollo were obviously traumatic, and they illustrate clearly how a child's prior experience can have a profound effect upon their learning in school. But even children who don't have such traumas in their past bring with them to the classroom experiences, traits and learning preferences that profoundly affect their learning.

In the previous chapter, we presented a model illustrating the relationship that we perceive (Figure 1) between a teacher's knowledge of his or her students and the teacher's knowledge of the curriculum. We see the integration of this deep knowledge of the student as learner with a profound knowledge of the curriculum as essential to designing learning tasks that will fall within what Vygtosky called the child's "Zone of Proximal Development", that frontier between challenges that are too easy and therefore boring and challenges that are too complex for the student's readiness level and therefore are either simply meaningless or paralytically stressful.

The Zone of Proximal Development (ZPD) is the zone in which maximal student learning makes place. It is the teacher's challenge to identify this zone and pitch learning challenges within it. It is therefore essential that teachers come to know their students as learners.

Teachers have long known intuitively about the importance of knowing their students as learners. All we need to do to confirm this is to think back to our own childhood and recall a teacher who had a profoundly positive impact on our learning. The chances are very good that this teacher made a personal connection to us and came to know us as learners at a deeply meaningful level.

While the most effective teachers have appreciated intuitively the importance of knowing their students as learners, as a profession we have not set about systematically and rigorously to gather data, frame probing questions and develop hypotheses about our students as learners. To our knowledge, very few teacher training colleges explicitly teach the classroom skills of clinical observation.

In the past, the ways in which teachers have gone about coming to know their students were not systematic, nor were they particularly rigorous. For the most part, the data was collected in a haphazard manner – tidbits from essays or student journals, a hint from an example of student art work, a guess from an overheard conversation in the corridor, or a comment from a parent or last year's teacher. Teachers for the most part did not self-consciously set out with the goal of coming to know their students. In some cases, teachers did come to know students as learners and personal connections were forged. This was often when the personality of the student and teacher were compatible or when they shared a common interest (more often than not in the subject the teacher was teaching.) In other cases, the teacher ended the school year in June with little more knowledge about a certain student than she had the previous August. Coming to know one's students was an optional, haphazard and arbitrary business.

We believe that such days are over. The business of coming to know our students as learners is simply too important to leave to chance.

Our friend and colleague from UCLA, Barbara Keogh (1998) is fond of saying that a very significant number -- perhaps even most -- of the problems and issues that we perceive with student learning literally disappear when we engage in systematic and rigorous observation of our students. There is something about the act of deliberate observation that changes the ways in which we perceive; alters the nature of those perceptions and, as a result, actually reshapes our relationships with students.

We believe that we can address the challenge of coming to know our students by developing student learning profiles. Teachers develop learning profiles over time as they compile information about their students as learners in five critical areas. We have labeled these five areas: Biological Traits, Societal Influences, Social and Emotional Characteristics, Academic Achievement and Learning Preferences.

Reasons Why We Need to Develop Learning Profiles for Our Students

When we consider the diversity of the children who fill our classes as learners, it seems foolish to think we could treat them all as a single entity. Children, especially in our international schools, come to us with a variety of stories and histories, cultures, languages, likes and dislikes, learning styles, and intelligence preferences. No two aches or pains are alike, and no two family experiences are the same. As such, each child presents us with a different opportunity for learning.

Specialist teachers in elementary schools (music, art, PE etc.) and high school subject area teachers often see more than a hundred students each week. Those teachers can understandably ask: *"How is it possible for me to come to know all these students as learners within the limited time available in the school day?"*

It is a reasonable question. However, knowledge of one student as a learner is often applicable to other students. While it is a truism to say that each child is a unique learner, it is often more helpful to think that each child is a unique combination of common learning attributes. So, by coming to know one child as a learner, we are actually coming to know the learning attributes of many children. In other words, by coming to know what works in the classroom for one kinesthetic learner, we come to know what works for many kinesthetic learners.

Developing an in-depth understanding of the learner allows:

1. The teacher to more accurately identify the child's Zone of Proximal Development and mediate the upward movement of that ZPD.

2. The teacher to design challenging units of study so as to maximize access to the curriculum for all learners, but perhaps most importantly for children who learn differently.

3. The teacher to develop rapport and trust so that he/she is able to juxtapose cognitive discomfort with psychological safety. We know that all children (and adults) need to feel physically and psychologically safe in order to learn. The lower levels of Malsow's hierarchy of basic needs must be catered for. However, we also know that deep learning results from cognitive discomfort – when we confront a new idea that challenges our pre-existing mental models. By developing a deep knowledge of our students, we can create the psychologically safe classroom environment that will permit the intellectual discomfort that maximizes learning.

Perceptions of Childhood

Even before we approach the challenge of coming to know the individual learners in our classrooms, we need to explore the perceptions of childhood that we bring to that process. In other words, we need to understand what assumptions we have about childhood and children in general. We know two important things about assumptions. The first is that they exert a very powerful influence over our belief systems and behavior, and secondly, that most of them are held unconsciously. It is therefore particularly useful for teachers to bring to the conscious mind some of these assumptions about the young people we teach daily.

Our perceptions of childhood determine to a considerable degree how we actually interact with the children and young adults in our classes.

For this purpose, we have developed five possible lenses through which childhood can be perceived. These are obviously broad generalizations and we readily acknowledge that there are other lenses and that no one person is a pure type. However, it is sometimes useful to have such models or lens before us as we explore the process through which we construct our perceptions.

The Hobbesian Lens: Named after the 17th century British philosopher, Thomas Hobbes, this perspective views education as the process of preparing children to live in a civilized society. Human nature is understood to be profoundly influenced by selfishness. Through the Hobbesian Lens, the moral order of civilized society is something which must be explicitly taught to children. When viewed though this lens, children are seen as potential 'savages' with a leviathan residing within them that must be brought under control. Accordingly, one of the most basic purposes of education is to socialize and domesticate children. Childhood is thus a period in which children learn to control their selfish urges and to master their destructive emotions.

At its best, the Hobbesian perception emphases that young children should be taught social skills such as turn taking, sharing, empathy and how to delay gratification. We see the influence of the Hobbesian lens in many of our international school missions statements that include the goal of developing young people into "responsible world citizens."

When taken to an extreme, the Hobbesian perception of childhood can be dehumanizing and cruel. It characterized a great deal of education during the Victorian era and early twentieth century. Teacher control of the classroom was considered of paramount importance. Children were to be "seen and not heard." Compliance was the order of the day and corporal punishment was routine. The "rod" in Proverbs 24 ("He who spareth the rod, hateth his son") was clearly interpreted to be the ubiquitous Malacca cane that hung next to the teacher's desk, not the comforting "rod" of the 23rd Psalm. Students were primarily motivated through fear.

Freud's model of the conscious mind (Ego) as a battleground between the bestial, amoral and pleasure seeking Id and our ever-restraining Super-Ego (conscience), can be seen as a permutation of the Hobbesian lens. Young people need to acquire self-control.

We can even see the influence of the Hobbesian perspective in the Behaviorism of 1970's and 80's. Teachers were heavily influenced by B.F. Skinner's operant conditioning and student self-control was to be engineered through the use of positive and negative reinforcements.

One of the most eloquent representations of the Hobbesian Perception of childhood is presented in William Golding's classic novel. *The Lord of the Flies*, in which a group of English choir boys are stranded on a deserted island following the crash of the airplane. Unlike the resourceful, resilient and morally upstanding *Swiss Family Robinson* or the school boy chums of *Coral Island* (from whence Golding took his inspiration) Golding's choir boys descend into savagery and order is only restored at the end of the novel by the entrance of an adult authority presence.

The Rousseauian Lens: Named after the French philosopher Jean Jacques Rousseau, the Rousseauian Lens perceives children and childhood very differently. The child is seen as an embodiment of primordial innocence – Adam before the Fall – a well-spring of natural moral order. Rousseau perceived the innocence of childhood as being systematically corrupted by the pernicious influences of a competitive, cruel and controlling society. He perceived this corruption taking place in the traditional schooling of his age. He believed that evil was not a naturally occurring phenomenon, but rather a learned state. In his treatise on education, *Emile,* learning (as opposed to schooling) is presented as a natural and gentle process that taps into the child's pre-existing curiosity, creativity and motivation.

In literature, perhaps the most passionate expression of this romantic view of childhood is captured in the poetry of William Wordsworth. The child is perceived to embody a natural wisdom and is described as *"father to the man"*. There is an almost divine quality to childhood and the child is described as *"trailing clouds of glory"*.

One of the most controversial examples of a Rousseauian perception of childhood was a school founded originally in Germany but later moved to Great Britain. Developed by A.S. Neill, Summerhill School was a truly radical experiment in which there were no adult-determined rules, punishments or negative consequences for anti-social or disruptive behavior. The organization of the school, the schedule of classes and the actual curriculum were determined by the students themselves. Like Rousseau, Neill believed that children were inherently good and that if provided with freedom they would naturally gravitate towards responsible and constructive behavior. The difficulty with any enclave community, such as Summerhill, that derives its identity and *raison d'etre* from attacking a corrupt and cruel external society is that its graduates had an extremely difficult time re-integrating into the society they had come to despise.

The Confucian Lens: As globalization is increasingly recognized as a reality, particularly in our international schools, it is very useful for Western teachers to understand something of the Confucian world view and this particular lens into childhood. While the word "Confucian" has a historical link to China and the Far East, many of the attributes of the Confucian Perception of childhood can be found in traditional societies around the world.

Confucian values include an emphasis on the collective welfare of group as opposed to our more Western focus on individual autonomy. Confucian collectivism is seen in the subjugation of individual needs and desires to the furtherance of the larger group. This might be manifest in profound loyalty to one's family, one's village or tribe, one's employer or even as an expression of nationalistic patriotism. Confucian societies are hierarchical with the elders occupying a revered position of respect. Ancestors and the accomplishments of past generations are greatly honored and stability and social cohesiveness are highly valued. Children are expected to honor and respect their parents and teachers. One of the greatest compliments that the young can pay to a highly skilled, elder craftsman or artist is to imitate the master. This focus on imitative learning often leads in Western oriented international schools to confusion about plagiarism.

In Confucian cultures, learning is perceived to be the transfer of the knowledge and values of the previous generation to the younger generation so that the collective good and stability of the society is preserved. Children are not expected to challenge ideas or think critically or independently. Such thought might prove disruptive to the common order.

What we are referring to as the Confucian Lens extends into many traditional, non-Asian societies. Recall Frank, the Tanzanian scholarship student at the International School of Tanganyika who spoke eloquently in his Valedictory Address about the enormous challenge he had encountered in his move from a traditional Tanzania school into the International Baccalaureate Diploma program. The challenge was not in the complexity of the content material, but rather in the expectation that he was to think for himself, to challenge ideas, to analyze and evaluate theories and concepts.

Confucian and other traditional societies have historically placed a greater value on boys than girls. We see this played out in the disparity in literacy rates in Asia, the Middle East and Africa and it makes for a significant challenge for educators in international schools. A few years ago a poster in the UNICEF office in Dar es Salaam read: *There is greater probability that an 18 year old African girl will have acquired AIDS than the ability to read and write.*"

In Confucian and other traditional societies, Western syllogistic thinking (if X, then not Y) is often replaced with an Eastern search for a "middle way". Richard Nisbett (2003) in his book *The Geography of Thought,* suggests that it is no accident that Algebra developed in Ancient Greece and Geometry in China. He theorizes that thousands of years of cultural values and behaviors have actually affected the way in which Eastern and Western students think. Western "either/or" thinking lends itself to the intellectual development of disciplines such as algebra, the experimental sciences, and precedent-based jurisprudence. On the other hand, Eastern thinking tends to be more expansive (as opposed to reductionist), more inclusive of both the foreground and the background, and more focused on social cohesion and stability.

Respect for teachers on the part of a child brought up in a Confucian or traditional culture can be manifested by what may appear to be quiet passivity. This often provides Western teachers with a challenge, particularly in the area of English as a second language where active engagement with the content is perceived to be a key to learning.

A sign in a Buddhist temple in Japan reads *"Speak only if you can improve on the silence."*

The Malthusian Lens: Thomas Malthus was the 19th century British economist who postulated that the supply of food increases arithmetically, whereas the population grows geometrically. Through the Malthusian Lens, children are perceived as either economic assets or liabilities. We see children viewed as economic assets in developing economies that are reliant on agriculture. In subsistence-farming communities, children are frequently viewed as critically important workers upon which the actual survival of the family may depend. Birth rates often reflect this perception. This is also borne out in the negative population growth rates in some affluent Western counties.

We even see the legacy of the Malthusian Lens in Western societies where our school calendar still contains a long summer vacation when a century or so ago the children were needed to work in the fields. In fact, much of the 20th century "industrialized" model of American education (the influence of Frederick Winslow Taylor and his Scientific Management) can be interpreted through a Malthusian Lens. In a century ushered in by Henry Ford's assembly lines, it was understood that most children would grow up to work in repetitive and mindless jobs in factories. What better training than the repetitive and boring rote learning of the mid 20th century school house!

The Malthusian perception of childhood manifests itself regularly in our school when we hear parents and board members talking about how students need to be prepared for the "real world of work" or when educational success is reduced to acceptance at a prestigious university.

The Deweyan Lens: At about the same time as Henry Ford and others were industrializing America, John Dewey was at Columbia and the University of Chicago, rethinking the 19th century perception of children and childhood. He radically challenged a number of cherished beliefs. First of all, he challenged the notion that childhood was somehow a "preparation for life". Dewey believed that childhood was not preparation for anything, but an essential part of life. When childhood is perceived as "preparation", it is construed as a means to an end, and it is seen as having little, if any, intrinsic value. It is a stage that one needs to grow out of as soon as possible. A natural consequence of this perception is that childhood is not respected (how many times have we heard children admonished not to act "like a child"?) and the period of time a child spends in school becomes a "quarantine" of sorts.

Dewey also challenged the prevailing notion that children were simply empty vessels that teachers would fill with facts and knowledge. He understood that for children (and adults) learning is fostered in active engagement with the concepts to be learned. Children need to work with ideas, to explore concepts and to apply them. It was Dewey and others in the Progressive Movement in education who set the stage for constructivism, active engagement, cooperative learning and many of the other elements that we frequently see in schools today. It was also Dewey who, like Jefferson before him, saw the critical link between high quality, universal education and the maintenance of democracy and freedom.

We readily concede that these "lenses" are generalizations and that there are numerous other ways in which children and childhood can be perceived. We also recognize that each of these perceptions have positive values embedded within them, but are also subject to abuse – particularly when one "lens" is embraced at the expense of the others. Accordingly, we believe that it is critically important for teachers to "uncover" their own perceptions of childhood as they will almost certainly color and shape the way in which we come to know individual students as learners.

Five Dimensions of Knowing Our Students

We suggest that there are five important dimensions that can come to comprise a meaningful learning profile of our students. These include: Biological Traits, Societal Influences, Socio-Economic Factors, Academic Achievement and Learning Preferences.

Biological Traits: *What can we learn about a child biologically, that will allow maximum accuracy in our interpretations of that child's behavior?*

Knowledge of a child's biological learning traits can help a teacher to accurately interpret classroom behavior. For example, it is all too easy for us to fall back on the labels of "laziness", "defiance" or "willfulness" when in fact there may be a biological cause for the child's behavior. The types of biological information that we might gather can include the child's medical history, family history, abilities (particularly those outside of school), disabilities and developmental progress.

We are learning now that even gender (which in the past some people regarded largely as a socio-cultural influence on learning) is a biological trait in that there are some distinctive physiological differences in the male and female brains (King & Gurian, 2006)[2].

Biological parameters for learning are defined to some degree; however they may be malleable with appropriate context and support. For example, it is certainly not uncommon now to see teachers wearing wireless clip-on microphones that are connected to a hearing device for a hearing impaired child. We also know that child with Attention Deficit Disorder (ADD), Autism and Aspergers' Syndrome are educable and our knowledge of these biological traits allows us to construct meaningful and worthy learning objectives for these children.

> *We cannot direct the wind, but we can adjust our sails.* ~Bertha Calloway

Societal Influences: *What do we need to be aware of (particularly within ourselves as teachers), in order to be sensitive to societal influences upon the child, such as economic status, race, culture and gender?*

A number of years ago, Bill was interviewing prospective IB scholarship students at the International School of Tanganyika in Tanzania. One student had already completed the first year of Sixth Form (equivalent to the first year of the IB Diploma). Bill was curious as to why the student had "dropped out" and he asked about the circumstances. The student replied that the food at the school was bad. Bill was incredulous. Tanzania was (and is) a desperately poor African country in which less than five percent of the population was privileged enough to get to Sixth Form education, and here was a student who turned his back on such a tremendous opportunity because he didn't like the food in the school canteen!

Following the interview, Bill commented to a Tanzanian colleague that he thought the interviewee immature and spoiled. The Tanzanian colleague gently reminded Bill that the student's previous school had been a boarding institution in a region of the country devastated by famine. The fact was that the school probably didn't have *any* food for its students.

---

[2] Please see Chapter 10: Differentiating for Girls and Boys for a more detailed discussion on the physiological differences in the brains of girls and boys and the implications for the classroom.

Societal influences play a significant role in learning. Research in social psychology (Aronson, 1999) confirms what most of us have known intuitively – that life is much easier for attractive, wealthy individuals who belong to the dominant culture and race. As a generalization, this is also true for students in schools – school success is easier if you are physically attractive, affluent and *belong to the dominant culture or race.*

Richard Nisbett proposes that students from different cultures actually think and to some degree learn differently. People hold the beliefs they do because of the way they think and they think the way they do because of the societies they live in. Historically, the West has had a focus on linear logic, on syllogism, on knowing through exclusion and reductionist thinking. This has been fertile intellectual ground for the development of disciplines such as the experimental sciences. It has also lead us in the West to be intolerant of ambiguity and prone to the creation of false dichotomies (e.g. either you hate communism or you are un-American).

In the East, on the other hand, the focus has been more on holistic thinking, understanding the larger or broader situation. There has been an emphasis on the "big picture", taking in the background as well as the foreground, and in seeking out multiple causes.

Nisbett (2003) relates the story of Heejung Kim, a Korean graduate student of psychology at Stanford University. Kim was exasperated by the constant demands of her professors that she speak up in class. Failure to speak up in class, her professors told her, might indicate a lack of understanding on her part. Failure to speak up in class limited the interaction in the class and therefore limited the learning of Kim and her classmates.

Kim wasn't buying it. She felt that she and her fellow Asian and Asian American students would not benefit from speaking because their fundamental way of understanding the material was not verbal. For Kim, this was the essence of the difference between Western analytic thought and Eastern holistic thought.

Kim tested her theory by having people speak out loud while solving various complex problems. This had no effect on the Western European students. They were just as good or just as bad at solving the problems regardless of whether they were speaking or silent. However, speaking out loud had a very deleterious effect on the problem solving performance of the Asian and Asian American students.

While we are not suggesting that it is unimportant for Asian students to participate in class discussions, we are suggesting that we who teach in international schools are wise to remember the words of Samuel Huntington (1996) in his book *The Clash of Civilizations and the Remaking of World Order*: "In the emerging world of ethnic conflict and civilization clash, Western belief in the universality of Western culture suffers three problems: it is false, it is immoral, and it is dangerous (p. 310)."

Social/Emotional Characteristics: *How can we recognize, honor and integrate a child's social/emotional characteristics in order to provide the child with the psychological safety that accompanies a sense of belonging and membership within the class?*

There are numerous social/emotional characteristics that impact learning, among them self-concept, temperament, emotional intelligence, ability and/or willingness to trust, motivation, status within peer group, interpersonal skills, culture (dominant culture vs. minority culture), previous school experience (familiarization with the culture of international school, etc.).

When Ochan was a child, many of her teachers operated on the clear understanding that the classroom was an academic setting and that student emotions were best "left at the door". We know now that such a notion is impossible. We know that it is impossible to separate our cognitive and emotional lives (Damasio, 1994; Pert, 1997; Ledoux, 1996). When a child has experienced an intense emotional experience, we must expect that to influence the youngster's ability to attend in school. These experiences can range from the grief of the departure of a friend (all too common in our very transient school communities), to the anxiety of a family member's illness to the terror of witnessing a violent altercation between Mom and Dad.

A child's academic and peer status can also have a profound impact upon his or her learning. In a typical classroom even in primary school, students rank themselves and each other in terms of how good a student each child is perceived to be (academic status) and attractiveness and popularity (peer status). Elizabeth Cohen (1998) writes "low status members (of the class) talk less than others, when they do speak up, no one takes their ideas seriously and other members may not even listen to what they have to say. Low status group members have trouble getting their hands on materials for the group task; they may even be physically excluded." Cohen has suggested that teacher awareness of student status within the classroom is a starting point to making cooperative learning groups equitable. By assigning group work that require multiple intellectual abilities (no one person will have all the abilities – e.g. art, role play, music), the teacher creates a learning situation that relies on group interdependence. The teacher can then deliberately search out opportunities to assign competence to low status students. "If the teacher publicly evaluates a low-status student as being strong on a particular multiple ability, that student will tend to believe the evaluation, as will the other students who overhear the evaluation." According to Cohen the effective assignment of competence must have three essential features: 1. the evaluation must be public, 2. it must be genuine and true, and 3. the skills of abilities of the low-status student must be made relevant to the group task. Cohen is clear that assigning competence to low-status students is not just about increasing or enhancing self-esteem. *It is also about modifying the expectations that other students have for the low-status student.* There is, however, a caution. The low status student knows what he or she has done, so a false or disingenuous assignment of competence will do more harm than good (Cohen, 1994; 1998).

We have found that a very simple way to assign competence to a low-status student is through the use of paraphrasing. Paraphrasing sends three important messages: I am trying to understand what you're saying. I value your ideas. I care about you as a person. These are messages that every student, but particularly a low status student, needs to hear.

Academic Performance: *How does a student's academic performance help us to ascertain the child's zone of proximal development, so that we can create lessons that are appropriately challenging?*

When teachers talk about academic performance, we often use the term "ability". We talk about the challenges of teaching to a mixed *ability* class or the delight of watching a high *ability* student go beyond our expectations. Given how frequently teachers use the term "ability", it was a surprise to Bill that Tomlinson & McTighe (2006) in their book *Integrating Differentiated Instruction and Understanding by Design* almost completely avoid the use of the word. Instead of the term "ability grouping" Tomlinson & McTighe use the phrase "readiness grouping".

Why would two bestselling authors deliberately use a phrase that would be unfamiliar to many of their readership?

Bill paused to examine his assumptions about the word "ability". What does ability really mean? Is it synonymous with the student's present level of academic performance? Or does ability imply natural aptitude and talent? Is there something about one's ability in a specific subject area discipline that suggests potential for future success or failure? How malleable is ability? What is the relationship between ability and potential? What is the relationship between a teacher's perception of ability and his or her expectations for a given student? What is the relationship between teachers' expectations and student performance?[3]

---

[3] Please see the description of the so-called "Pygmalion Study" later this chapter.

Another critical question that we need to confront is how well equipped are teachers to evaluate a student's ability? We suspect that teachers are much better able to judge a student's *readiness* for the next learning challenge than they are a student's *ability*. We would further suggest that *readiness* is the key concept in coming to know a student's academic achievement.

The importance of teachers evaluating student readiness is supported by a substantial body of research. Longitudinal research ((Hunt, 1971) establish two features of effective differentiated instruction. First of all, more effective learning takes places when the amount of task structure by the teacher matches a student's level of development. In other words, students who are functioning at a fairly concrete level of thought might require very explicit and sequential task instructions; whereas students who are thinking more abstractly might benefit from task instructions that are deliberately open-ended and 'fuzzy'. Secondly, there is a strong relationship between student achievement and a teacher's ability to diagnose student skill level and prescribe appropriate tasks (Fisher et al., 1980).

In a study of 250 classrooms, Fisher and his research team found that in classrooms where individual students worked at high success levels, the students felt better about themselves and about the subject they were studying, and learned more. Fisher went on to suggest that a success rate of about 80% is probably optimal for intellectual growth.

The last sentence is worth dwelling on for a moment. This suggests that students who are achieving at success rate significantly over 80% are probably being under-challenged. Put another way, student achievement is not likely to improve when teachers ask students to practice what they already know.

Csikszentmihalyi (1993) and others in a five year research study also found an important correlation between student readiness and student motivation. The researchers studied over 200 teenagers, pursuing the question of why some adolescents become committed to the development of their talents while others become disengaged and neglect talent development. The study findings show a strong correlation between the complexity of the tasks developed by the teachers for the students and the individual skill level of a student. Students whose skills were under-challenged demonstrated low involvement in learning activities and a decrease in concentration. On the other hand, students whose skills were inadequate for the level of challenge demonstrated both low achievement and declining self-worth. *Most destructive was the combination of low challenge task and low student sense of exercising skills* (emphasis ours). The researchers write: "This situation, which accounted for almost a third of the observed classroom activities, consisted mostly of reading, watching films and listening to lectures (p. 186). According to these researchers, teachers who are effective in developing student talents craft challenges commensurate with student readiness levels.

Typically, teachers differentiate instruction for student readiness levels by addressing content, product and process in four ways (Tomlinson & Allen, 2000):

- By varying the degree of dependence or independence of the learning activity (e.g. task complexity);
- By modifying the task clarity or "fuzziness";
- By varying the degree of structure or open-endedness of the learning task;
- Or, by teaching or re-teaching particular skills in small groups as students need them.

It is clear that teacher adjustments that accommodate student academic readiness enhance *both* student achievement and student attitudes about learning.

Learner Preferences: *How can we use various learner preferences to maximize access to the curriculum for all learners?*

The assumption here is that it is possible to identify individual student learning preferences and to modify our instructional practices to create a match with those preferences. As a result, the student will improve his or her ability to learn. We think of Learning Preferences in four broad categories: Intelligence Preferences, Learning Styles, Production Styles and Student Interests.

 Intelligence Preferences: Historically, schools have tended to recognize and reward two types of intelligence: linguistic and mathematical/logical. We now know that intelligence is not monolithic, but is more like a Periodic Table. Gardner has identified seven specific types of intelligence. We also know that intelligence is malleable and is subject to a wide variety of influences. Many teachers find Gardner's model of intelligence fascinating intellectually, but cumbersome when they come to actually attempt to apply it to classroom instruction. Sternberg (1985) from Yale University has also developed a model of multiple intelligences that teachers may find easier to apply in the classroom. Sternberg proposes three intelligence preferences. All people have and use all three intelligences but vary in particular preferences and in combination of preferences. These preferences may be shaped by brain "wiring", culture, gender, and personal experiences. It makes sense for teachers to support students as they develop their intelligence strengths while providing opportunities to expand their non-preferred areas. Sternberg's three intelligence preferences include:

- o **Analytical Intelligence:** This is the intelligence most often recognized and rewarded in schools. Students with strengths in this area learn well with traditional school tasks such as organizing information, perceiving cause and effect, logical analysis, note taking and predicting implications.

- o **Practical Intelligence:** Students with strengths in this area learn well when they see connections with the real world outside the classroom. They need to see how things work in the real world and how ideas and skills can be used to solve problems. They learn better by using ideas rather than just by learning them. Students with a preference for practical intelligence need relevance. They need to solve problems in a meaningful context.

- o **Creative Intelligence:** Students with a preference for Creative Intelligence tend to come at ideas and problems in fresh and sometimes surprising ways. They often prefer to experiment with ideas rather than "work" like everyone else. They include your divergent thinkers.

Sternberg's work is well researched with students from primary school through university. His findings point to important achievement gains for students when teachers permit students to explore ideas utilizing their preferred intelligences, encourage students to express their learning in their preferred intelligence and teach regularly in all three modes. Teachers who employ all three modes on a regular basis deepen student understanding and enhance retention.

Learning Styles: Often teachers will use the phrase "learning style" to indicate a modality preference (e.g. visual, auditory, kinesthetic or tactual). We know from research and experience that individual learners do have modality preferences. Each of us uses all four modalities when we learn, but in different combinations of preference. Generally, the largest proportion of the population tends to be visual learners (these are students who greatly benefit from a graphic display of the material to be learned.) The next largest groups are those which include those who prefer kinesthetic and tactual learning experiences. Interestingly, research out of the United Kingdom is suggesting that a very significant portion of boys with learning disabilities have a preference for kinesthetic learning (so asking them to sit still all day long seems counterproductive). The smallest proportion of the population tends to prefer auditory learning. (This is significant given our proclivity as teachers to fill the classroom with teacher-talk).

Beyond modality preference, Rita and Kenneth Dunn (1993) have spent almost thirty years developing a learning styles model that incorporates stimuli from the environment, emotions, sociological groups, physiology and psychology. The Dunn and Dunn model involves two main types of activities: (1) the identification of individual learning styles, and 2. the planning and implementation of instruction to accommodate individual students' learning strengths. Allowing students to use their preferred learning styles can include allowing them to choose when and where they will study (time of day, soft or hard furniture, in absolute silence or with background music); whether they will work by themselves, with a partner or on a team; or whether a learning activity is primarily visual, auditory, kinesthetic or tactual.

Figure 1

POSSIBLE OBSTACLES TO LEARNING

Everyone learns through all four sensory styles. However, sensory preferences can create possible obstacles to learning.

Kinesthetic Learners: Possible Obstacles to Learning	Tactual/Emotive Learners: Possible Obstacles to Learning
• Persisting with an activity for long periods • Developing neat handwriting • Expressing emotions without physical movement • Developing effective interpersonal skills • Achieving standardized spelling • Recollection of visual or auditory input • Listening to auditory stimuli, such as lectures • Sitting still • Interpreting nonverbal cues	• Learning when s/he perceives an absence of respect • Engaging when there is little or no opportunity to touch, feel or manipulate things • Working in groups in which student perceives him/herself to be disliked or dismissed • Performing/achieving without explicit teacher approval
Auditory Learners: **Possible Obstacles to Learning**	**Visual Learners:** **Possible Obstacles to Learning**
• Following written directions • Reading silently for long periods of time • Learning in an environment with distracting background noises or long periods of enforced silence • Taking tests with only written directions • Reading quickly and not being allowed to vocalize	• Working in classrooms with distracting background noise • Being compelled to listen to lectures without visuals • Working in sterile or uninteresting classroom environments • Working in an environment with too much visual stimulation

Carolyn Brunner, the Director of the International Center for Learning Styles at SUNY Buffalo sets out three non-negotiable rules for students using their preferred learning styles: 1) the student's grades must either remain the same (if they are already acceptable or good) or improve; 2) the student's behavior must remain constructive and appropriate (if it is already so) or it must improve; and 3) the student's use of his or her preferred learning style must not interfere with anyone else's learning.

Figure 2

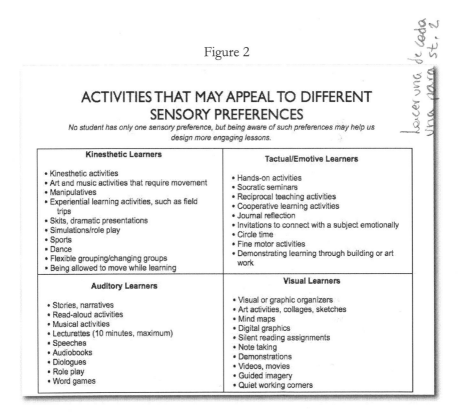

ACTIVITIES THAT MAY APPEAL TO DIFFERENT SENSORY PREFERENCES

No student has only one sensory preference, but being aware of such preferences may help us design more engaging lessons.

Kinesthetic Learners	Tactual/Emotive Learners
• Kinesthetic activities • Art and music activities that require movement • Manipulatives • Experiential learning activities, such as field trips • Skits, dramatic presentations • Simulations/role play • Sports • Dance • Flexible grouping/changing groups • Being allowed to move while learning	• Hands-on activities • Socratic seminars • Reciprocal teaching activities • Cooperative learning activities • Journal reflection • Invitations to connect with a subject emotionally • Circle time • Fine motor activities • Demonstrating learning through building or art work

Auditory Learners	Visual Learners
• Stories, narratives • Read-aloud activities • Musical activities • Lecturettes (10 minutes, maximum) • Speeches • Audiobooks • Diologues • Role play • Word games	• Visual or graphic organizers • Art activities, collages, sketches • Mind maps • Digital graphics • Silent reading assignments • Note taking • Demonstrations • Videos, movies • Guided imagery • Quiet working corners

 Production Styles: Allied closely with learning styles, production styles refer to the preferred mode in which the student expresses his or her learning. For example, an easily manageable model of production styles might ask the students to self-select into four different groups: the Writers, Performers, Builders and Artists. The students would then be given a learning task or activity that would correspond to their preferred mode of expressing their learning. Several years ago, Susan Baum and Hank Nicols led a differentiation workshop at the International School of Kuala Lumpur in Malaysia. They asked the entire teaching staff to take a quick individual inventory of their preferred and non-preferred production styles. The teachers were then grouped together in their *least preferred* production style and given the following simulation task: *Design a product that shows the social and economic structure of a medieval European town, illustrating the relationships between economic classes and different forms of power and authority.*

And so the reluctant writers were asked to write, the shy performers to perform and the clumsy builders to build. After about thirty minutes each group made a brief presentation. As can be easily predicted, the products were awkward, concrete, unrefined and lacking precision. The participants were also noticeably frustrated.

Susan and Hank then regrouped the teachers into their *most preferred* production style and assigned the same learning task. The change in the room's energy and enthusiasm was palpable. Thirty minutes later, the four groups presented their products with relish and pride. There was a richness and creativity and a depth of understanding that had been entirely absent in the previous products.

Had these teachers reached a greater understanding of medieval Europe in the previous half an hour? We suspect not. We suggest that there is a positive correlation between the complexity and sophistication of understanding and learning that a student can demonstrate and the degree to which he or she is permitted to use a preferred production style. We know that the anxiety and stress of being compelled to work in one's least preferred production style can actually serve as an obstacle to cognition.

If we as teachers focus on only one production style (for example, writing) we may be artificially limiting students to demonstrations of superficial understanding and knowledge. The medium can significantly affect the message.

Another significant learning that emerged from Susan and Hank's workshop was that teachers tend to be profoundly suspicious of their own *least preferred* production style. We heard a number of teachers express concern that it was simply not possible to demonstrate the depth of understanding in building, for example, that you could in writing an essay. Another teacher dismissed a visual representation of knowledge as a "soft option". However, when evaluated objectively against a precise rubric each of these production styles can yield products that are rich in conceptual understanding. We, as teachers, need to be aware of our own learning prejudices.

A caution: the choice of production style must match the teacher's learning objective. The social and economic structure of a medieval city can be illustrated in numerous different ways. However, if the teacher's objective is to have the student learn how to write a five paragraph essay, it would make little sense to allow the student to do other than write. The teacher might use a variety of production styles in the pre-writing activities, but each and every student would be required to write.

Student Interests: Considerable research has been done in the area of student interests and choice which indicates a strong correlation between the degree of student interest and levels of motivation, achievement, productivity and long term commitment (Amabile, 1983; Torrance, 1995). Collins & Amabile (1999) write: "The freedom to choose what to work on allows individuals to seek out questions that they are highly intrinsically motivated to pursue. This high level of intrinsic interest will lay the groundwork for creative achievement. Teachers may incorporate this approach into the classroom by allowing students to choose their own topics for individual or group projects (in Tomlinson & Allan, 2000)."

Csikszentmihalyi (1993) and others have also found that student interest was as critical to talent development as was the match between task complexity and student readiness for the task. Another important research finding was that students who were interested in what they were learning were motivated to pursue learning experiences of ever-increasing complexity and difficulty. There is also a significant correlation between student interest in the learning content and his or her *willingness to persevere in learning tasks that are momentarily not interesting.*

Another important correlation to emerge from the research on student interest and choice is that students who are engaged in work which interested them were overwhelmingly more able to see connections between their present work in school and their future academic or career goals. These connections form the foundation of commitment to future learning and foster self-directness.

> *The best learning environment is like a good cafeteria. It not only affords the essential staples but offers a large variety of choices to satisfy individual tastes. This allows children to discover their natural interests, proclivities and special talents.* ~A. Jensen, 1998

There are two basic categories of student interest and in each case the teacher's role is slightly different. The first case is pre-existing student interest, those areas of enthusiasm which the child or young adult brings to the classroom ready made (for example: antique cars, fishing, folk music, social justice, or community service). The teacher's role in this case is to search out the interest and find connections to the learning experience of the classroom. The second category includes the interests and passions that are mediated by the teacher. The teacher supports the student in finding connections between the work of the classroom and the child's "real life". The teacher mediates relevance and the students perceive the interdependence and interconnection of knowledge. This can be facilitated through authentic performance assessments. These connections provide for what Geoffrey and Renate Caine (1997) call moments of "hot cognition" (the visceral thrill of learning) that form the foundation of a life long love of learning.

Some Ways in Which We Can Come to Know Our Students as Learners

Most of us have not been trained in clinical observation. However, the fundamentals are not complex and the benefits of systematic and rigorous observation of students in the classroom can be truly remarkable. Ochan learned a very efficient way of using Clinical Observation from a first grade teacher at the International School of Tanganyika. Called "Post It Observations", the teacher records brief observation notes on specific children on sticky notes. In the elementary school the observations can be categorized into the various learning domains that the teacher is working on (e.g. fine motor skills, group work collaboration, sight word vocabulary, etc.). The "Post It Observations" in the secondary school can be categorized with regard to the teacher's learning objectives or grade level benchmarks. All the observation notes should reflect a time of day and should be dated. In this way, over time the teacher can monitor progress and celebrate successes. "Post It Observations" are also extremely useful data when teachers come to writing report cards or planning for parent conferences.

Another way to come to know a student deeply as a learner is to engage in a structured reflecting conversation about that student with a coaching colleague. Here we would highly recommend the work of Art Costa and Robert Garmston in Cognitive Coaching^{sm}(2002) in which the coach practices the skills of pausing, paraphrasing and probing (and withholds evaluation, advice and solutions). Please see Figure 4 on the following page which outlines a possible coaching map for coming to know a student deeply as a learner. Following such a coaching conversation, it is often helpful for the colleague to record his or her thoughts in writing. We suggest this because thoughts that are not recorded in writing remain in the ether. They are not editable. With the commitment to writing comes precision in both language and thought. We find the Student Analysis Instrument as illustrated in Figure 5 is often useful to teachers.

Figure 3

SOME CONSIDERATIONS FOR THE CLINICAL OBSERVATION OF STUDENTS

Student

Internal Influences	Sample Questions
Temperament & Style	How does s/he respond to different kinds of stimuli? What is his/her preferred way of learning?
Attention & Learning	What does s/he pay attention to, and for how long? Is there a learning disability? ADHD? Is the child a highly talented learner?
External Influences	Sample Questions
Background History	What is the family constellation; what are the circumstances of the child? Prior school history? Is the child a second language learner? Other languages?
Interactions & Transactions	How does s/he interact with adults and peers? How is s/he accessing and managing curriculum and instruction? How does s/he respond to environmental influences/distractions?

Consider

	Sample Questions
Curricular Area	In which curricular area is the observation taking place? Is the behavior the same in other classes?
Time of Day	Morning? Afternoon? After a recess break or lunch?
Environmental Factors	What are some of the influences of the grouping in which the child is working? What other environmental factors might be considered? (e.g. lighting, noise, temperature furniture etc.) What is the class climate?
Teacher	What is the teacher's instructional style, and how does it influence this student's behavior? What is the class teacher's relationship with the student?

Observation Pattern

1. Suspend Judgment: Identify existing conclusions about the student; suspend judgment to enable separation of perceptions from observable data.
2. Collect Data: Decide on recording style(s) and times; collect data.
3. Frame Questions: Look for patterns and connections; develop questions.
4. Look for Covariation of Data:

Observation Pattern, cont'd

- **Consistency:** Does the student always behave in this manner in other situations and at other times?
- **Consensus:** Do other students behave in the same way in the same situation?
- **Distinctiveness of Action:** Is s/he the only one to behave in this manner?

5. Consider All Factors:
- Student internal and external influences
- Environmental factors, including the teacher/instructional style
- Curricular area

6. Develop, Test Hypotheses

Figure 4

A Coaching Map: Knowing Your Students

✓ express empathy, reflect content, paraphrase for understanding

✓ probe for specificity about child's interests, strengths (What does s/he like to do? When have you seen him at his best? In what media have you seen her produce her best?)

✓ summarize child's strengths

✓ construct new learnings (what learnings do you want to take into future situations?)

✓ commit to application (So how might you apply your new learning?)

✓ reflect on the process (How has this conversation supported your learning?)

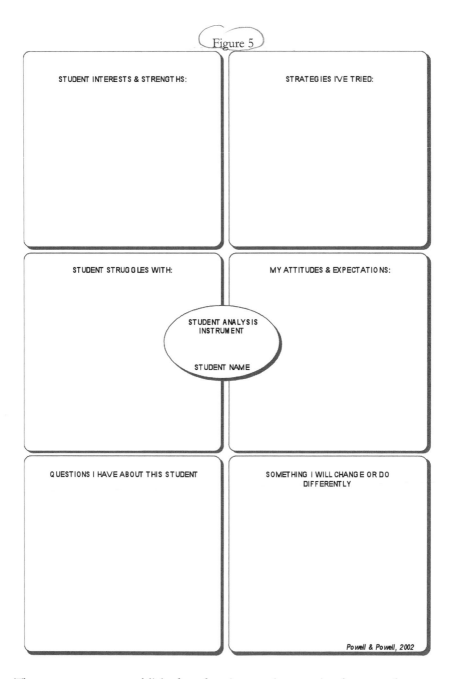

Figure 5

There are numerous published student interest inventories that a teacher can use to get a quick "read" on the areas of interest represented in a classroom.

These are particularly useful at the start of a new school year when a teacher may be faced with the daunting task of coming to know a relatively large number of new learners. One of the most student-friendly interest inventories that we know of is the Interest-A-Lyzer written by Joseph Renzulli (1997) out of the University of Connecticut. The Interest-A-Lyzer comes in versions specifically designed for primary, intermediate (middle school) and secondary (high school).

Conclusion

In closing this chapter, we would invite you to think back to the teacher you identified at the start of the chapter as having made an important positive difference to your learning. We would like to suggest that this teacher intuitively made a personal connection across two or three of these dimensions of knowing you as a learner. You are probably not the same person today that you would have been if you had not been taught by this individual. Such is the power of coming to know our students as learners.

While the goal of coming to know our students as learners is to support the teacher in designing and planning learning experiences that will provide an invitation to learning for all students and maximize access to the curriculum, there is another equally important objective. This is to support the student in coming to know him or herself as a learner. This is the gift of a lifetime. For as we come to know ourselves as learners, we can take control of the circumstances and influences under which we learn most effectively and efficiently.

4 KNOWING OURSELVES – THE STUDENT PERSPECTIVE[4]

At a recent workshop presentation, teacher participants were asked to close their eyes and to recall a particularly successful lesson that they had observed. The participants were then asked to write on a 3" x 5" card the source of their recollection. Not surprisingly, a large number of the teachers indicated that their recollection was from their own childhood. Some recalled instruction from a university professor. What did surprise us was how few of the teacher participants indicated an observation of outstanding instruction from a colleague. This absence made us ponder what maybe the greatest hubris of our profession: the fact that a remarkable number of teachers do not have recent models of teaching excellence to draw upon.

For decades educational researchers have bemoaned the privacy that has beset our craft as teachers. While collaboration has become a near universal goal of forward-looking schools, the sad truth is that most teachers continue to practice their craft in a large degree of isolation from each other. How then, in the absence of recent models of pedagogical excellence, can teachers strive to improve their craft? As we were reflecting on this question, we recalled a remarkable piece of research conducted by Rudduck, Day and Wallace (1996) and a different perspective on the question emerged.

Jean Rudduck and her colleagues examined student views of schooling and school improvement initiatives. They interviewed more than 800 secondary school students in the United Kingdom and looked for common responses to the question: *What are the characteristics of teachers who are most likely to increase student commitment to learning?* They identified 10 features of teacher behaviors and attitudes that students frequently associated with increased learning. Interestingly enough, it would appear that what the students knew intuitively about the effective classroom has been to a large extent borne out in recent

---

[4] Originally published as 'Seeing Ourselves: The Student Perspective,' in *International Schools Journal,* November, 2003.

research regarding how the brain works, how emotions are integral to cognition, and how differentiated instruction serves a crucial purpose in meeting the needs of diverse learners.

The students interviewed by Rudduck *et. al.* identified the teachers most likely to increase student commitment to learning are those who:

- enjoy teaching the subject;
- enjoy teaching students;
- make lessons interesting and link them to life outside school;
- will have a laugh but know how to keep order;
- are fair;
- are easy for students to talk to;
- don't shout;
- don't go on about things (*eg.* how much better the other classes are, or how much better an older brother or sister was);
- explain things and go through things students don't understand without making them feel small; and
- don't give up on students.

Let us spend a few moments looking at each of these attributes in turn.

Enjoy teaching the subject: It is a cliché to say that enthusiasm for one's subject or content material is contagious, but it is true nevertheless. A passionate interest on the part of the teacher for his or her subject is almost impossible to resist. This is a product of a deep knowledge of the curriculum (Kusuma-Powell & Powell, 2004) and a belief that the content will have an enduring importance for students to learn (Wiggins & McTighe, 1987). The specific content, however, is almost less important than the teacher's passion. It could be art, music, math, or history. What is critical is the enthusiasm. Take, for example, the remarkable popularity of Lynne Truss's (2003) bestseller: *Eats, Shoots and Leaves* in which the author transforms the inherently dry subject of punctuation into a delightful *tour de force* by virtue of her playful fanaticism.

Enjoy teaching students: Teachers most likely to engage students in active learning are those who authentically enjoy and value the company of young people. They make a deliberate and concerted effort to come to know students, both as social entities and as unique learners (Kusuma-Powell & Powell, 2004). These teachers understand that perceptions and emotions are integral to learning (Caine & Caine, 1997; LeDoux, 1996). Their classrooms are characterized by structure and purpose but also with a degree of playfulness. The climate is supportive and encourages risk taking. These teachers understand that students do not leave their emotions at the classroom door.

Several years ago, a high school aged girl was transferred from a boarding school in the United Kingdom to an international school overseas where her parents were living. The transfer was not Martha's choice and she arrived at her new school angry and sullen. For several months, she remained alienated from both classmates and teachers, with many of her teachers commenting on her negative attitude. But gradually, we began to see engagement in academic work and extra-curricular activities and greater achievement motivation. On closer inspection, Martha's integration into the life of the school began in her IB Theory of Knowledge class. The intellectual playfulness of her TOK teacher was irresistible to Martha. It was clear to the entire school community that this teacher thoroughly enjoyed being with students, and as a result, Martha began to as well.

Make lessons interesting and link them to life outside school: One of the cornerstones of constructivist learning theory is the teacher's mediation of relevance (Brooks & Brooks, 1993). The content may not necessarily have a pre-existing relevance to students' lives outside of school, but teachers need to make such content meaningful by assisting students in making connections between the classroom learning and their real life outside of school. When we do so, we actually forge new neural pathways in the brain. We also engage students in a "natural form of learning" that appears to students to be almost effortless as opposed to the artificial learning that is part and parcel of onerous "drill and kill" memorization.

We once encountered a teacher of mathematics who had assigned her entire class 30 math problems of exactly the same type for homework. We asked her to help us to understand the purpose of this repetition. She responded with the cliché: "Practice makes perfect." In our minds, this was an example of the kind of artificial learning that comes from confusing *onerous* with *rigorous* (Powell & Kusuma-Powell, 2000). We believe it is critical for teachers to recognize the signs of boredom and know what conditions produce it.

Will have a laugh but know how to keep order: Gentle, appropriate humor within the context of focused learning can do a great deal to establish a productive class climate. Effective classrooms are by definition stressful places. If the student is to be in the zone of proximal development (Vygotsky, 1986) the challenge must be appropriate. The learning task must be on the frontier between that which is too easy and produces boredom, and that which is too difficult, and produces frustration (Csikszentmihalyi, 1991). Humor is a superb tonic for stress. It helps to create in students the "relaxed alertness" that researchers Geoffrey and Renata Caine (1997) identify as optimal for learning.

One Middle School teacher we know uses a "People Search" strategy at the beginning of the school year in order to introduce students to each other. The eighth graders are asked to go on a hunt for other students who have similar hobbies and interests. This teacher always includes one zany item in the People Search. One year, the students were instructed to find a classmate who had 'snorted spaghetti up his/her nose'. This is, of course, exactly the kind of humor appreciated by Middle School students and gave students explicit permission to laugh in class.

Are fair: The perception of fairness is a complex issue for both children and adults and is often the source of conflict. Garmston & Wellman (1999) suggest that one proactive way of addressing the fairness issue is to define how we are using the term. They offer three commonly used definitions: equality, equity and merit-based fairness. Equality is often what young students mean when they use the term fairness. It implies that everyone is treated exactly the same. The pie is divided equally. Equity, on the other hand, implies that people are treated according to their individual needs (Lavoie, 1989). Providing a learning disabled student with additional time on an examination might be an example of equity-based fairness. Affirmative action programs are another. Merit-based fairness is providing individuals with rewards based upon the value of their individual contribution. Merit pay for teachers is an example of this definition of fairness.

Frequently, students will use the term "unfair" as a synonym for "unreasonable" and by this they often mean that they do not know or understand the reasons behind a certain decision. Many times, a teacher can become "fair" by simply sharing the reasons behind a decision or situation.

At the start of a new school year, the teacher adviser to the High School student newspaper was confronted with a dilemma. He had an eager and enthusiastic group of would-be journalists on his hands. They were keen to engage in investigative reporting but did not yet understand or appreciate the complexities of responsible journalism. Wanting to avoid a confrontation over censorship, the teacher engaged the students in a workshop. He presented them with 15 possible articles (some clearly appropriate, some clearly inappropriate, and some in that gray area in between) and asked the students to determine which articles were journalistically responsible, and why. Together, the students and teacher developed criteria for responsible journalism. The students could see that the criteria were reasonable and the teacher was perceived as "fair".

Are easy for students to talk to: Considerable research has been done in the area of developing and maintaining rapport (Costa & Garmston, 2002) and we know from experience that such rapport is vital in the classroom. One component of rapport is the congruence of verbal and nonverbal behavior on the part of the teacher. Michael Grinder (1997) has some particularly insightful work in this area. In addition, teachers with highly developed listening skills are likely to appear much more approachable to students. Cognitive Coaching^sm (Costa & Garmston, 2002) provides an extremely useful framework for developing active listening skills, particularly in the areas of pausing, paraphrasing and probing for greater understanding.

In a school community there is often an individual who is not in an ascribed position of counseling or other authority, but who is recognized informally by large numbers of students as being a trusted source of advice. In various schools that we have visited, this individual has been a teacher, a secretary, a receptionist, the nurse or even one of the serving ladies in the canteen. These individuals have been perceived by the students as being approachable and trustworthy because there is congruence between their verbal and nonverbal behaviors and they exhibit superb active listening skills.

Don't shout: The foundation of Daniel Goleman's concept of emotional intelligence is self-awareness that allows for emotional self-regulation (Goleman, 1995). More recently, Goleman, Boyatzis & McKee (2002) suggest that effective leadership (and we would argue: pedagogy) must include both emotional self-awareness and relationship management. Goleman et al. identify a series of personal and social competences that form the fabric of emotionally intelligent leadership and, we believe, are critical for the effective classroom teacher.

When negative, disruptive emotions intrude into the classroom, learning suffers. More often than not, outbursts of frustration and anger on the part of the teacher are perceived as highly threatening to the child and result in what Paul McLean refers to as "downshifting" (1978) in which our basic flight or fight instincts are evoked. In such a state, intellectual risk taking and creativity are greatly inhibited and higher level thinking is virtually impossible.

We would argue that there is a place for carefully managed anger in the classroom, but we would counsel that it is only constructive under some very specific conditions. In his Nichomachean Ethics, Aristotle writes: *"Anyone can become angry – that is easy. But to be angry with the right person, to the right degree, at the right time, for the right purpose and in the right way -- that is not easy"* (in Ross, 2000). We would add to strive to employ anger appropriately is the mark of a truly civilized person; to accomplish it with grace is more often than not an act of love.

We have also learned over three decades in the classroom that it is rarely a good idea to show anger while we are still feeling it.

A number of years ago, we worked with a colleague who was chronically unable to control his temper. There were frequent outbursts of frustration and anger in his classroom and the students came to expect this behavior from him. At first, the lack of emotional self-regulation intimidated the students. But as time went by, this teacher became the object of his students' secret ridicule and they sought deliberately to provoke such outbursts. On one notable occasion, a group of students actually visited his home and stole his underwear from the washing line in order to orchestrate yet another outburst. Ironically, the locus of the teacher's emotional control had shifted from himself to his students.

On the other hand, we once worked with a masterful Middle School principal who opened a brand new computer writing lab only to discover that some of the students had pinched all the marbles out of the computer mice. He summoned the Middle School students into an assembly and deliberately and firmly let the students perceive his anger and disappointment. He announced that the computer lab would remain closed until all the marbles were returned. The marbles reappeared within 48 hours.

Don't go on about things (eg. how much better the other classes are, or how much better an older brother or sister was): Implicit in this statement is a concern on the part of students about the potentially humiliating effect of competition and comparison. Researchers into the relationship between self-esteem and student achievement in school (Covington, 1989) suggest to us that while there is no strong correlation between positive self-image and superior school achievement, there is a powerful correlation between a negative self-image and failure in school.

Several years ago, Fatimah confided to her guidance counselor that her English teacher was constantly making unfavorable comparisons between her class and the class the teacher had taught in a previous school. The comparison resonated with Fatimah as she had a learning disability and relatively low self-esteem. Fatimah took the teacher's negative comments about her class personally and they confirmed her own poor self-concept as a learner.

The win/lose dichotomy that is inherent in individual competition can serve to undermine a child's self-concept and may even have a debilitating effect on students who are on the "winning" end of such competition. In such cases, competition reinforces the child's reliance on external motivators (Deci & Ryan, 1985). Whether the reward is tangible such as a prize or trophy or intangible such a public recognition or parental approval, the motivation is external to self. Alfie Kohn's (1999) *Punished by Rewards* makes a compelling case against reliance on such extrinsic motivators.

In their meta-analysis of educational research, Marzano, Pickering & Pollock (2001) point out that the learning Effect Size of individual competition between students as a learning strategy is virtually insignificant. On the contrary, the use of cooperative groups has a profound (ES .78) Effect Size and is therefore a much more powerful educational strategy.

Explain things and go through things students don't understand without making them feel small: Masterful teachers avoid condescension. They do not need to enhance their own status at the expense of their students. They have the ability to empathize with the ignorance of their students. They remember what it was like to struggle with some aspect of their learning.

Over the last several years, we have become very interested in 'stuckness' -- the state students often find themselves in when they are seemingly unable to mediate their own thinking. We have also become very interested in how teachers can assist students so that they become 'cognitively unstuck'. We have probably all encountered at one time or another, the student with the blank expression. We ask if the student understands the concept we are trying to teach and the student responds with a hesitant shake of the head. We then ask the student what exactly it is that they don't understand and the response is that they don't know what they don't understand! This is 'cognitive stuckness' and this is where skillful mediative questioning (Costa & Garmston 2002; Lipton & Wellman 1989) can be critically important.

Sonali had had piano lessons for years and she had cleverly hidden from a series of music teachers her inability to read music. She was gifted musically and managed to play even complex pieces by ear. In the sixth grade, Sonali met her match in a new piano teacher who saw through the young girl's deception. The teacher approached the discovery with understanding and empathy and was able to create with Sonali an enthusiasm for learning to read music. Her inability came to be perceived by both student and teacher as an opportunity. Sonali was now able to combine both sound as well as sight in playing the piano.

Don't give up on students: There is probably no more powerful influence in the classroom than the high expectations of a caring teacher. When those expectations are diminished – and we put it to you that *this cannot happen secretly*, that is, without the child's knowledge – we give the message to children that we do not care for them as much as we once did. We give the message that they are less capable and have less intrinsic value. We let them know that we are giving up on them and often under this powerful influence, they give up on themselves.

If, on the other hand, we increase our expectations, especially when a child is facing learning adversity, we send the opposite message – one of caring and affectionate support.

A teacher friend of ours recently shared with us a letter from Mark, a former student. The teacher was a special educator who had worked in a school for learning disabled and emotionally disturbed students in a suburb of New York City. The letter began: 'This letter has taken almost 15 years to write' and went on to describe the powerful influence our friend had had on this young man's life. The occasion of the letter was Mark's graduation with a Masters Degree from Teachers College, Columbia University. Mark had qualified as a special education teacher himself. This might not be a remarkable achievement had it not been for the fact that Mark had a severe learning disability, had been expelled from the public school system for appalling behavior, and that many of his former friends were now serving time in prison. Mark concluded his letter by thanking the teacher for 'not giving up on me'.

Conclusion

It may be that as a profession, our hubris is indeed our lack of first hand models of outstanding pedagogy. However, we have, as illustrated in the marvelously insightful student comments above, a tremendous source of professional knowledge in the children that we teach. We have only to listen to the expertise that surrounds us.

We suspect that the young adults who provided Rudduck, Day and Wallace the above observations, probably didn't understand or realize how tremendously challenging, complex and demanding the work of teachers actually is. However, reading between the lines we suspect, that these young people did understand, perhaps intuitively, how critically important and noble the work of an effective teacher can be.

5 KNOWING YOUR CURRICULUM

If the first key to differentiated instruction is knowing your students, the second is for the teacher to gain a deep knowledge of the curriculum that he or she will be teaching. This, of course, begs the question of what constitutes a "curriculum" and what it means to "know it".

Back when Bill interviewed for his first English teaching job in a public high school in the New York City suburbs, "knowing your curriculum" was synonymous with subject area mastery. Bill recalls an hour-long interview in the early 1970's during which the principal (who was remarkably well-read) rattled off a list of English and American authors to which Bill was supposed to respond by indicating which works he had read and what he thought of them.

There is no question that teachers need to know the content of what they are to teach. Jones & Moreland (2005) describe the perils of implementing a new curriculum for which the teachers do not have sufficient pedagogical content knowledge. Their study describes learning "activities" that had little or no conceptual substance, and teachers who were unable to give feedback to students beyond praise-based responses. It is clearly important for a teacher of English to know the various genres of literature or for a social studies teacher to understand how the great thinkers of one century influenced the events of the next. But mere content knowledge can no longer be synonymous with "knowing your curriculum". The specific content of an academic discipline, no matter how interesting or seemingly important, can be likened to the specific physical features of a landscape – for example a pond or meadow, a cluster of oak trees or the path of a stream. All of these are important physical features of a specific landscape, but none of them, in and of themselves, give us the big picture of the geography of the region. As teachers we need to be able identify the metaphorical geography of our academic discipline. We need to be able to construct the big picture -- to identify the primary concepts or enduring understandings that we want our students to take way from our classroom. We need to be able to synthesize what is truly important for students to know, to understand and to be able to do, and articulate these major learning outcomes and plan learning activities that are aligned to them. We also need to collect data and evidence that will indicate how successful our students are in achieving these learning outcomes.

This is not a simple or easy task. It is intellectually demanding. It requires time and energy. It also requires collaboration with valued colleagues. It is, in short, what we mean by "knowing the curriculum."

A paradigm shift in how we think about curriculum has come about in part because of the constructivist revolution.

Less than two decades ago, Brooks & Brooks (1993) described what the research suggested was the status quo of most American classrooms. (We suspect that there would have been similar findings in other countries and in many of our international schools). Five major points emerged.

1. Classrooms were dominated by teacher talk. Teachers were perceived to be the dispensers of knowledge and students the consumers. Student-initiated questions and student-to-student interactions were atypical.
2. Most teachers relied heavily on textbooks in lieu of a thoughtful, clear and coherent curriculum. Information was often presented from a single (non-controversial) perspective.

3. Most classrooms structurally discouraged cooperation and required students to work in relative isolation.
4. Student thinking was devalued in most classrooms. When teachers posed questions to students, more often than not they were not asking students to think through complex issues, but rather trying to determine if students knew the "right" answer.
5. Most schools had curriculum documents predicated on the notions that there was a "fixed world" that the learner must come to know. The emphasis was upon the students' ability to demonstrate mastery of conventionally accepted understandings – not on the construction of new understandings or connections (p.6-7).

Perhaps "revolution" is too strong a word to describe the impact of constructivism since there are some schools, perhaps many around the world, in which these descriptions still offer an accurate window into how teaching and learning are taking place. However, where it has been embraced, constructivism has radically altered how we think about the curriculum.

At the risk of oversimplifying a complex topic, constructivism is a theory about knowledge and learning. It suggests learning is not the passive absorption of information – the so-called "coverage of the curriculum" but rather the active search on the part of the student for intellectual connections that will promote the "construction" of personal meaning.

Three central tenets of constructivism impact profoundly on our understanding of curriculum.

First, all knowledge is tentative. We need to be prepared that whatever we teach as truth to our students today may be declared a falsehood tomorrow. There was a time when the very best minds believed that the earth was the center of the universe, that monarchs ruled by divine fiat, that people with darker skin pigmentation were inherently inferior, that women had prescribed domestic duties, and that children with disabilities were better educated in isolation from their "normal" peers – to name just a few.

The idea that knowledge is temporary has several profound implications for curriculum and instruction. First of all it suggests that knowledge is not a noun but a *verb*, an exciting and stimulating process, an intellectual adventure that generation after generation engage in and build upon. Even more importantly, the tentativeness of knowledge allows us to give equal time to what *we don't know* – those intriguing mysteries that never fail to captivate the curiosity of our students. It allows us to talk about how we tolerate and perhaps even come to appreciate uncertainty – a quality that Elliot Eisner (1998) finds woefully unappreciated in most schools. It also suggests that we need to approach our work as teachers with a degree of humility – always a good idea.

Secondly, there is altogether too much content to be taught. The rate at which human knowledge is expanding is nothing short of breathtaking. Experts estimate that the wealth of human knowledge is doubling in less than a year. (Other experts estimate that human ignorance is also expanding at a similar rate – particularly in the field of wisdom). Certainly the knowledge we have acquired in the last decade about the human brain and how learning takes place is much greater than that accumulated in all the rest of human history combined. There is now simply too much content to fit into a curriculum. Therefore, it becomes vitally important that we critically prioritize what goes into the curriculum and be willing to make thoughtful judgments about what needs to be expunged. This is easier said than done as we always seem to be adding to the curriculum, but only very rarely weeding our garden.

The conclusions reached by a recent ACT National Curriculum Survey 2005-2006 would seem to agree. While state-mandated curriculum standards may help high school teachers focus their coursework, the university faculty responding to the ACT Survey reported a "significant gap" between what high school teachers teach and what university professors think entering students need to know. "States tend to have too many standards attempting to tackle too many content topics…High school teachers are working very, very hard at following and teaching their state standards, but college faculty felt it was more important for students to learn a fewer number of fundamental but essential skills" a spokesperson for ACT concludes (*USA Today*, April 11, 2007).

Third, the structure of the curriculum affects its outcome (or in the words of Marshal McCluhan 'the medium affects the message'). If one of the goals of the curriculum is to promote an inquiry-based approach to learning, it would stand to reason that the curriculum would be designed around *questions* as opposed to knowledge statements, and that these questions would be central to what we want children to learn. In other words, the curriculum needs to be both thoughtful and thought-provoking. Very few students can resist genuinely thought-provoking questions.

So, how does a constructivist approach to learning mesh with a standards-based curriculum and where does differentiation fit into all of this?

In fact, differentiated instruction and a standards-based curriculum are not only complementary but are essential to each other's integrity and efficacy. A standards-based curriculum without differentiation renders what happens in the classroom merely standardized. The emphasis is on quality control and accountability, not on meeting the needs of the learners – particularly diverse learners. The voice of the student is lost no matter how thoughtful and thought-provoking the curriculum. This represents one of the many problem's associated with the No Child Left Behind (NCLD) legislation in the United States.

On the other hand, differentiation without clear learning standards is a journey without a destination – a cordial invitation that doesn't provide a date, time or venue. Without learning standards, either classroom instruction become "activities-based" without conceptual substance or lesson plan objectives are individualized out of existence. Either way, the curriculum loses rigor and credibility. Rather than success for all, we have confusion and mediocrity for many.

Clear and coherent learning standards need differentiation and vice versa. They support each other's integrity. High quality curriculum insures that what we are focused on in the classroom is worthy of student time and attention; that the content is meaningful and relevant; and that our approaches are intellectually challenging. Differentiation, on the other hand, ensures that the invitation to access the high quality curriculum is extended to *all* learners.

Tomlinson & Allan (2000) write: "We need to stress continually what best-practice curriculum and instruction look like, and then help teachers learn to differentiate it. Differentiation as a magic potion loses much, if not most, of its power, if what we differentiate is mediocre in quality... Excellent differentiated classrooms are excellent first and differentiated second (p.81)."

In conversations with colleagues, we have come to understand that at least part of the seeming conflict between a rich and stimulating curriculum and differentiation comes out of some conflicting ideas that teachers hold about student success. Many teachers perceive student success in school as monolithic. In other words, some teachers may be willing to concede that 'one size may not fit all' in terms of intelligence preferences or learning styles, but the successful outcome for a unit of study must look the same for all children. Equality (treating all children in exactly the same manner) is further reinforced when it becomes emotionally associated with a misguided sense of fairness. Our preferred definition of fairness is to provide each child with whatever he or she needs (eye glasses, hearing-aid, extra-time on tests, large print books, voice recognition software, etc.) that will allow them to achieve individual success.

In fact, this standardized vision of student success can actually prevent teachers from perceiving individual student growth. The worrying deficit in a child's achievement can actually blind us to a child's accomplishments and strengths. In some cases, particularly where a student is not meeting grade level benchmarks, individual student success literally needs to be *unmasked* in order to be celebrated.

Not unlike the other professions, teaching creates its own false dichotomies. Perhaps one of the most pervasive in our international schools is that since our curriculum is more often than not college preparatory, we do not have an appropriate program for students with learning disabilities or for students who are still struggling with basic skills. The pundits justify their selective admissions policies with platitudes such as "we can't be all things to all people". Such "either/or" analysis tells us more about the limited thinking of the individual than about the potential of schools to meet the needs of diverse learners. Certainly one of the greatest challenges, perhaps the greatest, that schools have faced in the last hundred years is to balance the demands for *excellence* and *equity*. Some schools choose to perceive these as conflicting demands, as mutually exclusive opposite ends of the spectrum. This is shallow thinking. Schools that deny access to students on the grounds of preserving excellence abrogate a moral responsibility to equity.

A number of international schools are moving beyond this exclusive mental model. One such school is the International School of Brussels with its 1400 very diverse learners. Its motto: *Everyone included, everyone challenged, everyone successful – 1400 ways to be intelligent.*

So, what are some of the implications of the marriage of a high quality, standards-based curriculum with differentiated instruction?

We see four dimensions to this integration: backward design, teaching to primary concepts, framing curricular objectives as questions, and clarity about what can be differentiated (and what should not be differentiated).

Backward Design

Backward design comes to us from the work of Wiggins & McTighe (1998) in their book *Understanding by Design*. It frames a logical three step process of lesson planning that starts with the outcome in mind. Steven Covey (1989) writes that "to begin with the end in mind means to start with a clear understanding of your destination. It means to know where you're going so that you better understand where you are now so that the steps you take are always in the right direction." Wiggins & McTighe identify three stages in backward design:

1. Identify desired results.
2. Determine acceptable evidence.
3. Plan learning experiences and instruction.

The first stage may seem obvious, but our experience has shown that it is not a given in all classrooms. Many teachers start their planning with a textbook chapter, old-favorite activities or lesson plans that have been taught many times before. This often results in an activity-based learning experience that has little conceptual substance. This can also be the case when the integration of subjects (social studies, science, math and language arts) is artificially forced.

Critics of linear models of lesson planning (John, 2006) such as backward design suggest that such models do not reflect the inherent complexity and dynamism of the classroom and that ends and means are isolated into successive steps rather than being seen as part of the same situation. Again, this criticism would seem to us to represent a false dichotomy. There is no necessary contradiction between a logical step-by-step approach to lesson preparation and the iterative, simultaneous creativity that is part and parcel of the real world of teacher unit planning. The former provides us with structure and accountability; the latter allows us to cater for the context of our specific classroom and our specific students.

It is hard to argue with the logic of starting the planning process with the end in mind.

Teachers often have more difficulty with the second stage and find it counter-intuitive. For most teachers, once a learning goal or objective has been identified the next logical step is to design a learning activity that will allow us to achieve that outcome. However, Wiggins & McTighe (1998) counsel that it is important for us to think of the assessment piece as an embedded component of the planning process and not simply as a summative event that occurs at the conclusion of the unit. We need to ask ourselves how we will know that students have achieved the desired results. What will we see our students doing that will indicate that they have mastered certain skills? What will we hear our students saying that will indicate understanding? What evidence will we come to accept as valid for the outcome of our unit of study? By placing the assessment evidence before the planning of the actual learning experience, we force ourselves to visualize the outcome of the unit, which in turn increases the likelihood of alignment between learning goal, assessment and actual instruction.

What follows as Figure #1 is a model of Unit Planning for Diversity. It follows the backward design structure and provides a meta-cognitive script for teachers. The script suggests questions that teachers might be asking themselves about the intersection of a high quality curriculum and the actual intelligence preferences, learning styles, strengths and weaknesses and content interests of an actual class of students. The model is presented in a linear format. However, teachers are encouraged to use it recursively so as to capture spontaneous ideas and capitalize on creativity, but at the same time not losing sight of the structure of the whole.

Figure 1

METACOGNITIVE SCRIPT	UNIT PLANNING FOR DIVERSITY
	CONCEPT
What is the big concept I want to teach? What is the enduring understanding? Why is it important for the student to know this 20 years from now? What question guides my planning? (Essential Question)	
	CONTENT
What are my learning goals and content objectives for teaching this concept? (Learning goals & content objectives should be linked directly to big concept/enduring understanding)	
	DECLARATIVE KNOWLEDGE LEARNING GOALS (specify one or two only)
What do I want my students to know and understand?	

	PROCEDURAL KNOWLEDGE GOALS? (specify one or two only)
What do I want my students to be able to do?	

How will I know that I have achieved my objectives? What criteria are most important to assess? What feedback will I use to monitor that the lesson is working? What will my rubric look like? Will students be able to access the language of the rubric? What formative assessment will I use? What tools will I use to judge whether students have learned what I set out to teach?	ASSESSMENT OF STUDENT LEARNING?

How will I activate students' prior knowledge about the content? How will I make the content meaningful and relevant to the students? Are there particular pre-teaching activities I need to consider for any special populations (ESL, LD, Highly Capable)?	PRE-TEACHING? ACTIVITIES?

What special populations do I have in my class (ESL, LD, Highly Capable)? What specific learner needs(learning styles, social needs) do I need to remember and consider in my planning?	DIVERSE LEARNER CHARACTERISTICS?

	DESCRIPTION OF INSTRUCTIONAL ASSIGNMENT
How does the task ensure that all learning goals are included? How have I ensured that a wide range of talents, interests and intelligences are required? How have I planned to engage all students in active learning? How do I anticipate the most "challenging" students in the class to respond to this activity/lesson? Check List for Task: ☐ open-ended ☐ interesting ☐ challenging ☐ there is more than one way to address it ☐ involves reading & writing	

	INSTRUCTIONS
What are the verbatim instructions that I will give my students for this task? (Having re-read my instructions to the students, what is the likelihood that students will be confused by lack of clarity or ambiguity?)	

	WORKING GUIDELINES
What materials will I need? What materials will students need? How will student learning be monitored during the assignment? How will student work be graded? What is the timeline for this assignment? In what way will grouping be formed?	

How will I synthesize and bring closure to the lesson? In what way will I return to the essential question or enduring understanding?

What homework will I assign?

BRINGING CLOSURE

REFLECTING QUESTIONS

How did the lesson go? *(summarize impressions)*

What connections are you seeing between the lesson you planned and the one you taught? *(analyze causal factors)*

What are some ideas that you want to take away from this teaching experience? *(construct new learnings)*

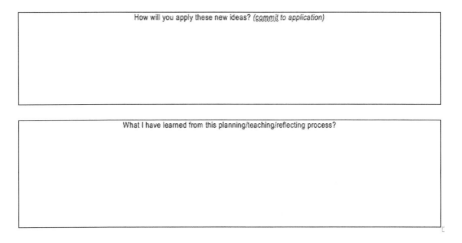

How will you apply these new ideas? *(commit to application)*

What I have learned from this planning/teaching/reflecting process?

Backward design is structured to ensure clarity of learning objectives and alignment of assessment and instruction to that learning objective (coherence). The importance of these elements was underscored in recent research undertaken in Germany. Seidel, Rimmele & Prenzel (2005) set out to measure clarity and coherence of learning objectives and to determine whether there were correlations to the development of student motivation and achievement. Clarity and coherence of lesson goals were measured by analyzing videos of physics lessons and rating the criteria on a Likert scale using specific indicators.

The researchers found a strong correlation between clarity and coherence of lesson goals and: 1) student perceptions of supportiveness of the learning conditions; 2) students' learning motivation; 3) types of cognitive learning activities; and 4) the development of student competence in physics over a one year period.

Teaching to Primary Concepts

Structuring curriculum around primary concepts is a critical dimension of constructivist pedagogy and an essential aspect of the Understanding by Design process. Structuring curriculum around primary concepts also provides for the possibility of differentiation.

By primary concepts we mean those "big ideas" that lie at the heart of the discipline. Wiggins & McTighe (1998) suggest a model for the structure of knowledge that involves three nested ovals or eggs. In the largest oval, they place knowledge that is "worth being familiar with". In the second concentric oval is knowledge that is "important to know and do". In the smallest oval resides what Wiggins & McTighe call the "Enduring

Understandings". These Enduring Understandings are the primary concepts or big ideas that Brooks & Brooks (1993) call the "quest for essence".

Most students find whole-to-part learning easier and more meaningful than a part-to-whole approach. Teachers facilitate student leaning when they present explicitly the big idea. "When concepts are presented as wholes…students seek to make meaning by breaking wholes into parts that *they* can see and understand. Students initiate this process to make sense of the information; they construct the process and the understanding rather than having it done *for* them (Brooks & Brooks, 1993)."

The understanding of a primary concept is enduring. It is not something that is simply memorized for a test. It makes sense to the student and a connection is forged to prior knowledge. Therefore, the student does not need to memorize meaningless, fragmented information.

Several years ago, Bill made a presentation to the parents of elementary school children on why the math curriculum was structured around understanding of primary concepts as opposed to the memorization of algorithms. At one point in the presentation, he asked all members of the audience to stand if they currently used algebra in their daily lives. About a quarter of the audience stood. Bill's comment was that those parents who used algebra in their daily life probably learned it conceptually. Their conceptual understanding was both *enduring* and *transferable.*

Teachers sometimes have difficult identifying "teachable concepts" as opposed to "topics to teach". There is a critical distinction here that is vital to differentiation. Topics to teach might include *Lord of the Flies,* green plants, World War Two, or ratios and percentages. The content of each of these topics is unquestionably important. However, when we teach *topics* we don't connect the content with the reason for learning it. In our workshops, we encourage teachers to move from teaching *topics* to teaching *concepts.* Figure #2 illustrates this movement from topic to concept.

Figure #2

ISOLATED TOPIC	TEACHABLE CONCEPT
Butterflies, frogs, green plants…	Life cycles – What similarities are there in the development of living things?
The Industrial Revolution	Human Progress – Who are the winners and losers of

	industrialization?
Pollution	Interdependence → What are some of the relationships between humans and their environment? *or animals around?*

We suggest that teachers "test" the big idea or enduring understanding for its worthiness and teachability against Wiggins & McTighe's (1998) four filters for understanding. The first filter is that the concept has enduring value beyond the classroom. We liken this to the twenty year test. What value will this understanding have for students in twenty years time? If we struggle to answer this question, it may mean that the concept we are exploring is not worthy of student time.

The second filter asks us whether the concept resides at the heart of the discipline. For English, a concept that might reside at the heart of the discipline could be that "literature is manufactured" – meaning that novels, short stories and poems are crafted by authors who have specific purposes and are using deliberate strategies and literary devices in order to achieve those purposes.

The third filter asks us to evaluate to what extent the concept requires "uncoverage". By this, Wiggins & McTighe (1998) are asking us to assess the potential that the big idea has for engaging students in analysis and deep critical thought. In order for students to translate isolated and fragmented information into personally meaningful knowledge they must engage in such higher order thinking. We also need to ask ourselves what aspects of the concept will the students have difficulty in grasping? What may be counter-intuitive? What are some common misconceptions?

Finally, the fourth filter asks us to what extent the concept has the potential for engaging students. The big idea does not need to have ready-made student interest. Not all students arrive at the classroom door interested the French Revolution, baroque music or conjugation of future tense verbs. However, skillful teachers can mediate relevance "by having student encounter big ideas in ways that provoke and connect to students' interests (as questions, issues, or problems) (p. 11)." For example, the question "How do we recognize justice?" not only serves as an essential question for a number of topics in social studies (the American Revolution, colonialism, racial persecution etc.) but also connects with the intrinsic preoccupation of Middle School and High School students with fairness and fair treatment.

In terms of differentiation, teaching to primary concepts opens up many more opportunities to differentiate for content, process, product, student interest and readiness, learning styles. *It is virtually impossible to differentiate the teaching of topics such as "green plants" or "The Industrial Revolution" or "Pollution" because the actual learning objectives are so vague as to make the desired results of the lesson nebulous or non-existent.* Differentiation is a means to an end. If the destination is unclear, the journey is at best confused. However, if we look at primary concepts, or as Wiggins & McTighe (1998), refer to them as Enduring Understandings, the possibilities for differentiation are many. If we are teaching "life cycles" the content can vary broadly. Students can produce different products to demonstrate their learning and these products can reflect their interests, learning styles and readiness levels.

We believe another critical aspect of teaching to primary concepts is that the process that the teacher goes through in identifying the enduring understanding (testing the teachable concept against Wiggins & McTighe's four filters) actually makes explicit to the teacher *why the topic is worthy of student time and attention* and as a result liberates within the teacher the energy and motivation for dynamic classroom implementation.

Framing the Curriculum Around Questions

If the curriculum is to produce genuine inquiry on the part of the students, it must be framed around questions. Wiggins & McTighe write: "Only by framing our teaching around valued questions and worthy performances can we overcome activity-based and coverage-oriented instruction, and the resulting rote learning that produces formulaic answers and surface-level knowledge (p. 27)."

Since questions are the most common instructional tool of teachers, we often have a tendency to take them for granted. Skillfully crafted questions don't just happen and are rarely the product of spontaneous classroom discussion. Not all questions are created equal and we need to give time and attention to crafting *valued* questions about which we can frame our curriculum and units of study.

A very counterproductive questioning practice stems from a misunderstanding and misuse of Bloom's Taxonomy. Bloom and others (1956) identified hierarchies of thinking skills. At the lowest level of most of these taxonomies are cognitive processes such as recall and rote memory. At the highest level are processes such as comparison, evaluation, synthesis and prediction. Some teachers mistakenly assume that students with processing difficulties, learning disabilities or students who are simply struggling with basic skills will find questions that rely on recall and rote memory "easier" and more accessible than those that demand higher order and more complex thinking. However, recall and rote memory questions usually have a single right answer. You either know it or you don't. Questions that embrace higher order thinking are often open-ended and have multiple entry points which students can access at their particular readiness level. For example, the question "Who discovered America?" requires a single right answer. You either know it or you don't. Whereas, the following question has multiple entry points: "If you were planning a voyage of exploration at the end of the 15th century, what might be some of the things you would want to consider?" A student can choose to address such a question at his or her own level of readiness (e.g. on a concrete level in terms of food and water needs or on quite an abstract and sophisticated level focusing on navigational difficulties – the lack of latitudes and longitudes or sailor morale on such a long voyage).

Bloom attempted to use "degree of difficulty" as the criteria for distinguishing between levels in his taxonomy. However, the higher levels are not always more difficult (Costa, 2001). Sousa (2001) perceives this difference as being between *difficulty* and *complexity*. We do well to remember that *arduous* tasks (tasks that require more effort or time) are not the same as *rigorous* tasks (tasks requiring more complex thought at high levels of Bloom's taxonomy (Dodge, 2005; Kusuma-Powell & Powell, 2000).

The other even more disturbing misconception held by some teachers is that students must master the basic skills of reading and writing *before* they engage in higher order thinking. Students who are struggling with basic skills have, just as much – *if not more* -- need for intellectual stimulation as their apparently more school successful classmates.

Wiggins & McTighe suggest that curriculum should be framed around Essential Questions. These questions have seven characteristics:

- "Have no one obvious right answer;
- Raise other important questions, often across subject-area boundaries;
- Address the philosophical or conceptual foundations of a discipline;
- Recur naturally;
- Are framed to provoke and sustain student interest; and,
- Have embedded in them enduring understandings." (p.10-11)

We would add that in our experience the most successful Essential Questions are ones that we took as teachers into the classroom without knowing the answer ourselves.

What can, should and should not be differentiated

Parents often ask us whether differentiation doesn't "dumb-down" the curriculum.

The question hinges on what it is that we choose to differentiate.

There are some things in school that are non-negotiable. For example, every student who leaves high school should be able to write a well-organized and coherent essay. Learning to read is another non-negotiable. With all our advances in technology and our so-called "digitally native" children, basic literacy and numeracy will continue to be the currency of individuals who successfully navigate the complexities of the 21st century.

As a general rule, the learning standards and instructional goals should not be differentiated[5]. Every student deserves the richness and stimulation of the enduring understandings and essential questions.

However, the content that we use to achieve those enduring understandings can be differentiated. When social studies teachers look at the sources of human conflict, students can study the Chinese Revolution, the American Civil War or the genocide in Rwanda and Burundi. When students come to explore "life cycles", they can focus on frogs or butterflies or human beings.

In addition to the content, the skills that we select to focus on can also be differentiated. One of the benchmarks for Ochan's Grade Eight Humanities class was writing a well-organized five paragraph essay. Several of her students were still working on constructing a well-organized paragraph. One student, who had a severe learning disability, was working on a well-organized sentence. The skill focus was differentiated in accordance with individual needs, but the standard (the five paragraph essay) remained the same for all. The fact that we do not differentiate the learning standard allows us to put our hand on our heart and tell parents that differentiation does *not* dumb-down the curriculum.

Assessment of student learning can be differentiated. We can invite students to demonstrate their learning in different ways. Some students can show their learning through a written piece of work; others can perform their learning through a skit or musical presentation; still others can show their learning graphically through a poster or in a piece of art work; and still others can build a model that shows their understanding. We know that the medium in

---

[5] An exception to this might be for a severely disabled student for whom the learning standards were clearly inappropriate.

which students work affects the quality of their demonstrated learning. Allowing students to use their strengths often produces much higher quality work. We are also aware that some media can be so anxiety producing that students put all their attention into the process of production and little into the content itself.

Again a caveat is in order: if the desired result is a quality piece of writing, it makes no sense to permit students to demonstrate their learning by way of a poster or a skit. In order to learn to write, students need to write.

While assessment can be differentiated, the criteria by which we evaluate the assessment should *not* be differentiated. We need to hold all students to the same high standards. For example, it is possible to have students demonstrate their understanding of photosynthesis by way of an essay, a model, a graphic design or a skit. However, the rubric that is used to evaluate each of these different learning products should be the same, because the enduring understandings that we are looking for are the same.

Finally, the learning experience itself should be differentiated. We need to build into the learning activities that we design for our students aspects of differentiation based on content, process, product, learning style, student interest and readiness level.

We close this chapter with Figure # 3 which suggests some observable indicators of both high quality curriculum and differentiation in the classroom:

 Figure 3 *importante*

Observable Indicators of High Quality Curriculum & Differentiation
• Units of study reflect a coherent design. Primary concepts (big ideas), enduring understanding and essential questions are clearly aligned with assessments and learning activities.
• There are multiple ways to access and explore ideas.
• Students are permitted to demonstrate their learning in various ways.
• Assessment of understanding is anchored by "authentic performance tasks", calling for application and explanation.
• All assessment (teacher, peer and self) includes clear criteria of evaluation. The teacher and the students share a common understanding of "high quality".

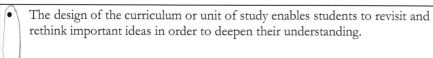

- The design of the curriculum or unit of study enables students to revisit and rethink important ideas in order to deepen their understanding.

- The teacher and students use a variety of resources which reflect different cultural backgrounds, reading levels, interests and approaches to learning.

Adapted from Tomlinson&McTighe,(2006),
Integrating Differentiated Instruction and Understanding by Design

6 DEVELOPING A REPERTOIRE OF STRATEGIES

"If the only tool one has is a hammer, all problems look like nails."

--Abraham Maslow

While we cautioned in an earlier chapter that differentiation isn't just a larger toolbox, there is no question that a broad repertoire of instructional strategies will serve students well in the classroom. In this chapter, we have selected seven strategies that lend themselves to differentiated instruction. Obviously these are not the only strategies that can be used to promote personalized learning in the classroom. However, these seven are research-based and time tested and generic enough so they can be used in virtually any subject area and at almost any grade level. We have included brief descriptions of each strategy and an example of how it might be used in the classroom.

Strategy One: Classification Activity

A classification activity asks students to identify similarities and differences. This can be on a very simple level in the primary grades or it can deal with complex and sophisticated ideas in the high school. Identifying similarities and differences is a very basic function of human thought and is the origin of all of our conceptual thinking. At the simplest level, concepts are clusters of similarities. Marzano et. al. (2001) describe the research-base and the efficacy of identifying similarities and differences as a learning strategy. There are several ways in which teachers incorporate this critical thinking activity in the classroom:

- Comparison: the process of identifying similarities and differences between items or ideas.
- Classifying: the process of grouping items or ideas that are similar or have like qualities.
- Creating metaphors: the process of finding patterns and perceiving similarities in things that at first appear dissimilar. Metaphoric

class. lo que ayuda y lo que no ayuda a que un animal sobreviva; 91 o viva bien.

thinking is one of the highest levels of thinking and represents an excellent informal assessment of conceptual understanding.

- Creating analogies: the process of perceiving relationship between pairs or concepts – seeing relationships between relationships.

There are numerous ways that teachers can use a Classification Activity. The Venn diagram provides a simple and accessible graphic organizer for students to work with. A "T" chart can fulfill a similar function.

Below is an example of how Colette Belzil from the International School of Brussels uses a classification activity with her Year 2 IB Standard Level Math class. The purpose for this particular exercise was to get students back into a 'math mode' at the beginning of the school year and review curricular topics from Year 1. She started by putting the students into randomly selected small groups and then distributed the following sheet (Figure 1).

Her instructions to the students included:

- Organize the concepts into 4-6 categories. No group should have fewer than 3 concepts.(absolute minimum) (20-30 minutes)
- Each group must come to consensus as to which concepts are to be classified together.
- Choose one of the categories. (Must not be your smallest category if you have one that only has 3 elements.)
- Identify the link between its concepts. This can be expressed in paragraph form or any form if you like, but must show how/why the different concepts are related to one another. In other words, why did you place them in the same category? It must show an understanding of each of the concepts and its mathematical link to the others in the same category. (20-30 minutes)
- Share your category with the rest of the class (possibly done the next day).

Figure #1

IB Standard Year II

Cut out the topics and categorize them in groups (no group should have less than 3)

$b^2 - 4ac$	increasing/decreasing	unit circle	growth and decay
Binomial theorem	Exponents and radicals	Periodic phenomena	System of equations
Trigonometry (right angle and non-right angle)	Matrices	Calculus	Quadratics
Σ	Expansion	transformations	normal
Intercepts	$\begin{pmatrix} 1 & 0 \\ 0 & 1 \end{pmatrix}$	Tangent	gradient
completing the square	Common ratio / common difference	Speed	maximum / minimum
Series	vertex	Asymptotes	inflection point
e	period	Derivative	inverse
Family of Functions	Rate of change	logarithms	Pascal's triangle

Colette uses this kind of activity as an informal assessment of student understanding. She pays special attention to the concepts *which do not get used by the students*. She assumes that these are the ones that the students are least familiar with and she focuses future instruction accordingly.

Strategy Two: 10-2

The strategy 10-2 comes to us from the work of the American science educator, Mary Budd Rowe. It is very simple to implement and highly efficient in terms of the use of classroom time. Rowe understood that the optimal concentration span for most young adults (and older adults) is between 9 and 12 minutes. She therefore suggested that teachers "chunk" their direct instruction into lecturettes of no more than about ten minutes. There is no question that brilliant lecturers can hold their audiences spell bound for longer periods. However, most of us are not brilliant lecturers.

She further suggested that following each of these lecturettes, students be provided with two to three minutes of processing time. This processing time provides an opportunity for students to identify the key idea(s), formulate questions, forge links to pre-existing knowledge or make personal connections to subject under examination. Mary Budd Rowe's research demonstrates conclusively that when students are provided with brief periods of processing time understanding and retention increase dramatically.

We use the 10-2 strategy regularly in our workshops. In terms of the processing time, we like to vary the instructions to include the following:

- **Turn to your neighbor:** Identify the key idea(s).
- **Stand-Up Conversation:** Have a stand up conversation with a person not sitting at your table and identify an important question that remains.
- **The 2-Minute Essay:** Write one or two sentences that capture the most important concept.
- **Give one – Get One:** With a partner share a personal connection to the subject that you are exploring.

Strategy Three: Centers

Teachers have been using Centers since the 1960's as they provide for great flexibility and many opportunities for personalized learning. Centers focus on student mastery (or enrichment) of specific understandings or skills. Center tends to be more exploratory and inquiry-based than other assignments.

Two Kinds of Centers:

- **Learning Centers:** Areas of the classroom that contains activities and materials that are designed to teach, reinforce or extend a particular skill or concept (Kaplan, Kaplan, Madsen & Gould 1980).

- **Interest Centers:** An area of the classroom that contains activities and materials designed to motivate students' exploration of topics they have a particular interest in.

Generally, Centers should have the following characteristics:

- Focus on important learning objectives;
- Contain activities that are directed linked to student growth towards those outcomes;
- Use resources and activities that address a wide range readiness levels (especially reading), learning styles, and student interests;
- Contain learning tasks and experiences that vary from structured to open-ended, abstract to concrete, and simple to complex;
- Provide clear and explicit instructions for students;
- Incorporate a record-keeping system at the center in order to monitor what students do at the center; and
- Include both a teacher assessment plan and a student self-assessment plan that will lead to adjustments in center learning activities.

Centers in Action: 20,000 Leagues under the Sea

Irving Sentosa teaches a combined sixth and seventh grade science class in an international school in East Africa. Irving recognizes that the school's proximity to the Indian Ocean offers his students a tremendous learning opportunity and he is keen to capitalize on the students' natural curiosity about the life that exists beneath the surface of the ocean. Specifically, he wants students to understand scientific concepts such as adaptation, eco-system, interdependence, classification and change.

To start out, the whole class listens to a story by a parent who is a professional diver and they watch a National Geographic video on under sea life. Irving has also arranged for a field trip to a nearby coral reef marine park.

He also uses a science center to ensure that students get individual practice with key concepts and skills. For the next month, all the students will visit the science center and have an opportunity to work like marine biologists in analyzing different aspects of under-sea life.

However, Irving has recognized that in his combined sixth and seventh grade classroom there are a wide variety of readiness levels. Students vary greatly in reading levels and in their complexity of thought. Some of Irving's students are also learning English as a second language, a couple have been formally identified as having Learning Disabilities and several are academic able and need to be stretched. Their previous knowledge about and interest in marine biology also varies greatly.

The science center contains a number of specimens of crustaceans, several (not-to-scale) models of sea creatures (a leather-back turtle, a sand shark and a moray eel), a variety of photographs of fish, samples of different kinds of coral and sea shells and three large salt-water aquariums with different varieties of coral fish. The center also contains a replica of a parrot fish skeleton and the jaw of a leopard shark. To augment the displays of marine life, Irving has also included his own diving equipment, a wide range books on marine life and a variety of art material and writing tools.

Students are assigned to the center over the course of the month of study. They may also elect to visit the center when it is not in use when they have student-choice-time or when they have finished other learning tasks before the rest of the class.

In the science center, Irving differentiates tasks and learning experiences by student readiness level. He varies that complexity of the task to match the students starting points. Irving allows students to select whether they will work in pairs, trios or quartets. He attends to their learning profile differences by presenting the material in both auditory and visual ways, and he has included both tactual and kinesthetic activities. He also includes an element of student choice. Students can pursue specific interests in marine biology. Predictably, a small group of boys want to research the Great White Shark.

Irving has crafted a number of different learning experiences for the science center that include:

- Select four inhabitants of a coral reef (must be approved by the teacher) and make a power point presentation to the class on how their survival is dependent on each other.
- Identify three sea creatures that illustrate the scientific concept of adaptation. Make a poster illustrating the different creatures and their connection to adaptation.
- Make a model of a specific fish (choice must be approved by Mr. Sentosa in advance) and illustrate how the body of the fish is specifically designed for its environment.
- Write a job description for a marine biologist that explains what this person does, what kind of training is required and why it might be a very important career in our world today.

Strategy Four: Entry Points

The strategy of Entry Points comes to us from Harvard Professor Howard Gardner (1993) who recognized that students bring to the classroom with them a vast array of intelligence preferences, learning styles, talents and strengths. Gardner has identified seven different types of intelligence (four additional types currently have candidate status). Each of us has all seven types of intelligences but to differing degrees.

Gardner describes Entry Points as a strategy for addressing the varied intelligence preferences that our students bring to the classroom with them. He suggests that students can initiate an exploration of a given subject or topic through five different channels or Entry Points:

Five Different Entry Points

1. **Narrative Entry Point:** This involves presenting a narrative or a story about the subject of topic.
2. **Logical-Quantitative Entry Point:** Using a scientific/deductive or qualitative (numerical) approach to the topic or concept.
3. **Foundational Entry Point:** Examining the philosophy or the big ideas that form the foundation to the subject or question.
4. **Aesthetic Entry Point:** Focusing on the sensory (aesthetic) qualities or features of the subject.
5. **Experiential Entry Point:** Connecting the topic or subject to the student's own personal experience. The student deals with the topic or subject in a real world setting.

Entry Points in Action: "Wanted Justice: Dead or Alive"

Mrs. Linda Polonsky is about to begin an exploratory unit with her eighth grade social studies students. Through the study of different periods of history, she wants them to develop a deeper understanding of social justice. She wants them to understand that governments and societies are not always "just" and that through-out history individual men and women have spoken out and acted, in some cases courageously, in the face to unjust laws and governments. She wants her students to make connections and identify some of the values and beliefs that underlie the concept of social justice. She also wants her student to be able to identify "real life" issues in the world today that are socially unjust.

The students in Linda Polonsky's class begin their unit of study by a whole class discussion of what they think of when they hear the phrase "social justice". This gives the students a chance to explore prior knowledge and previous understandings. It also provides Linda with an opportunity to get a sense of the students depth and breadth of knowledge, their understandings, and perhaps most importantly their misunderstandings.

Linda then allows each student to select one of the five Entry Point investigations. The students may choose to work individually or in groups (up to a maximum of four). Linda has also developed specific assignments for each of the Entry Points and she distributes explicit rubrics that contain the criteria for success.

Following are brief summaries of Linda Polonsky's five Entry Point Investigations:

1. **Narrative Entry Point:** Using the stories provided by the teacher (Rosa Parks and Aung San Suu Kyi), students analyze the issues and the specific reactions to social injustice. They develop a glossary of vocabulary words and design posters and graphic representations illustrating an historical protest against injustice. The students then select an individual who confronted an unjust government or system and write or tell orally the story of their protest.
2. **Logical-Quantitative Entry Point:** Students are asked to imagine a village of 100 people and to use it as a comparison to the world today. They are assigned a series of questions to answer. For example: if the world were a village of a hundred people, how many would live in the United States? How many would own televisions, computers, cars, Ipods? How many would complete primary school, secondary school, university? How many would have access to a fully qualified doctor? How many would live in a democracy? How many go to bed every night hungry? The students would then make a graphic representation (a mural or a poster) illustrating what they had learned about "their village" and social justice.
3. **Foundational Entry Point:** Students would be invited to watch the film "Gandhi" and listen to Martin Luther King Jr.'s speech "I Have a Dream". They would then relate the film and the speech to the United Nations' Universal Declaration of Human Rights. They would also prepare a power point presentation entitled "The State of the World Address" exploring how well implemented the Universal Declaration of Human Rights actually is.

4. **Aesthetic Entry Point:** Using the resource material provided by the teacher and others (librarian), the students will examine how art, literature and music have been historical expressions of social conscience. Students will be asked to examine how an artistic expression of protest is different from a political one.

5. **Experiential Entry Point:** Students will be presented with the example of two men who believed that they faced unjust laws (Socrates and Thoreau). After reading their stories, the students will analyze the men's values, beliefs and actions. They will then use newspapers, magazines and the nightly television news to relate these values and beliefs to the present world situation. The students will select an issue that is meaningful to them and writer a letter describing their feelings (eg. a letter to the editor of a local newspaper, a letter to the CEO of Philip Morris, etc).

Linda Polonsky has differentiated content by providing a range of different research materials for each group. She has differentiated process by providing a variety of different ways to think about social justice. The students can use a variety of different production styles (writing, drawing, building, performing) to demonstrate their learning. What stays the same for all students are the core concept of social justice and the exploration of the responsibilities of the individual.

Strategy Five: Tiered Activities

Teachers often ask about how to provide appropriate levels of challenge for a class of students with widely varying degrees of readiness while focusing on the same general learning goals. What strategies can we use when a class contains students with very different reading levels or students that have a difficult time with abstract thought and more advanced students who are clearly sophisticated in their analysis? Tiered Activities offers teachers a useful and efficient strategy to focus on common learning outcomes (understandings and skills) while providing for appropriate learning challenge for different learning needs.

Teachers employ Tiered Activities so that all students can acquire the essential understanding and skills, but at different levels of complexity. A simple example of a Tiered Activity would be when Ochan provided her Grade Eight Humanities students with several choices of essay questions. She would place as asterisk next to one or two of the questions, indicating that they were the more challenging questions. Students who wished to select the more challenging question needed to conference with Ochan about their ideas before starting to write. While student choice was the general rule, Ochan reserved the right to guide some of the more capable, but less confident, students into choosing the challenging essay topics. Student choice also mitigated against some of the negative stigma that is associated with "tracking" or so-called "ability grouping". What was crucial for Ochan was that even the basic level essay prompt met all the benchmarks for Grade Eight Humanities. Success on the basic level essay prompt was success in Grade Eight Humanities.

Designing a Tiered Activity[6]

1. **Clarify the essential learning outcomes/goals**
   - Concept/generalization (enduring understanding)
   - Skill or process
2. **Identify the learning profiles of your students:**
   - Readiness range (reading, thinking, prior knowledge)
   - Interests and special talents
   - Learning styles and intelligence preferences
3. **Develop an activity that includes:**
   - High level of interest
   - High level of thinking
   - Students using key skills to understand key idea
4. **Build a ladder of complexity and chart the activity:**
   - High skill or complexity
   - Medium skill or complexity
   - Low skill or complexity
5. **"Clone the activity along the ladder in respect to the appropriate challenge for your students:**
   - Materials – basic to advanced
   - Form of expression – familiar to unfamiliar
   - Personal experience – from personal experience to experience that is unfamiliar to the student
6. **Match the level of the Tiered Activity to the student based on student learning profile and task challenge.**

Tiered Activities in Action: "Troubling Deaf Heaven with Bootless Cries"

---

[6] Adapted from Tomlinson's (1999) *The Differentiated classroom: Responding to the Needs of All Learners,* Association for Supervision and Curriculum Development.

Mrs. Gina Gathercole has a very diverse group of students in her Grade Nine English class. Wendi and Diah are reading at a college level and Diah's essays have won prizes in international school competitions. Rhona, on the other hand, is reading on about a 7th grade level and is still struggling with the organization of a five paragraph essay. Steve and Geoff have been formally identified as having learning disabilities and Mrs. Gathercole suspects that Butch may have attention issues. Dunja, Ika, Dawi and Seung Hye are all recent graduates from the school's ESL program and are still developing fluency and competence in English.

Gina Gathercole is planning a unit on poetry. She wants all of her Grade Nine students to read quality literature and to come to understand that poetry is "manufactured" – that it is crafted by the poet for a specific purpose. She wants her students to develop skill at inferential reading, appreciate figurative language and understand metaphors. She also wants the students to come to appreciate some of the other literary techniques that poets employ. Ultimately, Gina would like her students to come away from the unit being intrigued by poetry and wanting to read more.

She begins the unit by asking the students what they know about poetry and what poems they may have read in the past. She then engages them in a whole class activity in which she reads to them Shelly's poem "Ozymandis". Trios of students then study the poem and draw a picture of the scene that the poet is describing. The trios then discuss the meaning of the poem and draft a single sentence that captures the essence of the poem.

Gina then divides them into task forces with the following assignments:

Task Force One (basic level): Reads Thomas Hardy's "During Wind and Rain". The students identify the structure of the poem and two of the literary devices the poet is using. The students discuss and identify the themes of the poem. Once the students have an idea of the author's purpose, they embark on the "photo safari" collecting digital images that will serve to illustrate their presentation of the poem to the rest of the class. They are also required to prepare a brief prose commentary on the poem.

Task Force Two (medium level): The students read Dylan Thomas' "Do Not Go Gentle into that Goodnight" and John Donne's "Death by Not Proud." They discuss in each case what might be the poem's meaning and what purposes the poet had in writing it. They identify three literary devices that are used in the poems. They select appropriate background music for each poem and accompanying visual works of art that will support their presentation of the poems to the rest of the class. They prepare a prose commentary for each poem.

Task Force Three (advanced level): The students read Shakespeare's "When in Disgrace with Fortune and Men's Eyes" and Marvel's "To his Coy Mistress". They identify the structure of the poems and four literary devices that the poets have used. They prepare a power point presentation comparing how the poets have dealt differently with the idea of romantic love. They incorporate visual imagery and music into their presentations and prepare an essay comparing the poems.

Strategy Six: Learning Contracts

Learning Contracts combine several aspects of differentiation that have been shown to be effective in promoting student learning. Learning Contracts are in essence a negotiated agreement between the student and the teacher regarding the tasks and activities that the student will complete in order that he or she develop the required understandings and acquire the necessary skills. The design of most Learning Contracts is teacher directed, but the student often works on the activities or tasks with considerable independence. Many teachers include in Learning Contracts a fair degree of student choice regarding what is to be learned (the content), working conditions (individual or group work) and how the learning will be demonstrated (production styles).

Like other learning experiences in the classroom, the assessment of Learning Contracts can take a number of different forms. One fourth grade teacher we know assesses her students Learning Contracts in three ways. First she looks had how well each student worked (goal clarity, on task behavior, perseverance towards the goal, use of feedback, revision). Secondly she checks one or two of the assignments to determine their completion, accuracy and overall quality. Thirdly, each student chooses two assignments (one must be a written assignment) for inclusion in his or her portfolio. Each assignment is self-assessed, assessed by a peer and finally assessed by the teacher against a rubric that was distributed to the class at the start of the unit.

A High Quality Learning Contract:

- Holds the teacher responsible for specifying important learning goals and outcomes and for making sure that the students acquire them;
- Presumes that students can take some responsibility for learning;
- Identifies the skills and processes that students need to practice and acquire;
- Ensures that students will use those skills in a meaningful context;

- Makes explicit the conditions under which the Contract will be executed (student behavior, deadlines, class work involvement in the learning Contract and homework);
- Establishes positive consequences for adhering to agreed working condition and for contract completion (continued independence, student choice, grades). Teachers can also set negative consequences if students do not adhere to agreed working conditions;
- Makes explicit at the start of the contract the criteria for successful completion and quality of work; and
- Includes the signatures of agreement of both student and teacher.

Learning Contracts in Action: "The Night of the Notables"

The Grade Five teaching team looks forward to their unit entitled "The Night of the Notables". Over the last three years it has evolved into a powerful learning experience for their students, and one that the students and their parents greatly enjoy. The teachers have identified three essential questions for the unit:

1. What are some common characteristics of heroes?
2. How does the passage of time change our perceptions of popular heroes?
3. What qualities make some heroes greater than others?

In terms of skills and processes, the teachers want their students to develop their research skills both in terms of print and electronic media, to hone their expository essay writing skills and to develop a sense of historical empathy.

The unit starts with the students watching a short film on the life of Harriet Tubman. Small groups discuss and identify the qualities that made Tubman a hero. The groups then read a short article on the suffragette leader, Emmeline Pankhurst. The teachers encourage the students to compare the two women. The groups prepare posters showing both similarities and differences.

The teachers then distribute to the students a long list of possible heroes for them to choose from. The students are asked to take the list home and consult with their parents about the selection of a hero to research. The choices range from heroes in sports, politics, science, medicine, exploration, art, music, literature, human rights, etc. Once the students have made their selection, the teachers give them their Learning Contract assignment card. The card states that they must research their "Notable" and answer a series of questions about him or her and the contribution that he or she made. The students must make a brief power point presentation on their "Notable" and write a five paragraph essay explaining why this person was truly notable (and how his or her personal characteristics matched those of a hero).

The students must then prepare for the "Night of the Notables". This is an evening event to which the students come dressed as their "Notable". The students gather in the gymnasium and the parents are held outside. At a specific signal, the doors of the gym are opened and the parents are permitted to enter. The students stand frozen in costume with props representing their "Notable". The parents move among the "statues" asking questions and trying to guess who each student is.

Strategy Seven: Curriculum Compacting

Curriculum Compacting was developed by Sally Reis and Joseph Renzulli[7] as a strategy for use with above average students who may have already mastered much of the content on offer, or with those who learn very quickly. The metaphor of the compactor helps us to imagine that the learning program will be compressed or condensed for these children, so that needless repetition can be eliminated and instruction can be streamlined to match the motivation of the children involved. Many gifted students come to school already knowing the material presented at their grade level, and consequently learn less than their peers.

Curriculum Compacting assists teachers in making appropriate program decisions for gifted children as well as to analyze curriculum content so that teachers are clear about what students need to learn. In addition, Curriculum Compacting provides time for learning enrichment or acceleration.

How to Use the Compacting Process

Define Goals and Outcomes: The first step of the compacting process is to define the goals and outcomes of a particular unit or segment of instruction. Although scope and sequence charts can offer much of this information, we recommend that teachers also look at their Essential Questions and Enduring Understandings that they want students to learn. Ask questions like: What's important for students to know, understand and do? What can be eliminated? What is new material (declarative and procedural) and what has been previously taught? This kind of analysis not only helps teachers to focus on what is important for students to know, but also illuminates how instruction might be streamlined.

---

[7] For further information, please see:
http://www.sp.uconn.edu/~nrcgt/sem/semart08.html

Identify Candidates for Compacting: The second phase of Curriculum Compacting is to identify students who already have an advanced mastery of the identified goals and objectives of the proposed learning unit, or who may learn the content very quickly. This step underscores one of the keys of differentiation; that is, Knowing your student as a learner. It is essential that teacher observations and comments form part of the assessment procedure. Some questions that teachers might ask include: Does the student complete work quickly and at a high standard? Do other students approach him/her for assistance? Is s/he bored during class instruction? Does the student score very well in specific areas, or wish to explore more advanced or other areas on his/her own? What is his/her reading/vocabulary level?

When compacting for specific skills (e.g. as in a math class), teachers may wish to administer pre-tests for each unit to determine which students have already mastered the skill and might benefit from compacting. If students have not mastered the skill, teachers need to be clear that students show the potential for learning it faster than would be expected for students of the same age.

When compacting for a content area, candidates for compacting would be those who are more likely to gain from opportunities for self-directed learning. Pre-assessing students is more complex with this type of compacting. Teachers may wish to set performance-based pretests (e.g. an expository or persuasive essay that can be analyzed for content), use observations of students (e.g. how they take notes, what questions they ask, what connections they are making), and review student portfolios or work samples that might indicate mastery of the learning objectives.

Provide Acceleration and Enrichment Options: Efforts should be made to identify possible enrichment options or replacement activities for learning the 'yet-to-be-mastered' objectives. Teachers and students can cooperate in the decision making for what would be an appropriately challenging learning experience. Some guidelines for such experiences include: the assignment must be of high quality and appropriate to the student's level; it must offer the potential of engaging students; and the students must have sufficient time to learn.

The formats for this type of learning are varied: students can learn on their own, in pairs or small groups. They can also be organized around seminars or work with a mentor. Students can pursue project work or conduct independent research on a high-interest topic. An important point is for students to be able to pursue self-directedness in their learning, and make appropriate decisions.

Curriculum Compacting can offer teachers rich opportunities for differentiating by student interest and learning style, and provide options for students to demonstrate their learning through a preferred production style. Teachers do need to keep documentation of the learning objectives and the basis on which compacting candidates were selected. Records should also be kept of student work and demonstrations of mastery.

7 KEEPING IT SIMPLE & SOCIAL - COLLABORATION

Walking through the Malagasy rainforest in search of the Indris Lemur can be a humbling experience. By about 10:00am we had spotted a troop high in the canopy overhead. Olivier, our guide, explained that the Indris Lemur, the largest of the Madagascar lemurs, have four distinctive calls – some of which are truly eerie and can be heard for miles in the dense undergrowth. Olivier explained that the Indris Lemurs have distinctive warning calls for the approach of both ground and aerial predators. The troop also has a communal territorial "song" in which each member has a designated part – the duration of which corresponds to the individual lemur's age and status. In addition, the troop has a distinctive "love song" which is sung to neighboring Indris troops advertising the first group's mating potential. But, Olivier explained, the loveliest and most mournful call of the Indris Lemur is the "song of reunification". This occurs when one of the younger members of the troop becomes lost and the elders join together in song to help the youngster find his way "home".

Ochan and I found stalking the Indris Lemur humbling in the sense that although simple, the Indris Lemurs' system of collaboration seemed in many respects so much more efficient, effective and established than those that we have traditionally found in schools.

In the early 1970's when Bill started his first teaching job in the suburbs of New York City, the Chairman of the English Department welcomed him to the school with the following words: "You will be working with a highly educated group of professional educators who are linked by a common parking lot."

In those early days, the parking lot and heating system were about all that teachers shared. Teachers went into their individual classrooms and closed the door (if the door had a small window in it – the teacher would often cover it over with a piece of construction paper to make his or her isolation

107

more complete). A teacher's classroom was his castle and territoriality was the rule of the day. Even the principal would not enter a teacher's classroom without tacit permission or prior warning. Peer observation was unheard of and peer coaching was still ten or fifteen years in the future. Lesson plans could be commandeered by the principal, but otherwise were not seen by others. Instructional strategies, like secret recipes, were considered private, intellectual property and for the most part were not shared. In many schools there was an unwritten rule that teaching and learning would not be spoken about in the Faculty Lounge. A novice teacher was unlikely to be mentored. Instead he or she was more likely to be given a baptism of fire by being assigned to the most difficult students or the class that no one else wanted to teach. When a veteran, master-teacher retired from the profession, she took her wealth of craft knowledge with her – as such, each new generation of teachers had, to some extent, to reinvent the wheel. It was an inefficient and ineffective system that even the Indris Lemurs would have found puzzling.

Teacher isolation was then and is now a major obstacle to the improvement of student learning.

Fortunately, we are seeing an increasing number of international schools trying to break down teacher isolation by emphasizing the importance of adult-to-adult collaboration. We see it when the high school when teachers sit together to moderate standards on internal assessment work and in the common planning of middle school learning communities. Teacher isolation is also breaking down in the collective assessment of student work in elementary school and in the increase in co-teaching situations. We also see it in the team approach that special educators and regular classroom teachers are developing.

One of the most stable factors in schools over the years has been the relative isolation of teachers from each other throughout their workday and work year. What sociologist Dan Lortie described in his groundbreaking 1975 study is still true in many schools today. In these "egg crate" schools, he observed a work life in which autonomous teachers were organized by a culture of presentism, individualism and conservatism. These teachers lived from moment to moment in their classrooms and sought routines that were efficient and energy conserving. They were careful not to tread on the territory of others and were proactively conservative about changes in curriculum and instruction.

Garmston & Wellman, 1999,

The Adaptive School: A sourcebook for developing collaborative groups

This paradigm shift is nothing short of a sea change. As a profession, we are slowly coming to recognize that our teaching colleagues are the most valuable educational resource we have – barring none. Some may treat this as a statement of the obvious. However, as a profession we haven't worked as though it were. And as we know from the work of the very greatest philosophers and scientists, the obvious isn't obvious until it is obvious.

We say that we "are coming" to recognize the value of our colleagues because schools are at different points on their journey towards professional interdependence – the union of individual teacher autonomy with a profound sense of school community.

The importance of the quality of adult-to-adult relationships within schools can not be over-estimated. In our professional development work with teachers, we visit more than thirty international schools each year. Within an hour or so of talking with teachers, we get a sense of the school culture, and the cultures vary dramatically. Some school cultures can be characterized by conviviality but little collegiality ("let's be pleasant to each other, avoid conflict, and maintain our own turf"). In other, healthier school cultures we see trust and generosity, a common vision and focus on student learning, and a collective emphasis on teacher professional development. These schools are truly a pleasure to work with. Occasionally, we enter a school with a toxic culture, where arrogance, insecurity, and competition between adults make for an atmosphere of fearfulness and suspicion.

In his classic work *Improving Schools From Within,* Roland Barth (1990) asserts that the quality of adult-to-adult relationships within a school is one of the most accurate barometers of school quality. He observes that the manner in which adults speak to each other, share ideas, form work partnerships and even manage conflicts is often a profoundly accurate predictor of the quality of learning within the classroom.

But what specifically do teacher-to-teacher relationships have to do with student learning and differentiation? For the past four decades, school people have been exhorted to be "child-centered". What has happened to the child in Barth's barometer?

Today's research is finding *the child* in the vital connections between high quality adult relationships and high quality student learning (Bryk, M. & Schneider, B. 2002; Garmston & Wellman, 1999; Seashore Louis, K., et al.1996). We have known this intuitively for some time. Michael Fullan goes so far as to say that "no school improvement initiative will be successful unless it also improves relationships within the school" (2000).

One incontrovertible finding emerges from my career spent working in and around schools: The nature of relationships among adults within a school has greater influence on the character and quality of that school and on student accomplishment than anything else. If the relationships between administrators and teachers are trusting, generous, helpful and cooperative, then the relationships between teachers and students, between students and students and between teachers and parents are likely to be trusting, generous, helpful and cooperative. If, on the other hand, relationships between administrators and teachers are fearful, competitive, suspicious, and corrosive, then these qualities will disseminate throughout the school community.

Roland Barth, *"Improving Relationships with the Schoolhouse"*, *Educational Leadership*, March 2006

The highest quality teacher-to-teacher professional relationship is collaboration. But it is a deceptively simple concept. We say collaboration takes place when members of a learning community work together as equals (irrespective of positions of authority) towards a common goal. Partnerships in a collaborative relationship may be between students as they work in groups, between students and teachers, and between teachers as they work to assist students to succeed in the classroom. Irrespective of whom it is between, collaboration is based upon mutual goals and shared responsibility for participation and decision-making. Individuals who collaborate share accountability for outcomes (Friend, 1992; Kusuma-Powell & Powell, 2000).

Garmston & Wellman (1999) write "collaboration is the norm in high performing and improving schools and results in increased student achievement . . . However, collaboration skills need to be taught explicitly." For many of us, this is a new and rather novel idea. Our unexamined assumption has been that we would *naturally* know how to work effectively and efficiently in a partnership or as a member of a team. Experience has shown that, for the most part, this is a hit or miss proposition. Sometimes when the chemistry is right it works. Some people have natural gifts in the areas of interpersonal and intrapersonal intelligence. Many don't. Sometimes collaboration happens naturally, but many times it doesn't. When it doesn't work, it is almost always the fault of someone else – arrogance, egotism, autocratic leadership style, communication problems, defensiveness, rigidity, sarcasm, hidden agendas, poor listening skills…the list could go on and on.

Teachers are not alone in needing to learn collaboration skills. Olivier, our guide in the Malagasy rainforest, described to us how the elder Indris Lemurs explicitly train the youngster in behaviors that are critical to the collaboration of the entire troop.

Whether in the rainforests of Madagascar or within the schoolhouse, collaboration is too important to be left to chance or the individual whim of the players involved. The commercial world has known this for many years and business invests many millions of dollars annually in helping employees learn how to work together in teams. The good news for schools is that, like emotional intelligence, collaboration skills can be learned. But they need to be deliberately developed and self-consciously practiced. Because we are not used to thinking about collaboration skills as something to be explicitly learned, this process can make us feel awkward.

What is the specific link between collaboration and differentiation? Why would "keeping it simple and social" form one of the four foundations of differentiated instruction?

The answer is that education has become one of the most complex, if not *the* most complex, profession. Every week, we see the publication of more and more research findings in education, psychology, neuroscience, medicine and anthropology that have implications for our work in classrooms. This barrage of information serves to both enlighten and confuse our work as teachers. In addition, we are regularly battered with competing educational claims. "This software package rewires the brains of dyslexic children." "This phonemic approach to reading will raise standardized test scores by 20%." "The adoption this math scheme will increase our children's conceptual understanding." The sheer volume of information and misinformation is enough to produce confusion in even the clearest thinking individual.

The explosion of knowledge in the last twenty years about the human brain and the ways in which children learn compel us into collaboration. We would have little confidence in a doctor who refused to consult with colleagues on a diagnosis or treatment. The same standard needs to be applied to education.

Designing high quality, thought-provoking unit plans and then devising ways of differentiating them to meet the needs of a multitude of diverse learners is highly complex and highly cognitive labor. Given the complexity of our work, it is unreasonable, unfair and counter-productive to ask teachers to go it alone. The days of flying solo are over.

Lipton and Wellman (2004) identify four forces that are driving constructive change in education. The change forces are actively driving us away from the isolation of the so-called "egg crate" school. In fact, these mega-trends are the vanguard of the movement towards creating Professional Learning Communities. Figure #1 identifies these four forces driving change:

Figure # 1

Four Forces Driving Change in Education[8]

FROM	TO
A teaching focus	A learning focus
Teaching as private practice	Teaching as collaborative practice
School improvement as an option	School improvement as a requirement
Accountability	Responsibility

Professional Learning Communities (Louis, Marks & Kruse, 1996) are the vision of what schools that embrace collaboration can become. These are schools that share common norms and values, have a collective focus on student learning, actively practice collaboration, deprivatize teaching practice and encourage reflective dialogue. Professional Learning Communities are places in which the challenge of differentiated instruction is embraced collectively.

However, it would be unrealistic to deny that some obstacles exist to developing collaboration in schools. Some of these obstacles are suggested in Figure #2. Most of these road blocks can be removed by effective and committed leadership. In order to genuinely improve learning for students and implement effective differentiation, school leadership needs:

- to provide time for collaboration *within the working day* (time for common planning, collective assessment and analysis of student work, etc.);
- explicit training in the specific norms and skills of collaborative work; and,
- the unwavering expectation that collaboration is the norm of how we do business in this school.

---

[8] From Lipton,L & Wellman, B. (2004). *Data Driven Dialogue,* Miravia Press.

The time teachers need for collaboration, in most cases, represents a significant budgetary increase. Nevertheless, we would argue that few budgetary expenditures are as important as providing teachers with the time to deliberately work on improving student learning. In our experience, the competing demands on teacher time and attention – particularly in high quality schools – means that collaboration simply will not happen unless schools provide faculty members time to engage in it.

However, time by itself is not enough. Teachers need to be trained in the skills of collaboration and the school leadership needs to have a steel resolve in insisting in a partnership or team approach to every aspect of student learning. The response of Melville's quixotic character, Bartleby - the Scribner: "I prefer not to", is no longer acceptable.

School leadership also needs to insist that the skills that are learned within a collaboration workshop are actually transferred to the workplace. This means that the administrators need the same training and they need to serve as role models. In some schools we work in, the administrators join the teachers in being participants in the professional development workshops. The message about collaboration that these school leaders give to their teachers is profound -- we are *all* learners. We are *all* here to focus on student learning. The effect on school culture is transformational.

Common Obstacles to Effective Collaboration

- Toxic school culture (unhealthy adult-to-adult relationships)
- Territoriality
- Fear of criticism or judgment of colleagues
- Fear of change ("What does collaboration look like anyway? What will I need to give up – classroom autonomy?")
- Perception that collaboration is optional – for those who want to embrace it.
- Absence of training in the skills of collaboration
- Absence of leadership support for collaboration
- Lack of planning/reflecting time
- Scheduling/time tabling problems
- The increased cost

--adapted from Kusuma-Powell and Powell, 2000

From our perspective, co-teaching offers enormous promise in the area of differentiation and improving learning for all students, but particularly for those students for whom school learning is a struggle. When two or more teachers plan together, execute instruction together and then reflect on the experience together, we see dramatic improvements in student learning and significantly increased teacher professional fulfillment. We see teachers sharing responsibility and accountability. We see genuine learning partnership emerging – both between adults and between teachers and students (Kusuma-Powell, Al-Daqqa & Drumond, 2004). We see teachers complementing each others' strengths and compensating for each others' weaknesses, and exploring new insights and perceptions about students and learning. We see school cultures moving towards Professional Learning Communities. There is little in education that holds as much promise for differentiation and improved student learning as teachers working together to plan, implement instruction and then critically reflect together.

The following figure includes a rubric which suggests some of the possible relationships between the Dimensions of Co-Teaching and the Levels of Collaboration.

In some situations, the increased cost of co-teaching opportunities can be offset by larger class sizes. At the International School of Kuala Lumpur, Grade Eight Humanities is team taught by three teachers who plan, teach and assess together. (All three teachers have a solid grounding in the Humanities content area. In addition, one has a background in ESL and another in Special Education. Their combined expertise makes unit planning and the analysis of student work a particularly rich and valuable experience.) The class size in Grade Eight Humanities over the last few years has ranged between 45 and 55, but since the physical space is available and virtually all classroom work is done in small groups, the large size is not an impediment to student learning.

DIMENSIONS OF CO-TEACHING

LEVELS OF COLLABORATION	ROLES & RELATIONSHIPS	ATTITUDES	PLANNING & DEVELOPMENT	DELIVERY OF INSTRUCTION	ASSESSMENT OF STUDENT LEARNING	EVALUATION OF LESSON EFFECTIVENESS
4	• co-equal partnerships; students perceive teachers as co-equal • trust in relationship allows for self-criticism, good humor & spontaneity • interaction between planning partners energizes both, strengths are complimentary • mutual coaching is evident & ideas are shared openly	• classroom space is perceived as shared space • joint ownership of the lesson is valued & celebrated • positive intentions are presumed • mutual trust is evident • partners disagree without being disagreeable	• co-equal contributions in development of lessons & materials • lessons scripted with learning objectives in mind • think time silence respected • inquiry & advocacy balanced • active & reflective listening skills evident	• seamless, integrated co-delivery from both partners • sufficient trust & rehearsal of the script allows for spontaneity • constant evaluation of lesson effectiveness during delivery	• partners both engage in clinical observation of student learning • dynamical & continuous assessment is aligned with instruction • co-teachers moderate assessment of student learning, achieving high inter-rater reliability • assessment informs future instruction	• structured, regular & joint reflection on content & process of lesson • constant effort to improve reflective self-criticism on both parts • student feedback regularly sought & considered
3	• co-teacher roles clearly defined, following a pre-arranged script • there is trust in the relationship, although spontaneity may be missing • partners volunteer to do tasks, although most tasks are done individually • some coaching is evident & ideas are shared	• classroom space is shared when second teacher is present; second teacher feels welcome & comfortable • some joint ownership of lesson • positive intentions presumed • tasks are shared, but not responsibility	• one or other partner dominates in development of lessons & materials • lessons usually referenced to learning theory & objectives • some probing for understanding evident • inquiry & advocacy usually balanced • some pausing & reflective listening	• primarily a tag-team approach, one "on stage," one "off duty" • interaction between co-teachers sometimes present during instructional delivery • some simultaneous assessment of lesson effectiveness during lesson	• some clinical observation of student learning • assessment is aligned with instruction • co-teachers sometimes moderate assessment of student learning, achieving some level of inter-rater reliability • assessment usually informs instruction	• frequent reflection on content & process of lesson by individual teachers • efforts to improve usually present • reflective self-criticism usually present • student feedback sought periodically
2	• there is clearly a hierarchical structure in the relationship • trust & spontaneity have not developed • one partner prepares material for approval & use of the other • one-way coaching is evident	• classroom space is shared with second teacher • second teacher does not feel totally at ease • there is some uncertainty about each other's intentions	• one partner usually dominates in development of lessons & materials • lessons at times referenced to learning theory & objectives may be clear to one partner • more advocacy than inquiry • little pausing/paraphrasing/probing • active/reflective listening inconsistent	• instruction delivered primarily by one teacher; other takes on special topics or assigned to tutor special students • infrequent interaction between teachers during lesson • little simultaneous assessment of lesson effectiveness	• assessment is usually aligned with instruction • co-teachers rarely moderate assessment of student learning; low level of inter-rater reliability • assessment does not always inform instruction	• infrequent reflection of content & process of lesson • some efforts to improve • insufficient trust prevents reflective self-criticism • student feedback rarely sought
1	• one teacher is directive towards the other • currently no scope for trust or spontaneity in the relationship • materials are not shared • no coaching takes place	• classroom clearly belongs to one of the teachers with other teacher a temporary guest • resistance to partnership may be evident • conflict may be personalized as positive intentions are questioned	• consultant partner provides ideas to other • lessons frequently based around activities or isolated topics rather than primary concepts; learning objectives unclear • advocacy dominates • almost no silence; partners interrupt each other • N.V language may be dismissive	• instruction is delivered by primary teacher; the other acts as assistant or subordinate • infrequent or no interaction of co-equal value between teachers during lesson • one partner may not be physically present during the lesson	• assessment is not aligned with instruction • assessment of student learning is not moderated • there is no clear link between assessment & instruction	• reflection of content & process lacking • efforts to improve missing or not evident • fear that self-criticism may be perceived as weakness • student feedback mistrusted

Powell & Powell, 2002

In terms of developing a culture of collaboration, explicit training for teachers is vital. The Adaptive School Model, developed by Bob Garmston and Bruce Wellman (1999) is one of the most effective that we know of. In their book by the same title, Garmston and Wellman identify seven norms of collaborative work. Norms are behaviors that have become habits – in this case positive habits that when carefully employed will create opportunities for groups to undertake their work in an atmosphere of relaxed alertness (Caine & Caine,1991;1997). Relaxed alertness is the state that permits individuals and groups to experience low threat and high challenge simultaneously. Research has shown that threat and fatigue inhibit brain functioning (LeDoux, 1996), whereas challenge, accompanied by safety (but not comfort) and a sense of personal or group efficacy leads to peak performance (Caine & Caine, 1997; Jensen, 1998).

The Seven Norms of Collaborative Work[9]

Pausing: Pausing actually slows down the number of "frames per second" of a conversation or discussion. It provides for precious "wait time", which has been shown in classrooms to dramatically improve student critical thinking. Pausing creates a relaxed and yet purposeful atmosphere. It gives tacit permission for participants to think. We do not need to come to the conversation or meeting with all our thoughts and ideas ready-made and well-rehearsed. Pausing also signals to others that their ideas and comments are worthy of our deep thought. It can serve to dignify the contributions of other and can encourage future participation. Pausing greatly enhances the quality of both enquiry and decision making and can serve as a powerful preventative to personalized conflict.

Paraphrasing: To paraphrase is translate into one's own words the comments or thoughts of another person. The paraphrase maintains the intention and the integrity of what has just been said while using different words. Paraphrasing helps team members understand each other as they analyze and evaluate data and formulate decisions. Paraphrasing can also serve to deepen thinking. "The paraphrase is possibly the most powerful of all non-judgmental verbal responses because it communicates that 'I am trying to understand you' and that says 'I value you' (Costa & Garmston, 2002. p.49). There are few classroom strategies as powerful as the teacher's skillful use of paraphrasing.

Probing: Probing seeks to clarify something which is not yet fully understood. More information may be required or a phrase may need more

---

[9] From Garmston & Wellman, (1999), *The Adaptive School: A Sourcebook for Developing Collaborative Groups.*

specific definition. Clarifying questions can increase the precision of a group's thinking and can contribute to trust building. It is often useful to precede a probing question with a paraphrase.

Putting Forward Ideas: It takes self-confidence and a degree of courage to offer an idea for a group's consideration. It is vital that collaborative groups nurture such self-confidence and courage. Ideas are at the heart of meaningful discussion. Groups must be comfortable in processing information by analyzing, comparing, predicting, applying and drawing causal relationships. Skillful facilitators will recognize when participants put forward ideas and will explicitly value the contribution.

Paying Attention to Self and Others: Collaborative work is facilitated when each team member is explicitly conscious of self and others – not only aware of what he or she is saying, but also how it is said and how others are responding to it. "Understanding how we create different perceptions allows us to accept others' points of view as simply different, not necessarily wrong. We come to understand that we should be curious about other people's impressions and understandings – not judgmental. The more we understand about how someone else processes information, the better we can communicate with them (Costa & Garmston, p. 59)." As Daniel Goleman (1985) has described in his work on emotional intelliegence, social awareness is the key to healthy and constructive relationship management.

Presuming Positive Presuppositions: Of all the seven norms, this one may be the most important, for without it a foundation of trust cannot exist. Simply put, this is the assumption that the other members of the group or team are acting out of positive and constructive intentions (however much we may disagree with their ideas) and are making the best decisions they can with the knowledge they have. Presuming positive presuppositions is not a passive state, but needs to be actively integrated into our work together. It permits the creation of such sophisticated concepts as a 'loyal opposition' and it allows one member of the group to play "the devil's advocate". It builds trust, promotes healthy cognitive disagreement and reduces the likelihood of misunderstanding. It is also one of the most powerful antidotes to destructive, personalized conflict.

Pursuing a Balance Between Advocacy and Inquiry: Both inquiry and advocacy are necessary components of collaborative work, and yet they have very different functions. The purpose of inquiry is to create greater understanding. The purpose of advocacy is to make decisions. It is often very helpful for collaborative groups to explicitly identify which process they are engaged in. This can often avoid misunderstanding and frustrated participants. A common mistake of work teams is to bring to premature closure the problem identification stage (inquiry for understanding) of the discussion and rush into possible solutions (advocacy for specific remedies). While meeting time is always in short supply, a rush to advocacy can often lead to decisions that need to be remade a few weeks or months later. Maintaining a balance between advocacy and inquiry inculcates the ethos of a Professional Learning Community.

One of the highest forms of collegiality and collaboration is represented in professional coaching. This is when an individual deliberately sets out to use specific coaching skills to support the thinking of a valued colleague. While we have also used Cognitive Coaching[sm] (Costa & Garmston, 2002) to support the thinking of students (Kusuma-Powell, Al-Daqqa & Drummond, 2004; Powell & Kusuma-Powell, 2007), the majority of our coaching work has been done with professional colleagues.

We have found coaching to be particularly helpful in the complex field of differentiated instruction. Cognitive Coaching[sm] provides three different conversation maps: the Planning Conversation, the Reflecting Conversation and the Problem-Resolving Conversation. Each of these different conversations offers practical ways to explore the complexities of differentiated instruction; practical ways that we can support colleagues in coming to know the diverse learning styles and intelligence preference of their students; practical ways of coming to know the primary concepts and essential questions of the curriculum; and practical ways of matching learning strategies to specific student needs. High quality differentiated instruction is contingent on high quality, on-going teacher learning. Coaching provides the vehicle for such learning. For this reason, we embed Cognitive Coaching[sm] into virtually all our teacher workshops.

Conclusion

Teachers are often either over-whelmed or under-whelmed by the prospect of differentiation. Either reaction is problematic. The over-whelmed teacher perceives the demands and complexities of differentiation as beyond his or her ability. There are simply too many balls to keep in the air. Thus differentiation is dismissed as an interesting theory but an unrealistic expectation in the real world of *my* classroom.

The under-whelmed teacher selects particular aspects of differentiated practice (e.g. specific instructional strategy or approach) and says to him or herself "I'm doing all that already." From the opposite end of the attitudinal spectrum, differentiation is similarly dismissed.

In order to avoid being either over or under-whelmed, we counsel teachers when they are setting professional differentiation goals to be realistic and kind to themselves. We suggest that the incremental steps on the journey of differentiation be *kept simple and social.*

As teachers redefine what it means to work together and as we collectively journey toward the vision of a Professional learning Community, we are wise to take a humble lesson from the Indris Lemurs of the Malagasy rainforests.

8 SETTING CONDITIONS FOR LEARNING: META-STRATEGIES FOR DIFFERENTIATION

BACKGROUND

Among the projects that Bill embarked upon with Susan Napolliello, Elementary School Principal at the International School of Kuala Lumpur, was the use of walk-through observations as a means of raising the profile of differentiation and to improve instruction in the school. The idea of walk-through observations is to get a snapshot or picture of what is going on within the school, by walking through and observing for very short periods (3 – 5 minutes) what goes on in a series of classrooms. Put together over the course of a year, the walk-through observations provide administrators and teachers a fuller, more extensive picture of the quality of education taking place within the school[10].

In preparation for those walk-through observations, Susan and Bill and others brainstormed a list of indicators that might be present in classrooms where differentiated instruction was present. In determining the criteria for these indicators of differentiation, Bill and Susan were guided by specific principles: they sought to identify those strategies that would support student learning and improve student opportunities for success. The long list of brainstormed strategies included diverse items such as flexible student groupings, the use of wait time, smooth transitions, non-verbal routines, and patterns of questioning during a lesson. Using an inductive process, Susan and Bill then categorized and refined their lists, looking not only at teacher behaviors, but also at the impact of those behaviors on student learning. They further identified student behaviors that would become evident when those approaches or strategies were in place, and also identified the learning theory and research bases for the strategies.

---

[10] For a fuller discussion of the walk-through process at the International School of Kuala Lumpur, please see Chapter 15, "How Administrators Can Support Differentiation: Using Observation to Improve Instruction," reprinted from *Educational Leadership.*

The results of their efforts are the following five meta-strategies, broad or super-categories of strategies or approaches which we now see as developing a classroom culture and setting optimum conditions for learning:

- Purposeful use of non-verbal cues
- Mediation of student thinking
- Deliberate creation of a constructive learning community
- Promotion of self-directed learning
- Use of student responses to inform instruction

While these are not specific differentiation strategies, they provide us with large patterns of classroom behaviors and interactions, and set conditions which encourage learning. Out of these patterns, specific differentiation strategies will evolve – hence the term *meta-strategies*. Teachers who employ these meta-strategies weave them into their instruction; they form the background architecture of differentiated classrooms, the structure of norms and values that provide scaffolds for all students to challenge themselves at appropriate levels. These meta-strategies also provide support for students who may be struggling (even momentarily) with learning.

THE META-STRATEGIES

Purposeful Use of Non-Verbal Cues

Students know when their teachers are pleased or irritated, can sense if their teachers like or dislike them, and even if their teachers have a preference for working with girls or boys in the class. Students usually make these inferences, not from anything the teacher has said, but rather from the nonverbal messages that their teacher sends.

Since Darwin's 1872 publication of *The Expression of Emotions in Man and Animals,* nonverbal communication in humans has been an area of scientific study. Our tone of voice, facial expressions, posture and gestures, even the way we dress, signal messages to those around us. Estimates vary as to the percentage of our communication that is expressed nonverbally, and range anywhere from 65% (Birdwhistell, 1970) to 95% (Mehrabian, 1971). While these estimates are hard to verify, it is apparent that most of our communication is expressed nonverbally. This makes evolutionary sense since as a species we have been communicating nonverbally for hundreds of thousands of years, while language is only thirty or forty thousand years old – a relatively new innovation. Since so much of what we communicate is nonverbal, it is important, then, to recognize and be conscious of the effect as well as the potential of nonverbal communications in our day-to-day interactions, and particularly as they influence student learning in the classroom.

Ralph Waldo Emerson, the 19th century American essayist, is credited with saying, "Your actions speak so loudly, I can't hear what you're saying." We have all experienced situations in which the verbal and nonverbal communication of the person we are speaking with is incongruent, or out of *sync* with his behavior. What is being said just doesn't seem to match the speaker's behavior. At such times, we tend to believe what we *see* rather than what we *hear*. Neuroscientists suggest that our nonverbal communication is processed in older parts of our brains such as the brain stem, the basal ganglia and the limbic system, areas that pre-date brain centers used for speech; this may be why our nonverbal processing overrides the verbal when there is a mismatch with the person's nonverbal signals.

The purposeful use of nonverbal cues in a classroom contributes to a learning environment that is safe and predictable. In visiting classrooms, it becomes immediately apparent whether students understand expectations for behavior, for learning and for interacting with one another, or whether they are confused because no routines, or inconsistent or poorly understood routines are in place. It is also clear when teachers have been thoughtful about furniture placement in order to construct efficient traffic and work patterns within the class. The use of nonverbal cues is much more than classroom management. It sends the message to all students that "I have tried to anticipate and be thoughtful about all aspects of our work environment in order to make learning as efficient and enjoyable as possible."

Teacher behaviors in this category might include the appropriate use of silence, adjustments in lesson pacing; the thoughtful and purposeful use of space; and the use of predictable routines; e.g. establishing patterns within the class so that students know what is expected of them when they "finish" a piece of work. Other teacher behaviors in this category might include the appropriate use of the approachable or credible voice[11], and a determined congruence between the teacher's verbal and nonverbal behaviors. Thus, as teachers, not only do we carefully select the words and phrases of our content

---

[11] The approachable voice is one in which a sentence or question might be delivered with a wide range of modulation, usually curling upwards at the end of the sentence. An example of this might be when a teacher asks, "Would you like me to read a story to you?" The credible voice has a narrower range of modulation and usually curls downwards at the end. It is the voice of authority and is often used by teachers in giving instructions. For more information on approachable and credible voice patterns, please see Michael Grinder's (1997) work, *The science of non-verbal communication.*

delivery and our instruction, but we also deliberately choose the nonverbal behaviors that will support our message.

Teachers sometimes ask if nonverbal communication is culturally bound, and whether the use of specific tones and gestures in one culture may be different to another. They want to know if our use of nonverbal communication might therefore be confusing to the ESL student or the student new to international schools. While it is true that the meanings and emphatic use of some gestures are culturally shaped or even culturally specific (e.g. hands on hips are perceived as an aggressive stance in some Asian cultures), Ekman & Friesen's (1975) work on the expressions of primary emotions suggests a universality in how we show emotions such as joy, anger, sadness or disgust. In other words, although some of our nonverbal communication is culturally bound, others are universal, and we can teach students in our classes to understand our meaning and intention.

Mediation of Student Thinking

Like the purposeful use of nonverbal cues, the mediation of student thinking relies on the development of a classroom culture in which thinking is *modeled, respected,* and *expected*. Our use of the word 'mediate' comes from the Latin, meaning 'in the middle' and describes our intervening role as teachers in setting conditions that promote thinking in our students. 'Thinking' here refers not only to the application of cognitive processes such as analysis, synthesis, or evaluation, to specific content, but also to the development of habits or routines that identify opportunities to apply such thinking. In other words, we need to develop the habit of thinking. None of this happens in a vacuum, and all of it requires deliberate and focused training. We have been influenced here by the work of Feuerstein (1980), Costa (2000), Perkins (2000), and Lipton & Wellman (2004).

In order to teach thinking, teachers themselves have to be regularly engaged in it. Modeling specific cognitive processes, or making thinking visible (Tishman & Perkins, 1997) makes thinking accessible to students at the same time as it provides them with routines that will help them to adopt and develop such habits for themselves. Specific suggestions for modeling thinking include:

1. **Use the language of thinking, and teach thinking skills explicitly.** When teachers thoughtfully use words such as *recall, infer, evaluate* or *analyze*, and teach students how to perform these cognitive operations, students gain insights into how to think in context. Students also have the opportunity to observe teachers in the act of thinking. We visited one 7th grade classroom in which the teacher

displayed Bloom's Taxonomy on her notice board with accompanying verbs that might be used in each category. This teacher also deliberately taught each of the cognitive operations explicitly, and gave her students practice in framing questions. Marzano and his colleagues (2001) note that teaching students to identify similarities and differences, to compare and contrast, is a strong research-based strategy that really does make a difference in children's learning.

2. **Develop the use of thinking routines within the classroom.** Simple and elegant patterns of thinking can be used over and over again and become part of the fabric of classroom life, making the practice of thinking public, shared and expected, at the same time as they provoke student thinking (Ritchart, 2002). The work of the Visible Thinking in Action[12] group from Harvard suggests a very simple routine that involves two questions: "What's going on here?" and "What do you see that makes you say so?" Repeatedly using such a routine gives students practice in thinking aloud: describing what they see or hear, and then developing the habit of citing data to support their conclusions.

Several years ago, in our Grade 8 Humanities study of industrialization, we used photographs taken in Vietnam, a country that is in transition from a primarily agricultural to an industrialized country. The photographs were varied in content, with pictures taken in cities as well as in the countryside. The cue to the students was, "What's going on here in terms of national development?" and when students had made a judgment, the follow-up question was, "What do you see that makes you say so?"

3. **Explore multiple perspectives as you examine events, concepts and ideas.** Ask students to deliberately take on and speak from different roles and perspectives in order to develop flexibility of thought. Adults, as well as children, often leap to one or perhaps two different points of view. As a deliberate habit, ask, "What other ways might we look at this issue? What other ways are there to interpret this data?" One favorite question from the unit of study on industrialization was one originally framed by Jay McTighe: *Who are the winners and losers of industrialization?* According to social

[12] For more information on Making Thinking Visible and suggested thinking routines, please see
http://www.pz.harvard.edu/vt/VisibleThinking_html_files/01_VisibleThinkingInAction/01a_VTInAction.html

psychologists, humans are cognitive misers (Fiske & Taylor, 1984); that is, we tend to take shortcuts in our thinking, leading us to make erroneous decisions or form inaccurate perceptions. Training students to explore multiple perspectives gives them the tools needed to form and express their own viewpoints; it also sends the message that critical thinking often takes time, and it is expected in *this* classroom.

4. **Craft thoughtful, mediational questions that invite intellectual risk-taking.** So often, we signal to students that thinking is unimportant when we frame questions that have a single right answer. Walter Plotkin, Director of the American International School of Dhaka, calls this the *"Guess what I'm thinking game."* When our questions are framed with a single right answer in mind, we give preferential treatment to students who know the content and can recall it quickly and with precision; we place a premium on fact knowledge; we send the message that "you can stop thinking" once we acknowledge the right answer; and we confirm the low status of students whose strengths are not in this area.

Rather than asking questions with a single right answer, we recommend asking mediational questions that are open-ended, and that open up more response possibilities. Costa and Garmston (2002) tell us there are five characteristics of mediational questions. They:

a. **Use the approachable voice[13].** We know that using the approachable voice makes the question invitational, rather than interrogatory. We know that differences in tone and emphasis, when asking a question such as, "Why did you do that?" produce different types of responses in the listener. If we want students to take risks, we need to invite them to do so by deliberately choosing the approachable voice.

b. **Use plural forms.** Using plural forms, e.g. "What are some reasons . . ." suddenly opens up the possibilities of responses. Particularly for students who are insecure when participating in classroom discussion, the use of plural forms is more invitational than if they need to focus on a single, correct answer. For students who are high-achievers, this question form also implies that there are other ideas that may not yet have been spoken.

c. **Use tentative language.** Tentative language, such as "might", or "hunch" or, *"What ideas are you **considering** at*

---

[13] See previous note on approachable and credible voices, and reference to Michael Grinder's work.

this time?" send the message that nothing is set in stone, and it's OK to take a guess.

d. **Are open-ended.** Open-ended questions, by their construction, state from the outset that there are many possible ways to answer a question, many different pathways to consider.

e. **Embed positive pre-suppositions:** This is the aspect of question crafting that lends the most self-confidence to the person receiving the question. When we frame a question that begins, _"What ideas are you considering . . ."_ we make explicit our trust that the listener _is_ considering ideas. Contrast this with the question, _"If you were to do that homework assignment over again, what might you improve?"_ which embeds the negative pre-supposition that something, in fact, needs improving. Positive pre-suppositions build self-confidence, are encouraging, and promote intellectual risk-taking.

5. **Explore authentic, real-life problems or tasks.** Thinking skills like mediational questions, rarely operate within a vacuum. We are much more likely to cluster and apply different skills depending on the task in front of us. We need to provide the context for this kind of thinking to take place. We suggest that real life, authentic situations that require deliberate and sophisticated thinking are more likely to engage students in a meaningful way, than artificial ones.

In developing a classroom culture for thinking, teachers support student risk taking and help them to develop cognitive self-confidence.

Create a Constructive Learning Community

In creating a constructive learning community, we set norms and expectations for our behavior and our interactions with one another. Highly effective teachers deliberately set out to develop a community culture that is characterized by interdependence, where all members of the class are mutually responsible for one another and supportive of each others' learning.

Parents sometimes complain that the learning of their highly talented children maybe negatively affected by the presence of ESL or lower achieving students within the same class. And, while this may be true if the teacher is unable to differentiate instruction to meet the needs of all learners, the research on cooperative learning is clear: cooperative learning has a powerful effect on learning, more powerful than strategies that employ individual student competition, or individual student tasks (Marzano, Pickering & Pollock, 2001). In many respects, the values and practices of cooperative learning embody the development of a constructive learning community.

There are many decisions that teachers can make if they wish to create a constructive learning community:

1. **Explicitly teach the norms of collaboration** (Garmston & Wellman, 1999), making them 'age-friendly' for the grade level you are teaching. For example, students need to learn what it means to share ideas and pay attention to self and others; if a group member isn't participating, what might other group members do to invite participation?

   Explicit instruction in pausing, paraphrasing and probing also gives students powerful tools to be active members within a group: to listen actively; to ensure comprehension of the group discussion, and to ask questions that will support deeper thought. Collaborative structures allow students to support one another in non-competitive ways.

2. **Use flexible grouping strategies to organize students into different configurations for learning** – pairs, small groups, whole class direct instruction, grouping around interest, or seeded grouping for problem-solving[14]. In addition to the positive research base for cooperative learning groups, flexible grouping helps to develop the expectation that during the course of the year, each student will work with every other person in the class. This is important in breaking down any notion of an 'in group' (high status) and an 'out group' (low status) for learning. Flexible grouping also offers opportunities for lower achieving students to negotiate status, especially when the teacher carefully architects the grouping and the tasks to give students a chance to "shine" in front of his or her peers (Cohen, 2002)[15].

3. **Use instructional strategies such as Jigsaw or Complex Instruction that support learning and interdependence.** The jigsaw strategy was developed by social psychologist Eliot Aronson in the early 1970s in Austin, Texas, when he was asked to help the authorities diffuse a potentially explosive situation in the Austin

---

[14] Please see *Making the Difference: Learning Guide* for a discussion of considerations for grouping, as well as for ideas for different grouping strategies.

[15] We have also found paraphrasing to be very powerful in helping low status students negotiate upward status in the classroom. A well-placed paraphrase can serve to dignify the student who made the original comment without the use of praise, which students often see as disingenuous or false.

schools after desegregation. Jigsaw[16] is a cooperative learning strategy in which each student plays an essential part in solving a problem or completing an assignment. And because each person contributes an essential part, each student is also essential. Likewise, Complex Instruction[17], designed by Elizabeth Cohen, is designed to develop higher-order thinking skills using tasks that require a wide array of intellectual abilities at the same time as it requires students to work interdependently in groups. Cohen's background in sociology prompted her to look specifically at how problems of unequal status within the classroom might be treated; the treatment of status problems is a key feature of Complex Instruction. Using instructional strategies like Jigsaw or Complex Instruction allows teachers an opportunity to craft a culture of interdependence, and not leave its development to chance.

4. **Set reflection as a regular feature of classroom life.** In our busy lives as teachers, the first thing to get cut from our schedules is often structured reflection. And yet, reflection is a necessary practice to help us understand the effect of our actions and behavior. From Plato to Solzhenytsin, writers and philosophers have emphasized that human beings do not learn from experience alone. We learn, not from experience, but from reflection on experience. Reflection is the difference between 20 years of teaching, and one year of teaching repeated twenty times. Just as teachers need structured reflection to continue to grow, so do students need frequent and varied opportunities to reflect on their academic performance as well as how they are performing as members of a group.

• Promote Self-Directed Learning

Ultimately, what we would like to teach our students is that learning is lifelong and isn't confined to the four walls of a classroom; that each individual develops the drive and responsibility for that learning. Self-directed learning is what we see when individuals take the initiative for their own learning, for example, when a Middle School student suddenly develops a keen interest in learning everything there is to know about computers – and emerges after a few short months as a self-confident computer geek! We would like to be able to harness this enthusiasm for

---

[16] For more information on Jigsaw, see http://www.jigsaw.org/

[17] For further information on Complex Instruction, see http://cgi.stanford.edu/group/pci/cgi-bin/site.cgi

learning, and train all of our students to develop that internal locus of control.

Teachers who help students develop self-directedness in their learning demonstrate great understanding of learning theory. They help students to gain deeper self-knowledge of their learning styles, strengths and interests and develop strategies to determine their readiness levels in different content areas. They help students develop a sense of their own identities as learners.

Specific suggestions for helping students develop and internal locus of control for learning include:

1. **Engage students in goal setting.** While teachers must establish curricular goals, Marzano et al. (2001) warn us not to make these goals too specific (e.g. as in behavioral objectives) and allow students opportunities to personalize these goals. Strategies such as K-W-L often illuminate to the teacher and the student what the student wants to learn from a specific unit. Personalizing goal setting provides opportunities for students to determine where they are in the learning journey in relation to the curricular goal: that is, at what level of readiness they are. This kind of goal setting also provides students with a chance to think about a context for their own learning.

2. **Provide students with opportunities to learn about themselves as learners.** What are their strengths and preferences as learners? In what media do they prefer to show their understanding or achievement of learning? How does a "least favorite" production style interfere with a demonstration of learning? When we provide students with choices in learning – whether it is on the specific topic, how they learn it, how they might present their learning, we are differentiating instruction. This helps students to know themselves as learners and develop independence in the learning process.

3. **Train students in self-assessment.** Although assessment in many classrooms usually comes from the teacher, there is a sound research base for student self-evaluation and assessment (Wiggins, 1993). Teachers can prepare exemplars for student review and train students to monitor their learning and achievement. This helps students to develop more realistic perceptions of their learning and align their concepts of quality work more closely with that of the teacher.

4. **Provide timely and corrective feedback.** In order for feedback to be effective, it needs to be descriptive and provide students with meaningful information: where they are in the learning continuum,

and what they need to do in order to make progress. The feedback also needs to be timely![18]

5. **Use Cognitive Coaching[sm] techniques.** The coaching techniques of pausing, paraphrasing and probing are highly effective in working with students, especially as we craft questions that help them to reflect on their progress and articulate what they have learned.

Use Student Responses to Inform Instruction

There are a number of different areas in which soliciting feedback from students can provide us with important data: student responses give us a window into what they have understood and learned from our instruction; and their feedback on our teaching allows us to see how we are doing as instructional leaders. Worked into a feedback loop, both kinds of data allow us to improve instruction for students at the same time as it affords us opportunities to grow professionally.

Teaching for understanding requires that we do less didactic teaching and ask more questions (Wiggins & McTighe, 1998; Perkins,1993). While lecture is an efficient means of delivering content, we recognize that adult (and student!) attention is generally no longer than 10 minutes; while brilliant lecturers can hold our attention for a longer period of time, very few of us are brilliant lecturers. Thus, it is necessary to check frequently for student 'understanding, in light of the problems of misconception, predictable misunderstanding, and apparent understanding (Wiggins & McTighe, 1998; p. 160).' Student responses will tell us what we need to review, revise or re-teach.

Students are also experts in being students. They know what works for them and what doesn't. Their feedback on our teaching can let us know how we're doing in terms of our presentation, our instructional methods, our pacing, and what we may need to do more/less of. Teachers who make it a practice of soliciting feedback on their teaching from students often make the purpose explicit: "Your comments and suggestions will be used to improve the learning and working conditions for all of us." Of course, the variety in student responses ("more homework;" "less homework;" "more assignments using visual skills;" "less assignments that have anything to do with drawing") also presents opportunities to help students become more aware that a variety of styles, interests and preferences are represented among the students in the class.

---

[18] Please see Chapter 13 on assessment, for a fuller discussion of effective feedback.

Exit cards are an efficient and effective way to get a quick sampling of student thinking. Students are asked to write on an index card their responses to one or two questions. The questions can be constructed to help the teacher focus on any aspect of the lesson that s/he wants to collect data on, for example:

1. What was your big learning of today?
2. What questions remain?
3. What was most helpful about today's instruction?
4. How does today's lesson connect with our Essential Questions for this unit?

Conclusion

The five different meta-strategies:

- o   Purposeful use of non-verbal cues;
- o   Mediation of student thinking;
- o   Deliberate creation of a constructive learning community;
- o   Promotion of self-directed learning; and
- o   Use of student responses to inform instruction

provide us with a framework around which we can develop classroom cultures that differentiate instruction and support student learning. When teachers weave these strands into their thinking and planning, students are more likely to feel the invitation to learn.

Meta-Strategy	IMPACT ON STUDENT LEARNING	TEACHER BEHAVIORS	STUDENT BEHAVIORS	RESEARCH/RESOURCES
Use non-verbal cues	• Predictable/safe trusting learning environment • Optimal use of learning time • Equal access for our students including those with special needs, including ESL • Enhanced understanding of learning objectives	• Use silence appropriately • Adjust lesson pacing • Use visual paragraphing • Use space purposefully • Use signals for transitions/behavior cues • Differentiate visual cues with color • Use predictable 'routines' • Use credible and approachable voice • Demonstrate congruence between verbal and non verbal behaviors	• Demonstrate automatic behaviors • Use learning time efficiently • Understand classroom routines • Read and respond appropriately to teacher non-verbals • Recognize and respond appropriately to non verbal cues, in general	Costa, A.L & Garnston, R. (2002). Cognitive coaching: A foundation for renaissance schools. Norwood, Mass.: Christopher-Gordon Publishers, Inc. Grinder, M. (1991). Righting the educational conveyor belt. Portland, Or.: Metamorphous Press. "Managing the Differentiated Classroom" ASCD Video. Marzano, R., Pickering, D.J. & Pollock, J.E. (2001). Classroom instruction that works: Research-based strategies for increasing student achievement. Alexandria, Va.: Association for Supervision And Curriculum Development.
Mediate student thinking	• Focused and active engagement of all students • Emotional and cognitive support for thinking • Self-regulated learning behaviors • Risk-taking in learning • Increased cognitive confidence and efficacy	• Craft questions that are invitational, with a specific topic and a cognitive focus • Craft open-end questions that can be accessed at multiple level that will generate higher order thinking • Control wait/think time (.3 types) • Use mediational paraphrases including the speaker's content, emotional and logic level (3 levels; clarify, organize/summarize, conceptual) • Use praise selectively • Model meta-cognitive reflection	• Paraphrase, summarize, elaborate • Generate 'deep questions' • Employ meta-cognition to guide understanding • Exhibit higher-order/divergent thinking • Demonstrate respectful dialogue/discussion • Construct knowledge focused on lesson objectives • Control impulse	Lipton, L.E. & Wellman, B. (1998). Pathways to Understanding: Patterns & Practices in the Learning-Focused Classroom, 3rd Edition. Sherman, Ct.: MiraVia, LLC. Costa, A.L. & Garnston, R. (2002). Cognitive coaching: A Foundation for renaissance schools. Norwood, Mass.: Christopher-Gordon Publishers, Inc. Costa, A. (1991). The school as a home for the mind. Andover, Ma.; Skylight Publishing Marzano, R. (1997). Dimensions of learning. Alexandria, Va.: Association of Curriculum and Supervision Development. Marzano, R., Pickering, D.J. & Pollock, J.E. (2001). Classroom instruction that works. Research-Based strategies for increasing student achievement. Alexandria, Va.: Association for Supervision and Curriculum Development. Wiggins, G. & McTighe, J. (1987). Understanding by design. Alexandria, Va.: Association of Supervision and Curriculum Development. Brooks J. G. & Brooks, M. G. (1993). In search of understanding: The case for constructivist classroom. Alexandria, Va.: Association for Supervision and Curriculum Development.

* Originally developed at The International School of Kuala Lumpur by Susan Napolitano and William Powell

Meta-Strategy	IMPACT ON STUDENT LEARNING	TEACHER BEHAVIORS	STUDENT BEHAVIORS	RESEARCH/RESOURCES
Create a constructive learning community	• Predictable/safe/trusting learning environment • Interdependent learners	• Teach cooperative learning strategies explicitly • Conduct class meetings regularly to teach social skills and resolve issues • Develop class norms with students • Practice active and reflective listening • Teach the norms of collaboration • Ask students to reflect on their participation in group work • Use jigsaws and other strategies that rely on interdependence	• Demonstrate respect for the needs and skills of peers • Exhibit positive and productive attitudes towards cooperative learning	Garmston, R. & Wellman, B. (1999). The adaptive school: A sourcebook for developing collaborative groups. Norwood, Mass.: Christopher-Gordon Publishers, Inc. Barth, R. (1990). Improving Schools from Within. San Francisco: Jossey-Bass, Inc. Ruddock, J., Day, J. & Wallace, G. (1997). Students Perspectives on School Improvement. In A. Hargreaves, (Ed). Rethinking educational change with heart and mind: ASCD Yearbook. Alexandria, VA.: Association of Supervision and Curriculum Development.
Promote self-directed learning	• Independent/self-motivated learners • Internal locus of control and efficacy • Internationalized self-assessment and goal setting • Development of student self-regulation with regard to academic work	• Construct thoughtfully instruction and directions • Provide assessment models and criteria in advance • Teach and infuse self-assessment and goal setting throughout the learning process • Provide opportunities to practice self and peer assessment • Differentiate instruction (content/process/product) • Insist on follow-up and closure on student assignments • Use cognitive coaching techniques • Teach explicitly rubrics ahead of assessment • Know students well/conduct interest inventories • Use clinical observation strategies • Encourage student choice • Use conferences and regular feedback to promote extended learning	• Use self/peer assessment and goal setting • Self-direct work habits/projects • Generate 'deep questions' • Understand expectations for assignments as per rubric	Costa, A. L. & Garmston, R. (2002). Cognitive coaching: A foundation for renaissance schools. Norwood, Mass.: Christopher-Gordon Publishers, Inc. "Count Me In! Developing Inclusive International Schools" "Internalized... Classroom" ASCD 'Multiple Intelligences in the Sternberg's Intelligence Preferences' ASCD Video Dunn, R. & Dunn, K. Teaching students through their individual learning styles: A practical approach. Tomlinson, C. A. (1997). How to differentiate instruction in mixed-ability classroom, 2nd ed. Alexandria, VA.: Association for Supervision and Curriculum Development.

[handwritten note in right margin:] D llamar a un niño o dos para que modelen los 5 reglas de la clase

Meta-Strategy	IMPACT ON STUDENT LEARNING	TEACHER BEHAVIORS	STUDENT BEHAVIORS	RESEARCH/RESOURCES
Use student response to inform instruction	• Targeted and differentiated learning • Constructive learning community • Development of academic interests • Teacher/student learning partnership	• Align planning with S & B based on student needs • Align record-keeping of student achievement with curriculum and performance standards • Analyze common assessments to inform instruction • Use a variety of student grouping • Target 'mini lessons' • Plan using a reflection/inquiry cycle • Obtain feedback from students on instruction • Analyze/anticipate misunderstandings • Balance teacher/student talk (interactional analysis) • "Uncover" student thinking so that it is explicit • Provide students with exemplars/models of work • Uncover student thinking so that it is explicit and can be used to plan instruction	• Learn in ZPD • Learn in flexible groups • Think out loud • Is familiar with examples and exemplars of grade level expectations • Is able to use rubrics in self-assessment	Powell, W. & Kusuma-Powell, O. (in press). Seeing Ourselves: The Student Perspective.

9 DIFFERENTIATING FOR SPECIAL POPULATIONS

Our Purpose

Several years ago, an anxious young mother went for an interview with the school psychologist. Her seven-year-old son was finding school hard and was behind grade level in learning to read. He had been referred for a psycho-educational evaluation and his mother had been called in advance of the evaluation to give information on the family background. At the end of the interview, the psychologist asked if the mother had any further questions.

"Only one," she said, "What do I tell my son about why he's coming to see you?"

"Tell him that we're going to find out how to tailor things at school to fit him better, so that school can be a more interesting and meaningful experience," the psychologist replied.

Making school fit better for all students so that it can be an interesting and meaningful experience is the purpose of differentiation. Whether students exhibit gifted behaviors, or have attention deficit or are learning English as a new language, we want to make sure that we find ways to engage each one in the learning process. We do this by making the curriculum accessible so that each student feels invited to learn and knows s/he can succeed.

Why Differentiate?

Sometimes, we have been asked by participants in our workshops whether differentiating instruction isn't doing a disservice to students. "Of course it makes learning more interesting and fun for kids, but when they get to the real world, the truth is that they will have to sit through boring meetings and do work they don't like. Are we raising expectations that will make them fail later on in life?"

Thankfully, we don't get those questions very often. We would hope that the purpose of education would be much, much more than training the next generation for a life of boredom. We feel very strongly that the purpose of education has to do with inculcating a love of learning; helping students to identify and develop their interests into talents; learning how to think critically about the problems of the world; and developing a sense of efficacy and interdependence as they enter adulthood. Differentiating instruction helps us to facilitate this growth in students. When we find ways to vary our instruction and adapt it according the needs of different individuals or groups of children in our classes, we are much more likely to engage all students in learning and maximize growth.

A recent report from the United Kingdom (DfES, 2006) suggests the need for personalizing learning as a way to ensure that all children are able to progress, achieve and participate. Personalizing learning is a highly structured and responsive approach to teaching and learning that takes into account and pays close attention to the learner's knowledge, skills, understanding and attitudes (p. 6). In this report, the 2020 Review Group suggests that work needs to be varied and pitched at the child's *zone of proximal development* and supported by assessment *for* learning. There is clearly a growing perception internationally, of the need to differentiate instruction.

How Do We Manage When All Students Are So Different?

Teachers are often overwhelmed at the thought of differentiating instruction when the children in their classes exhibit such different learner characteristics. Differentiation can be daunting, especially when we come to think of the diversity in culture, languages, educational background and experiences that our international school students come to us with. When we put those together with differences in readiness levels, differences in style and learner preferences, differentiating instruction for any class full of students is at least challenging, if not intimidating.

Having said that, differentiating instruction is not the same as the individual instruction of the 1960s and '70s; it doesn't mean having to think of 24 different lesson plans for 24 different students in our classes! In Ochan's Grade 8 Humanities class at the International School of Kuala Lumpur, the teaching team made a promise to the students as well as to their parents at the beginning of each school year. We said, "To the best of our ability, we will craft lessons that will appeal to your particular learning style or strength at least once in every four-day rotation (our Middle School was on a four-day schedule at the time). We would also ask that you stay with us during those assignments that you may not find immediately interesting, and we promise you that by the end of the year, those areas that you don't currently consider to be strength areas, will also improve. And who knows, some things that you thought were boring may become more interesting or even fascinating!"

What we tried to do in the Grade 8 class was to provide instruction in a variety of ways and design assignments that would tap into different learner strengths – so that each student would feel *invited* to learn. For example, we endeavored to provide a balance between visual, tactual, kinesthetic and auditory assignments. We also used a variety of grouping strategies so that students would have experience working individually, in pairs, in small groups, and with the whole the class. By varying our instruction and our assignments, we hoped to meet the needs of different learners in our classes.

In other words, while students *do* have individual learning characteristics, they also exhibit *clusters* of learner characteristics that may be shared by other children in the class. We can apply what we know about teaching to a particular style preference to groups of children who exhibit the same style. For example, what we know about working with one kinesthetic learner – the need to move about during learning tasks – can be applied to other kinesthetic learners.

Teachers ask us about differentiating for special populations. "What about the ESL kids in my class? Do I have to do anything else special for them, if I'm already differentiating instruction?" "How about the ADHD student? How do I handle *him* and teach the rest of the class?"

The motivation behind each of these questions is the same. Teachers want to know how they can ensure success for each child. We suggest that as teachers become more experienced at differentiating instruction, the answers become clearer. Many of the approaches and strategies of differentiation are reflective of good teaching practice for *all* students, and rely on a deep knowledge of our students as learners. The underlying principle for differentiating instruction for special populations – English Language Learners (ELLs), Learning Disabled/Special Needs, the Highly Capable, children with Autism Spectrum Disorders, and children with Attention Deficit (and Hyperactivity) Disorder – begins with exactly the same key. We need to develop a firm knowledge of our students as learners – who they are, what backgrounds (and baggage) they bring to class, what preferences they have for learning, and what their interests are.

We further suggest that our colleagues are our own best resources for differentiating instruction, and that collaboration between professionals – the fourth key – can make the process less overwhelming. Collaboration between specialists (special needs or ESL teachers, teachers with expert knowledge in working with the Highly Capable) and mainstream teachers; between teachers in the same discipline or on the same team; across disciplines, or even across grade levels can provide rich opportunities for professional growth and improved student learning. Although we have framed it as a suggestion, we have found that when teachers get "stuck" – in working with a student, in trying to think of new ways to present instruction, in rehearsing for a parent meeting – there is no better way than to have the benefit of working closely with a colleague.

We know that the decision to admit – or not admit – a child with special needs is one of the most difficult decisions a school can make, and is influenced by a number of variables. Much depends on staffing levels, professional preparation and training of teachers, class size, community resources, parental expectations and available medical support. Much also depends on the attitudes of the school leadership (Kusuma-Powell, 2002). As such, a school that is unable to serve one type of special need student today may find itself in the future able to take in a broader range of students. This is often based on a collective vision and the development of a *will* to serve.

In this chapter, we address suggestions for working with those specific, special populations most likely to be represented in international schools. Although there are still some international schools that have no program for children with special needs, the range of special populations in our schools is broader today than in 2000, when we published *Count me in!* This represents an ongoing shift in demographics and parental determination to travel with their children.

We write this chapter with the knowledge that in our international schools, "pure types" rarely exist; we are likely to find students with overlapping conditions, or children who are "twice exceptional": children who are gifted and learning disabled, ELLs with ADD[19], or ADD students who also exhibit some autistic tendencies.

We also recognize that the suggestions contained in this chapter are not the "be all and end all" of suggestions for working with special populations, but may serve as a point of reference for working with some of the typical issues that arise in our international classrooms. Having said that, we hope the suggestions will open up avenues for teachers as they try to meet the needs of all learners.

Differentiating for Special Needs Students

Students with special needs in our international schools may or may not come to us with diagnoses of learning disabilities or dyslexia, but may exhibit real difficulties with learning. Although the learning issues for each student will be

---

[19] We are using the terms ADD and ADHD interchangeably in this chapter.

unique, there are several characteristics demonstrated by learners which may indicate a learning disability. These may include difficulties in one or more of the following areas, and are not due to hearing/vision problems, environmental or educational deprivations:

- Organization – personal, spatial, time   *Sarah*
- Short/long term memory
- Attention   *London*
- Language development   *Sarah*
- Information processing
- Reading[20], writing, mathematics   *Roberto*
- Motor skills   *Asher*
- Social skills   *Felix vergüenza de bailar, buen constructor*
- Esteem issues stemming from poor school performance

Teachers often notice a difference between the child's academic performance and ability; that is, the teacher senses that the student is capable of a better standard of performance than s/he is currently achieving, and may be puzzled by the discrepancy. Our friend and colleague, Nancy Robinson[21] offers this sage advice: "When a student 'just seems lazy' – be suspicious. *Very few are born lazy.* On the top of your list should be a suspicion of hidden learning disabilities but also suspect depression, Attention Deficit Disorder without the hyperactivity, even poor vision or hearing that has gone undetected."

Nancy also offers us a sound 'problem solving approach to teaching learning disabled students' who have difficulties in reading:

---

[20] Sally Shaywitz (2003) offers a good discussion on the structural and functional differences in the neurological make-up of learning disabled and non-disabled children. Her studies, using magnetic resonance imaging (MRIs) point to a neurological basis for dyslexia.

[21] Dr. Nancy Robinson is the former director of the Halbert and Nancy Robinson Center for Young Scholars at the University of Washington. We are grateful to her for her many contributions to this chapter and book.

A Problem-Solving Approach to Teaching Learning-Disabled Students

- There is *no single best way* to help learning disabled students because there is no single syndrome of reading disability.

- The best thing you can do is to observe and listen carefully to how students speak, how they read aloud (and whether they do better reading silently than aloud), and try to figure out what will be helpful. Are there times they are successful? Use your own sleuthing skills. *Be specific and objective.*

- Start by looking at *very basic skills* such as ability to analyze words into components, get alphabetic-sound linkage right. Sometimes it seems so simple that it's hard to believe that the otherwise smart student can't make the connection. Seems impossible, but it's true.

- In the regular classroom, it is always helpful to *try to get around the disability* in teaching anything but reading
  - *Lighten the reading load* – shorten selections, use same words every time for assignments, etc.
  - Use *technology* wherever it will work (new programs will read material aloud including material from the internet, anticipate spelling, etc.) (www.donjohnson.com is a good place to start). Some programs will enable teacher to *scan the test in* – to read the test to student and record the student's oral response so the teacher can grade it later.
  - Use many *different media* – get books from reading services (see www.rfbd.org) or have parent tape text, let parent read longer homework selections to students, use videos, etc. For true dyslexics, keep complexity of material high; for those with language-learning disabilities, try to simplify or at least repeat material and let parent/buddy interpret if needed.

- Your best approach is often through the student's *own interests* and material that is challenging, keeping their engagement and motivation high.

- *Be a believer.* Some problems students have seem so simple – like linking letters and sounds – that it is almost impossible to believe that they continue to have these problems, day after day, year after year. They can be exasperating – even more for the student than for the teacher/parent. Keep your cool!

A good reference for working with special needs students can be found in Eide and Eide (2006). Their book, *The mislabeled child: How understanding your child's unique learning style can open the door to success*, explains many kinds of difficulties and offers practical strategies to address them.[22]

Differentiated instruction is an excellent approach to meet special needs students where they are and take them where they need to be in the educational continuum. Other suggestions for working with children with learning disabilities or special needs include the following:

1. **Relationships are everything.** Children with learning disabilities often have poor experiences of school and consequently have difficulty developing trust in new settings and with new people. Spend time to make sure you know the student behind the mask. It is likely that teachers will make little progress with these students until a relationship is established. If students are behaving poorly, try to find reasons for the poor behavior. If a learning situation is not working for a child, s/he will usually let us know.

2. **Focus on student strengths instead of deficits.** Because many of us entered the teaching profession to be of service to others, we often make the mistake of focusing on a child's difficulties, problems and deficits, and how to fix them, rather than focusing on his/her strengths. However, we are rarely able to help a child improve by focusing on deficits. Instead, when we are able to identify a strength and build on it, we can often use the strength to improve a weakness. For example, if a child who is experiencing difficulty in learning to read is a kinesthetic learner who needs to move around, capitalize on this style preference by using large cardboard cut-outs of letters that need to be placed on the ground like a giant jigsaw.

3. **Develop strong home-school relationships.** Many students with special needs have difficulty organizing themselves. They forget their

---

[22] See also the following internet resources for more suggestions, advocacy and support: www.texasreading.org (a number of resources that can be downloaded)

www.nifl.gov/partnershipforreading/publications/Cierra.pdf (good source for teaching beginning reading and/or checking basic skills)

www.ldanatl.org (National Learning Disabilities Association of America) offers a variety of resources.

www.ldonline.org A parent resource with numerous articles about specific disabilities, good links.

www.interdys.org (International Dyslexia Association)

www.nlda.org (Nonverbal Learning Disabilities Association)

homework, they forget to write it down, and they lose personal belongings. Having a good relationship with the child's parents is often helpful in getting the child organized. Keep the parent's e-mail address or phone number handy.

4. **Ensure that feedback is timely.** Prompt feedback helps students see the relationship between cause and effect. Sometimes students with special needs require a lot of reassurance from teachers that they are on the right track. Students with learning disabilities also may easily forget the learning objective that was meant to be the focus of the assignment, unless feedback is given in a timely manner.

5. **Teach collaboration skills explicitly.** So often, students with special needs have difficulty in social settings. They don't learn from social cues and often have to learn explicitly how to cooperate within a small group setting. Teaching collaboration skills explicitly (turn taking, sharing ideas, coming prepared, etc.) gives students tools to work cohesively as a team member.

6. **Use multiple modes of presentation.** We need to give students with special needs multiple forms of input in order to ensure their comprehension. We really should not expect students to "get it" on the first round of instruction and should include a recursive pattern in our planning so that we swing back to a concept using a different mode of presentation each time.

Differentiating for Students with Attention Deficit Disorder (ADD or ADHD)[23]

Working with ADD students may provide us our most frustrating – and rewarding – experiences as teachers. Because their attention can sometimes be so erratic, it is difficult to superimpose a pattern of behavior on these children. Their distractibility and poor attention, however, often result in late assignments, lost personal belongings and poor organizational skills. Although descriptions of children with ADD have occurred in medical literature for over a hundred years, our own profession's understanding of the condition as a neurobiological disorder is much more recent.

---

[23] We are using the terms ADD and ADHD interchangeably in this section.

> *Brown (2007) compares having ADD to having a symphony orchestra in the brain in which an effective conductor is missing. Despite having individual parts that work well, there is no "master coordinator" to pull all the efforts together. ADHD affects the brain's cognitive management system (executive functions) and affects one's ability to:*
>
> o Organize and get started on tasks.
> o Attend to details and avoid excessive distractibility.
> o Regulate alertness and processing speed.
> o Sustain and, when necessary, shift focus.
> o Use short-term working memory and access recall.
> o Sustain motivation to work.
> o Manage emotions appropriately.
>
> *Brown, 2007, p. 22*

To date, three different subtypes of ADD have been identified (NIMH, 2006):

o **Predominantly inattentive**: students with this subtype are inattentive, but do not show significant signs of hyperactivity or impulsivity. Signs of inattention may include difficulty screening out irrelevant sights or sounds, poor attention to detail, poor organization, e.g. losing personal belongings or inability to follow directions, or skipping from one activity to another with poor rates of work completion. We sometimes think of these children as "day dreamers" because they seem to be lost in their own world.

o **Predominantly hyperactive-impulsive**: these children do not show significant signs of inattention, but are hyperactive and impulsive. These children seem to have excessive energy and are in constant motion, dashing around the classroom, tapping pencils or fidgeting in their seats. They may also have great difficulty restraining their behavior, have difficulty thinking before acting, blurting out inappropriate comments in the classroom, or have difficulty waiting their turn.

o **Combined type**: these children show signs of inattention as well as hyperactivity and impulsivity.

Not every student who has difficulty paying attention or who shows signs of impulsivity or hyperactivity necessarily has ADD. A diagnosis of ADD is based on the severity and duration of symptoms, and the extent to which they interfere with everyday life (Hallowell & Ratey, 1994). However, because ADD has to do with neurological impairments that effect executive functioning, and because executive functioning does not usually mature in humans until late adolescence, the disorder itself may not be easily diagnosed until an individual is in his/her late teens.

Brown (2007) has identified six components of executive functioning. These components help us to function in our daily lives, often without our own conscious awareness:

- *Activation:* organizing, prioritizing, and activating for work.
- *Focus:* focusing, sustaining and shifting attention to tasks
- *Effort:* regulating alertness and sustaining effort and processing speed
- *Emotion:* managing frustration and modulating emotions
- *Memory:* using working memory and accessing recall
- *Action:* monitoring and self-regulating action

There is no single best treatment for ADHD. Although some children may have adverse reactions to specific medications, in many cases, the use of fine-tuned, stimulant medication is often helpful in providing the child with a window of opportunity for learning. *Medication on its own, however, does not solve the issue of learning.* Interventions for ADHD children are best handled in partnership between home, school and medical practitioner.

Some suggestions that may be useful in working with children with ADHD include the following[24]:

---

[24] See also www.chadd.org (Children and Adults with Attention Deficit Disorder) – for information and resources.

1.**Recognize that ADHD is *not* a lack of willpower.** It is a neurobiological condition that interrupts the development of self-management skills and it often continues into adulthood. ADHD is not simply another word for "behavior or attitude problems." It is important for teachers to understand this point, so that our own frustration levels don't get in the way of educating and supporting these children. Hallowell (1994) suggests that historically, it was probably the excited, excessively energetic child who was drew many of the punishments at school. Most children want to do well, and don't want to attract the ire of adults in their environments.

2.**Provide organizers and organizing support:** Because they are so easily distracted, and because their attention can be so erratic, anything we can do to help organize the ADD child will serve him well. This may mean separate, colored folders for homework, or different binders for each curricular area. It may also mean packing the child's backpack the night before school, so that everything is ready and in place for the morning. Home – school relationships are very important to develop and maintain. Communication between the two serves to provide consistency in our expectations for the child.

3.**Be consistent in behavior and expectations, and maintain rules that can be understood and followed**. When individuals go in and out of attention, life can be very difficult for them to predict. Consistency in adult behavior and expectations will help to keep students grounded and not cause daily school routine to be such a guessing game.

4.**Look for the 'lost' student.** Become aware of the quiet child who seems lost – this may be your quiet ADD student (quite often female), who will otherwise disappear into the background of the class. Because these children look like they are attending and focusing on their work, and because they are so quiet, their inattention and lack of understanding may slip our detection for some time.

Differentiating for Children with Autism Spectrum Disorders (ASD) [25]

We are seeing increasing numbers of children with autistic characteristics or with diagnosed Asperger's syndrome traveling with their parents overseas and

---

[25] Autism and Asperger's syndrome were formerly seen on a continuum as part of the same disorder. Although they share some similar characteristics, Asperger's syndrome has been listed as a separate diagnosis since 1994 in the *Diagnostic and Statistical Manual of Mental Disorders (DSM-IV-TR)*. In this section, we have focused on those symptoms that are similar between the two disorders.

seeking admission to international schools. As such, we felt it important to include a section on differentiating for autistic children.

Autism is defined as a developmental disability that significantly affects a person's ability to communicate and use nonverbal cues, e.g. facial expression or tone of voice (IDEA, US Department of Education, 2006). This impacts any social interaction they may have. Autistic children also have difficulty with language development, academic learning, play, and motor development. They are very sensitive to sensory input; many are hyper-sensitive to sound, contributing to difficulties in developing receptive language, while others are hyper-sensitive to visual input (e.g. flickering lights).

Autistic children are easily overwhelmed by new and unpredictable situations as they find it difficult to apply knowledge gained from earlier experiences to new settings. They also have difficulty learning through imitation, and are often engaged in repetitive actions and verbal repertoire. There is some current research in neuroscience that suggests autistic children may have a breakdown in their *mirror neuron systems*, the neurons which allow us to learn through imitative behavior (Altschuler, Pineda & Ramachandran, 2000).

The following are very general descriptions of autistic children and it is misleading to think of them as *typical*. We recognize that each child comes to us with his/her own unique combination and degree of learning issues.

The National Education Association in the United States has recently published a list of key indicators. All autistic children share the same early characteristics (NEA, 2006):

- o Lack of direct eye-contact. Autistic children use peripheral, rather than central vision, which causes them to appear to look at an object with eyes averted.
- o Lack of joint attention (i.e., attention to the same item or topic as another person)
- o Lack of reciprocal conversation (i.e., ability to engage in verbal turn taking)
- o Atypical sensory/motor processing

In addition, people with ASD exhibit core deficits of varying degrees and combinations in the following areas:

- o Difficulty with identifying important global concepts and elements of tasks
- o Difficulty processing auditory information—understanding, retaining, and retrieving;

> o Difficulty generalizing skills—skills must be taught in context;
> o Difficulty with sequencing information or steps in a task;
> o Difficulty transitioning between different activities;
> o Difficulty with time concepts and time management;
> o Atypical and/or uneven academic, social, or emotional development (e.g., high functioning in some academic areas, low functioning in others).
>
> *National Education Association,*
>
> *The Puzzle of Autism,* (p. 3)

Temple Grandin (2007), a university professor and industrial designer with autism, offers the following suggestions for working with children with ASD. At the elementary school:

o **Give the student time to respond**. When speaking to students with autism, teachers will notice that they take a long time to process auditory information and then produce responses to them.

o **Avoid long strings of verbal directions**. Because of difficulties with auditory processing, children with ASD will get lost in long instructions.

o **Respect sensory sensitivities**. Be aware that the child's heightened sensitivities make him/her easily overwhelmed by regular school experiences such as loud or excited classroom discussion or even the ringing of the school bell. Teachers may need to help ASD children develop coping skills.

o **Avoid vague language**. Autistic children think concretely, and instructions such as, "It's time for P.E." will need further elaboration (i.e. that work needs to be put away and the class tidied up, that children need to line up and walk to their PE class).

o

For middle and high school students with autism:

o **Develop the student's strengths**. Help students to learn how they learn best, whether it is through visual, auditory, kinesthetic or tactual means, and then help them make the link between the strength area and learning new material.

o **Develop social skills through shared interests**. Special classes or activities clubs such as chess, computer programming, or book circles can be positive and safe environments for students to learn social skills.

o **Find – or be – a mentor**. Autistic children need advocates who will help them to broaden their range of interests or deepen an existing one. They are often fixated on repetitive activities, and helping them to turn these fixations into useful activities will also help autistic children to be successful in life.

   o **Make a gradual transition from school to employment**. Although this is not always easy in international school settings, there are some schools such as the International School of Brussels and Western Academy in Beijing, already leading the way with work – school programs (p. 30 – 31).

   o **Differentiating for Highly Capable Children**

Interestingly, the idea of differentiating instruction was originally developed for use with gifted and talented or highly capable children, students who required greater challenge than the curriculum on offer. Strategies recorded elsewhere in this book (e.g. curriculum compacting) were created specifically for use with gifted children.

There are a number of definitions of giftedness or gifted behavior. One theory that has been influential in shaping policies and programs for gifted children in the United States as well as in the United Kingdom[26], Western Australia[27] and New Zealand[28], is Renzulli's (1998) 'Three-Ring Conception of Giftedness'. In this model, Renzulli discusses the dynamic nature of gifted behavior as the interaction between well-above average intelligence, high levels of task commitment, and high levels of creativity.

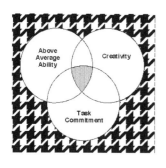

Well-above average intelligence is evidenced by high levels of abstract thinking, verbal and numerical reasoning, rapid information processing and an ability to apply learning to novel situations and make connections to real life situations. Renzulli also includes the application of these skills to specific areas of knowledge or human performance; making appropriate use of knowledge; and the ability to sort relevant from irrelevant information.

Task Commitment can be thought of as the capacity for high levels of focused attention, enthusiasm, interest and involvement in a particular area and the capacity to sustain that interest, persevere in the endeavor and work hard. Setting high standards for one's work. We recognize this aspect of Renzulli's definition is often difficult to fulfill, particularly in adolescence.

---

[26] http://www.nagcbritain.org.uk/giftedness/conceptions.html#renzulli

[27] http://www.det.wa.edu.au/education/Gifttal/provision/provtris.htm

[28] http://www.tki.org.nz/r/gifted/handbook/

Many gifted individuals will not exhibit task commitment until they are in the right environment, and as a result, may present as serious under-achievers.

Creativity is demonstrated by originality of thought, flexibility in thinking, reaching out for new and different connections, being mentally playful; and a willingness to take risks.

Individuals who are gifted and talented are capable of developing the interaction between these three areas, and applying them to potentially valuable areas of human performance. Renzulli (1998) warns us against limiting identification of this special population to the top 2 – 3% of students who show "school smarts" alone, or receive the highest marks on standardized or IQ tests; historically, he writes, it is the *producers* of knowledge, those who have found new connections in thinking, who have been considered to be truly gifted, rather than those who were only *consumers* of knowledge. As educators we need to be oriented towards developing gifted behaviors in certain students at certain times and in certain circumstances.

Giftedness can also be thought of in more general terms as being advancement in some areas of development that we value, whether in academic or some other domain (Robinson, 2007, personal communication). We need to be *hopeful* as well as *flexible* in our perception of giftedness and acknowledge that the demonstration of gifted behaviors doesn't need to be established on the first day of school and may include students who are not successful academic learners. None of these are neat or tidy definitions!

In working with gifted children an optimal match approach (Robinson & Robinson, 1982) may work best; that is, to strive towards an appropriate fit between readiness and opportunity (Robinson & Robinson, 1982). For highly capable learners, this may involve:

- Acceleration, either within the classroom or between class levels (there are many accelerative options, including escaping the Tyranny of the Birthdate through early school entry).
- A combination of compacting (pre-assessing so you don't waste time "teaching" what the child has already mastered or could master with a simple demonstration) and, with the time saved, deepening and extending the curriculum through substitute assignments, independent work and projects with other highly capable students(Robinson, 2007, personal communication).

Be aware that gifted learners may end up taking a great part of the load in a cooperative learning situation – because they often care more about the end product. In such instances it becomes very important to teach explicitly the norms of collaboration and the expectations for group work – and then closely monitor the group process.

In *Teaching gifted students in the regular classroom,* Susan Winebrenner (2000) provides us with an indispensable reference for teaching gifted students in the regular classroom.

Other suggestions for working with this population follow.

1.**Beware that gifted students may be at risk**. Because certain areas of academic work come so effortlessly to them, they don't develop the problem-solving heuristics *or* the resilience to face sudden new challenges. Many of them think so quickly that they often can't explain *how* they arrived at their answer. School work may come so easily to them that it won't be until they are much older that they face failure and, as a result, suddenly break down with self-doubt. They may not have developed the approaches to problem-solving that their contemporaries have. Gifted students are often looking for greater stability, loyalty and intimacy than their age mates are prepared to give them, and as a result are also at-risk emotionally.

2.**Don't be misled by academic achievement** (or the lack of it). Many gifted students may be underachieving. Prolonged experiences with boredom in the classroom may have produced negative attitudes to school.

3.**Help students to learn about themselves:** Help them learn about their strengths, interests and preferences. Who are their heroes? What are their hobbies and leisure time interests? Being flexible in our teaching approaches, and providing students with choice may help them identify and develop special interests.

4.**Look for prior knowledge** – Gifted students sometimes learn less than others because they already know more to begin with. Listen to the questions they ask, the inferences and connections these students make, and provide opportunities for them to grow. Continue to probe, using medative questions that will allow them to think deeply. Teach students to self-assess, so that they learn how to judge their own work. Beware that curricular standards don't dictate "minimum" competencies for gifted students.

5.**Watch out for gifted girls!** Many cultures produce unspoken pressures for girls to be obedient, submissive, attractive and downplay intelligence.

6.   **Don't over-use gifted students as tutors.** Gifted students can be very helpful in explaining concepts to classmates in age-appropriate language. However, it is important not to over-use them as assistant teachers.

7.   **Provide opportunities for these children to work with their intellectual peers, even adults.** These opportunities may include grade acceleration, after-school interest groups and clubs, or special projects.

Differentiating for English Language Learners (ELLs)

Sometimes when we design programs, it is convenient for us to think of ELLs as a single, specific population. However, when we come face-to-face with them in our classrooms, we know the only similarity they share is in not speaking the language of instruction. Even with same-country backgrounds, ELL students are not a monolithic group. They are as varied and diverse as any group of international schools students, and thus, differentiating for ELLs is not an issue of choice.

New ELLs in any international school face the daunting task of adjusting and adapting to a new community (and finding a sense of belonging there) at the same time as they must balance language learning with content learning in a new language (Nordemeyer, 2007, in press). When working with ELLs, it is important not simply to use words easily understood by the students. Krashen (1988) and others have written on the importance of Comprehensible Input, that is, setting receptive language targets just beyond what students can easily understand. Comprehensible Input, in low stress situations, helps ELLs acquire informal language, particularly important for beginning level ELLs. However, by itself, Comprehensible Input is insufficient to help students develop academic English. It is for this reason that class teachers need to become knowledgeable about language development – trends, expectations and plateaus – for students in the grade level they teach. Scarcella (1990) indicates the need for direct language instruction, followed by supportive instructional feedback to develop academic language.

Some suggestions for working with ELLs are as follows:

1.**Develop a broad understanding of the socio-cultural contexts of your students** – perhaps a brief history of their countries, their values and traditions, and attitudes towards education. Students and parents always appreciate it when teachers have taken the time to get to know something about their national identities.

2.**Become familiar with the types of errors made by specific language groups.** Quite often, teachers will find that typical linguistic errors are made due to interference from native languages. For example, in Bahasa Indonesia, there is only one pronoun used to refer to the third person (he, she), and it is gender-neutral. Consequently, when students from this language group speak English, they will often make mistakes in gender references. Adjectives in Bahasa Indonesia are also placed *after* the noun, so students from this language groups often have difficult with correct English syntax; instead of saying: "a big car," they may say, "a car big".

3.   Become knowledgeable also about the English language as well as most effective ways to teach it. Courses in ESL or ELL instruction are available in many locations, and teachers are wise to develop up-to-date knowledge of theory and practice.

4.**Become knowledgeable about expectations for language development of students at the grade level you are teaching.** This includes knowledge of how language is transferred and how to recognize it when it has reached a plateau – and how to move it forward again.

5.**Use multiple sources of input**: gestures and other nonverbal communication, dramatization, pantomime, visuals, and technology. All over the world, a common response to not being understood is to repeat what we've just said, only in a louder voice! All of us, ELLs, as well as other students, benefit from multiple sources of input. When we select other sources of input to support our spoken message, chances of it being understood are greater.

6.**Check frequently for comprehension!** ELLs may sometimes give nonverbal expressions of comprehension for what is being said or what they are asked to do, expressions that belie the confusion they may actually be feeling. Especially if these children were successful students in a previous school setting, not knowing or not being sure of what is going on can be a new and difficult experience in which they feel the need to mask discomfort. In addition, in some cultures, the idea of 'face' is sufficiently important that children would rather hide their lack of understanding rather than be embarrassed by showing uncertainty.

Jon Nordemeyer (2007) has prepared suggestions for mainstream teachers to integrate language and content learning:

Five ways for mainstream teachers to integrate language and content learning

1. *Use graphic organizers.* Give students a visual (e.g. timeline, diagram) which relates information and helps to organize new concepts. Graphic organizers also provide a "visual grammar" by allowing common language patterns to be connected to key concepts (e.g. smallpox vaccine was developed in 1796, the Red Cross was founded in 1864).

2. *Teach vocabulary.* Provide students with thematic lists of difficult words before a new unit, and return to these words throughout the unit. Pay attention to how common words (i.e. *table)* may be used differently in an academic context. Teach students to use prefixes, suffixes and roots to understand and remember new words since approximately 60% of English words have Latin or Greek origins. Practice with fun activities

---

like bingo, pictionary, or crossword puzzles.

3. *Use dialogue journals.* Have students write back and forth with other students, with their family or with the teacher. They can describe what they have done in class, articulate what they have learned and share any questions that remain.

4. *Teach discipline-specific genres.* Identify and explain different text types (e.g. lab report, newspaper article) by modeling patterns of organization, text structures and transition words. Provide writing frames or sentence starters to scaffold students' writing in the genre.

5. *Reverse the lesson.* Instead of introducing a new idea through a reading and <u>then</u> following it with application activities, reverse the sequence. Start with a lab, video, demonstration or other hands-on activity, then use the text to reinforce both content and key academic language.

Nordemeyer, J. (2007).Balancing Language and Content:

Teaching English Language Learners in the 21st Century

Nordemeyer echoes the need for collaboration between ESL and mainstream teachers so that instruction is seamless and supportive of ELLs learning. This means that collaboration needs to intentional, and take place in the planning, instruction and reflection stages of the teaching cycle – and that time in school needs to be given for teaming. Having said that, as skills in collaboration don't come naturally to most of us, each member of a teaching partnership needs training in collaborative practice. This will enable full participation from all members in the process of teaming.

10 DIFFERENTIATING FOR GIRLS AND BOYS

The trouble with conventional wisdom is that, more often than not, it is just that -- *conventional*. In other words, it is generally accepted without much critical examination, which on reflection, may be counter to just about everything we know about the pursuit of wisdom.

We believe that the education of boys and girls over the last century has been a victim of conventional wisdom.

Take, for example two children -- a girl and a boy -- born sixty years apart with their childhoods spanning the twentieth century: Myrna and David.

Myrna was born in the 1920s, the only child of a successful middle class family in Britain. Myrna's father was a dentist and her mother a housewife. The family was seen as a pillar of middle class respectability. Myrna was a bright, imaginative and sensitive child with considerable musical talents, who loved stories. But at school she was definitely an average student, frightened of the nuns who ran the Roman Catholic school she attended. While she enjoyed the opportunity to socialize with her friends, none of the school subjects really captured her interest. When Myrna turned sixteen, her parents presented her with a choice. She could go to university and follow in her father's footsteps as a dentist or she could go to secretarial school. The choice divided the family. While her father was keen to have Myrna enter university, her mother felt strongly secretarial training was more appropriate for a girl and would better suit *her* perception of Myrna's cognitive abilities. "Myrna's just not the academic type," her mother would say to anyone within earshot, including Myrna herself. Myrna's mother may also have been concerned about the perceived difficulty that well-educated young women had in finding husbands. Perhaps predictably, Myrna chose to enter secretarial school.

David was born in the mid 1980's to a successful middle class family living in the suburbs of Baltimore. His father was a financial analyst and his mother was an elementary school teacher. As products of the 1960's and 70's, Mom and Dad were very conscious of traditional gender stereotypes. In college Mom had been active in a feminist organization and Dad shared her sympathies regarding the historical subjugation of women. They were determined to raise David in such a way as to avoid what they perceived as the parenting errors of the past. The new born baby's room was painted yellow instead of blue. His toys included stuffed animals. Toys that replicated weapons or were associated with violence of any form were strictly banned from the household. David entered the Hobby Horse Play School at the age of three and had two happy years there. The trouble began in kindergarten.

David struggled with the alphabet and was confounded by phonemic awareness. He had great difficulty retaining "sight words." By October of his kindergarten year, David told his mother that his teacher was "mean" and that he didn't want to go to school. Mom visited the class to observe the interaction and could see nothing wrong with what the teacher was doing. She began to worry about David. In November, the teacher called in both parents to communicate her concern about David's impulsivity, lack of concentration, and aggressive behavior towards the other children. The teacher supported her concerns by showing evidence of David's lack of academic progress and sharing with his parents a series of drawings that David had made illustrating scenes of violence (a train crashing into a building, a spaceship attacking the school, and a dinosaur munching an airplane). David's down-hill spiral continued into first and second grade. By third grade he was referred for full psycho-educational testing and in the middle of grade five David started taking Ritalin. Middle School saw David constantly in disciplinary trouble for his impulsivity. He was suspended for skipping classes, for vandalism and stealing. The prognosis for David's high school career was not good.

It so happened that both Myrna and David emerged into adulthood successfully – albeit with little help from their formal schooling. Although she had nothing more than a tenth grade education, Myrna rose to be the director of a mental health clinic at a major American East Coast hospital. In her fifties, Myrna was touring the US making speeches at medical conferences on specialized therapies for the treatment of phobias. By any standard, she had emerged as a successful, self-educated career woman. David left high school during his tenth grade year and went into the job market – working first in a carpet factory and then on a fishing boat in Alaska. By his nineteenth birthday David had recognized his need for more education. He took the GED high school equivalency examination and entered a community college. Two years later he transferred to the state university.

Today, David has two masters' degrees and is teaching high school social studies in New Mexico.

Some of the difficulties that both Myrna and David encountered in school can be traced to conventional wisdom about the education of girls and boys.

For most of the 20th century educators have operated on faulty and sometimes very misguided assumptions regarding how gender affects learning. For the first half of the century, most teachers accepted that there were gender specific learning characteristics of boys and girls. Boys tended to be louder, more aggressive, more impulsive and more competitive than girls. Accordingly, schools offered boys different (and often many more) sporting opportunities than they did girls. On average, girls were able to concentrate on a given seat task longer than the more restless, more disruptive boys. In high school, however, boys tended to outperform girls in the areas of math and science and greatly out-numbered girls in terms of university admissions. For the years leading up to the feminist movement of the 1960's and 70's, teacher perceptions of how boys and girls learned differently were based on actual classroom observations *and* preconceived gender roles. It was *natural* for young boys to play with trucks and blocks and soldiers; just as it was *natural* for girls to play with dolls and stuffed animals. It was *natural* for boys to out perform girls on university entrance standardized testing. Girls were, after all, destined to be mothers, housekeepers, nurses or secretaries. Boys, on the other hand, had competitive corporate careers in front of them.

By the mid 1980's the pendulum of conventional wisdom, at least in the United States and Western Europe, had swung in the opposite direction. Traditional gender roles had come under fierce attack from the feminist movement. The historical subjugation of girls and women had become a widely accepted political reality and sexual chauvinism associated with bigotry and ignorance was widely scorned. In essence, the new conventional wisdom told us that traditional gender stereotypes had served as societal straight jackets for both girls and boys – but to the considerable detriment of girls. Historically, girls and young women had been the educational victims of a self-fulfilling prophecy. Myrna's lack of educational self-confidence had led her to choose a career as a secretary as opposed to a dentist.

The conventional wisdom that emerged from the 1980's would have us believe that while boys and girls start life with the same cognitive raw material, the traditional manner in which we raise and educate our children serves to transmit gender stereotypes from one generation to the next and perpetuate the subjugation of women.

This was a politically attractive notion since attitudes and perceptions, while difficult to alter, are considerably easier to change than physiology. The generally accepted idea was that by cleansing the upbringing and education of children of repressive gender stereotypes, we would nurture boys who would be more empathetic and sensitive and girls who would be more assertive and ultimately more self-fulfilled. Accordingly, we set about pruning our classroom libraries for sexually chauvinistic literature and encouraged boys to engage in imaginative and empathetic role play. Single sex home economics and woodworking classes disappeared. We offered girls more competitive sports options.

In our efforts to avoid the errors and injustices of the past, we engaged in the business of trying to create "gender neutral classrooms". In these classrooms, teachers ignored gender specific learning differences in girls and boys either because they were unaware of them or out of an attempt to be egalitarian. Nurture eclipsed nature.

However, recent research strongly suggests that as a profession we need to review and revise our perceptions and attitudes towards gender differences in learning. When we ignore the natural learning proclivities that boys and girls bring to the classroom, both genders suffer. There is increasing evidence that boys like David and girls like Myrna would learn more effectively in classrooms that included "gender-friendly" learning activities.

Some writers (Sax, 2005; Gurian, 2001) go so far as to suggest that because the "gender neutral classroom" does not take into account the real physiological differences in girls and boys brains, it inadvertently perpetuates the hurtful and pernicious stereotypes that it was designed to eradicate. There is also considerable evidence that the supposedly gender neutral classroom is particular damaging to the learning of boys. In the United States we have witnessed a dramatic drop over the past two decades in the academic performance of boys (Conlin, 2003; Newkirk, 2003). The so-called "new gender gap" has also been documented in the United Kingdom, Australia, New Zealand and Canada. According to a US Department of Education study (2000) the average 11th grade boy is now writing on the same level as the average 8th grade girl. The population of high school dropouts is predominantly male and the number of girls entering university in the US is now greater than boys. In fact, the National Center for Educational Studies predicts that by the year 2011, 60% of all earned degrees in the US will go to women.

Research over the last two decades in the medical profession, neuroscience, psychology and evolutionary biology strongly suggests that boys and girls do not start life with the same cognitive raw material. Researchers have identified more than a hundred structural differences in the brains of girls and boys (King & Gurian, 2006). These differences coupled with what we now know about chemical and hormonal differences in the male and female brains make it imperative that gender feature prominently in our efforts to differentiate instruction in order to maximize learning.

We are not suggesting that there isn't significant learning over-lap between girls and boys. Of course, there is. And often what works for boys also works well for girls and vice versa. Most importantly, we are not suggesting that there is a difference in what girls and boys can do, but rather in how they may most efficiently learn how to do it.

> *The differences between what girls and boys can do are not large. But the differences in how they do it can be very large indeed. For example…you can teach the same math course in different ways. You can make math appealing to girls by teaching it one way, or you can make it appealing to boys by teaching it another way. Girls and boys can both learn math equally well if you understand the gender differences* (Sax, 2005, p.33).

This was a message that the teachers at Douglass Elementary School in Boulder, Colorado took to heart. The results of the 2005 Colorado State Assessment Program revealed a significant literacy gap in the 470 student school. Boys, who represented at least 50% of the total school population (and 75% of the special education population) underscored the girls by average of 13 points in Grades 3-5. It became clear to the teaching staff at Douglass that the gender literacy gap had serious implications for the school and, of course, for the future of its students. The teachers placed this gender gap on the proverbial front burner and sought out recent research that actually supported much of their intuition about how boys and girls learn differently. They implemented deliberately "boy-friendly" teaching strategies in the classroom and within one year Douglass was able to close the gender gap (the boys experienced a 24.4 percentage point gain in reading and writing). At the same time, the girls' performance in reading and writing also improved significantly (King and Gurian, 2006).

The research suggests that it is time for gender learning differences to feature prominently in our differentiation of classroom instruction. What then are some of these biologically based gender differences that influence learning in the classroom?

The answers will surprise very few veteran teachers or observers of children. There are differences in the ways that male and female brains are organized. There are differences in verbal and spatial capacities as well as in the optical, neural and auditory systems of girls and boys. These differences have profound implications for the classroom.

Male and Female Brains are Organized Differently

Studies in the 1970's and 80's showed that the male brain is much more asymmetrical than the female brain. In other words, the brains of men are more regionally specialized -- more compartmentalized than the brains of women. In men, the left hemisphere of the brain is clearly specialized for receiving and generating language. In the female brain such asymmetry is much less noticeable. For example, men who have a stroke involving the left hemisphere suffer a drop in verbal IQ of about 20% (from 111.5 to 88.7). On the other hand, men who suffer a stroke centered in the right hemisphere see virtually no drop at all in verbal IQ. The message seems to be clear. If a man's left hemisphere is damaged, the language function will be damaged; while damage to the right hemisphere does not appear to affect language.

The female brain is significantly less compartmentalized. Women who suffer a stroke affecting the left hemisphere see drop in verbal IQ, on average of 9%. Women who suffer a stroke affecting the right hemisphere see a similar drop of about 11%. Women, unlike men, use both hemispheres of their brains for language (McGlone, in Sax, 2005).

Recent research seems to suggest that the female brain has, on average, a thicker corpus callosum than the male brain (Dubb et al.; 2003, Shin et al. 2005). Some claim it is up to 20% thicker in females (Gurian, 2001). The corpus callosum is the connecting bundle of tissue between the left and right hemispheres of the brain. The speculation is that this thicker corpus callusum permits greater cross hemispheric communication in the female brain. Newsweek[29] recently speculated that this might account for "female intuition" and that women tend to be better at multi-tasking than men. While this is still in the realm of reasoned scientific speculation, there is no question that as teachers, we often see that boys are more single-task oriented and have greater difficulties with transitions between activities or subjects than girls do.

There is also speculation that the male tendency to lateralize its activity, that is to compartmentalize activities into discrete areas of the brain, may be linked to the preponderance of learning disabilities found in boys as opposed to girls. This may be particularly true for attention deficit disorders. In other words, if there is a dysfunction in a highly specialized region of the male brain, it is probably more debilitating in terms of learning and much more noticeable to teachers and parents than a dysfunction in the more integrated

---

[29] http://www.msnbc.msn.com/id/9120157/site/newsweek/, accessed 18/5/07.

regions of the female brain. In addition, females also produce less of the neurotransmitter serotonin than do males and so are less inclined to hyperactivity disorders (Gurian, 2001).

Recent research is suggesting that differences in how male and female brains function is *not* solely the result of hormonal influences. In the 1990's studies out of Harvard University suggested that differences in how male and female brains functioned and how they organized themselves was primarily the result of hormonal differences, leading to the belief that since prepubescent children don't manufacture sex hormones in large quantities, the sex differences in the brains of young children must be small and virtually insignificant. We are now questioning whether, indeed, sex differences in the brains of males and females are the result of sex hormones. In 2004, a team of fourteen neuroscientists from the University of California, the University of Michigan and Stanford University published their findings demonstrating a significantly different expression of proteins derived from the X and Y chromosomes in the male and female brains (Sax, 2005). These scientists examined brain tissue from thirty different individuals and in each case they were able to identify the gender of the donor. While hormones may certainly play an important role in how males and females learn differently, it is now clear that the actual brain tissue of girls and boys are genetically programmed to be different.

Another important distinction in the brains of boys and girls is that their respective development is *sequentially different*. Any veteran teacher will have noticed that girls tend to mature cognitively (in areas that we tend to value highly in schools) earlier than boys. However, this is something of an oversimplification. Researchers at Virginia Tech studied the brain activity in 508 normal children (224 girls and 284 girls) ranging in age between two months to sixteen years. Their results demonstrate that various regions of the brain develop in a different sequence in girls as compared with boys. Sax writes that these "researchers found that while the areas of the brain involved in language and fine motor skills mature about six years earlier in girls than in boys, the areas of the brain involved in targeting and spatial memory mature about four years earlier in boys than in girls. These researchers concluded that the areas of the brain involved in language, in spatial memory, in motor co-ordination, and in getting along with other people develop in 'different order, time and rate' in girls compared with boys (p. 93)."

Implications for the Classroom

The significance of these findings for teachers is threefold. First, it clearly demonstrates that, in general, developmentally appropriate learning challenges may be somewhat different for boys and girls. This does not mean a two tier structure for academic standards. But, it could mean that boys and girls may need to follow different pathways to achieve the same standards.

Secondly, and no less importantly, the gender specific sequential nature of brain development strongly suggests that the sex differences in the brains of children are more influential to learning than sex differences the mature brains of adulthood.

Thirdly, because a girl's prefrontal cortex is generally more active than a boy's at an earlier age, girls tend to be less impulsive than boys and are usually better able to sit still and focus on a literacy task (reading or writing) than boys are.

Teachers can also increase the use of experiential and kinesthetic learning activities. Both boys and girls need physical movement – boys perhaps even more than girls. Activities that require movement actually help boys to focus and concentrate.

Verbal/Spatial Differences in the Brains of Girls and Boys

Generally, male brains have more cortical areas that are specialized to spatial-mechanical functioning than female brains do. This may account for boys tending to prefer toys that move in space (balls or trucks) or sports that rely on spatial orientation. This may also provide for the proclivity that males show in spatial abilities in areas such as mechanical design, navigation, geometry, measuring, geography, and map reading. It may also have a connection to the statistically higher proportion of boys who select and succeed at higher level math and science courses.

Girls' brains, on the other hand, generally have a greater cortical emphasis on verbal and emotional processing (Blum, 1997). Girls tend to develop elaborative language earlier than boys. They tend to use a broader vocabulary than boys do and they tend to think more verbally than boys. This has very significant implications for classrooms which tend to be language dominated.

The superior verbal ability of girls has been linked to emphasis that they placed upon the use of language in fostering and maintaining relationships. Sax (2005) describes friendships between girls as *face-to-face* in that these relationships focus on being together, talking together, developing a vocabulary for the emotions and engaging in a degree of self-disclosure. Sharing personal secrets is a measure of the girl-to-girl bonding that takes places in friendship groups. Girl friendships tend to be more intimate and personal and more reliant on conversation and oral language (Tannen, 2005). This emphasis that girls place on language development and use may be connected to the fact that girls outperform boys in reading and writing throughout elementary and middle schools.

Boy friendships, on the other hand, can be described as *shoulder-to-shoulder* (Sax, 2005) in that boys tend to socialize not around conversation but around a group activity – for example, a sport or a video game. Boys tend not to use language as a means of bonding friendships. Extended conversation among boys is not common and, as a general rule, boys do not tend to value emotional self-disclosure.

Researchers at Harvard using MRI brain imaging techniques have revealed some startling data about how males and females process emotions differently (Killgore, Oki & Yurgelum, 2001, in Sax 2005). Children from the age of seven to seventeen were exposed to negative or unpleasant visual images in order to ascertain which part of the brain was activated. In young children, the negative emotional activity was localized in the amygdala – a phylogenetically primitive portion of the brain that hasn't changed much through evolution. Thus it is not surprising that when we ask a six or seven year old about the source of his or her emotional reaction (e.g. "why are you looking so sad?") we are often greeted by a confused silence. The source of this confusion is that there are very few direct connections between the processing of the emotional reaction (in the amygdala) and the language generative portions of the brain (the cerebral cortex).

In adolescence we see a shift in the area of the brain associated with the processing of negative emotions. We see the processing of negative emotion moving from the primitive amygdala up into the cerebral cortex – that area of the brain which is associated with our higher order thinking such as language production, critical thinking and reasoning.

The startling revelation of this research is that this shift takes places *only in girls*. The processing of negative emotions in adolescent boys remains in the amygdala. In terms of our evolutionary past, this may have made sense in terms of survival. The amygdala is the seat of the male "fight or fight" response and twenty thousand years ago the processing of negative emotion could easily have been caused by the appearance of a saber-toothed tiger. However, it may put boys at a considerable disadvantage when a high school English teacher asks the class to write their emotional reactions to novel or short story.

Implications for the Classroom

Perhaps the most significant implication for the classroom is simply the awareness of the teacher that girls and boys bring to their learning different proclivities in the verbal and spatial arenas. In the service of gender friendly-instruction, we can increase our use of visual and spatial representations. These can include tools such as graphic organizers, illustrations, manipulatives, and the skillful use of technology.

We can also vary our use of production style preferences. In other words we can provide students some choice in how they demonstrate their learning (e.g. by writing, drawing, building or performing). In addition, employing nonverbal planning tools (such as story boards, etc.) are often very useful as introductions to activities that are predominantly verbal (writing activities). These non-verbal planning activities can be particularly valuable for boys.

In terms of the differences in how boys and girls process emotion, it is probably important for teachers to recognize that girls and boys are looking for different types of relationships with their teachers. Gurian (2001) explores this in some depth and suggests that the gender-specific needs for student/teacher bonding can be an important determinant of teacher behavior in the classroom.

Gender Differences in Our Optical and Neural Systems

We are now aware that the anatomy of the human eye is different in males and females and this has an important influence on how we perceive the world around us. In both girls and boys, the retina of the eye translates light into neurological signals. The retina contains the photoreceptors, the so-called "rods" and "cones". Rods are sensitive to black and white; cones are sensitive to color. The rods and cones transmit their neurological signals to the ganglion cells. There are two types of ganglion cells, usually referred to as M cells (magnocellular – very big) and P cells (parvocellular –very small). The M cells, principally detectors of motion, are wired primarily to rods and receive very few neurological signals from the cones. They are distributed throughout the retina so that we can track moving objects anywhere in our field of vision. P cells, on the other hand, are wired to cones and transmit extensive information about color and texture.

Microscopic examinations of the human eye over the last few years have revealed that the male retina is significantly thicker than the female retina. This is because large M cells predominate in the male retina while the female retina is richer in the small P cells. This means that boys are much more sensitive to motion and movement and girls more discriminating in terms of color and texture. This makes evolutionary sense when we consider that for the past several hundred thousand years males were the primary hunters and females had responsibility for identifying and gathering edible plants, fruits and roots.

163

Implications for the Classroom

These visual differences in girls and boys are borne out in the study of the art work of young children (Kawecki, 1994) Girls tend to draw pictures of people, pets, or colorful objects such as flowers, employing ten or more colors. Boys, on the other hand, tend to draw an action situation (e.g. a car crash, a rocket –taking off, a spaceship attacking earth) using a much narrower range of colors (gray, black. silver and blue). The difference in the distribution and density of M cells and P cells may have contributed to the stereotype that "art is for girls," and underscore the comparative ease with which girls are able to include visual details in their narrative and expository writing. Thus the importance of specificity in the construction of assessment rubrics (e.g., in an art rubric we might specify: "uses 4 or more colors" or in a writing rubric: "uses adjectives and adverbs to describe color, texture and motion").

Perhaps most significantly, girls and women have been shown to be able to "read" facial expressions better than their male counterparts (Hall, 1985; McClure, 2000). Given what we now know about the importance of non-verbal communication and how reliant we are (even unconsciously) on our intuition (Gladwell, 2005), the ability to interpret facial expressions represents a crucial dimension in any relationship building exercise, from parenting to teaching, from supervising a business associate to leading a work team.

Gender Differences in Hearing

In addition to seeing things differently, girls and boys actually hear differently. Extensive research on newborn girls and boys (Sax, 2005) has shown clearly that the average girl baby had an acoustic brain response about 80% greater than the response of the average boy baby. The researchers used sound in the range of 1,500 Hz because hearing in that range is essential for the understanding of human speech. Other studies have confirmed that girls' hearing is significantly more sensitive than boys'. In addition, this gender difference in hearing sensitivity appears to grow larger as the children grow older. This may have some significant implications for teachers in classrooms.

Implications for the Classroom

This gender difference in hearing may account for the perception of many teachers that boys tend to be "louder" than girls and are more inclined to shout. It may also be responsible for some of the difficulties boys may have when faced with a soft spoken female teacher. In addition, the greater hearing sensitivity of girls may contribute to the perception of the teenage girl that her adult male teacher has "yelled" at her, when the teacher believes he has used his normal conversational volume. There is also much room for mis-perception of non-verbal cues such as tone of voice. The greater hearing sensitivity of girls (and female teachers) also results in much greater auditory distractibility in girls than in boys. The British psychologist Colin Elliot (1971) demonstrated that eleven year old girls are distracted by noise levels ten times softer than noise levels that boys find distracting. Obviously, this is also true for the female teacher in a classroom with exuberant, foot-tapping, pencil-drumming boys!

Neural Rest State Differences

Each day the brains of girls and boys going into what the neurologists call "neural rest states". However, according to recent evidence from Single Photon Emission Computed Tomography (SPECT) these neural rest states are very different in girls and boys (Gurian & Stevens, 2005). As teachers, the neural rest states of boys are fairly easy to recognize. We see boys day dreaming, staring off into space, zoning out, drifting off or, on occasion actually slipping off to sleep in class. Some boys will fight against these neural rest states by becoming fidgety, by flicking paperclips across the room or by poking their neighbor with a pencil. For a few boys, these distracting and disruptive behaviors *may* indicate an attentional problem or hyperactivity. However, for many boys these self-stimulating activities may simply be an attempt to stay alert in a classroom that is not suited to their learning needs.

When boys enter a neural rest state, some areas of brain functioning actually shut down (King & Gurian, 2006). Boys lose the ability to focus and concentrate. Learning and academic performance suffers accordingly.

While girls also enter neural rest states, these are very different for girls than they are for boys. When girls get bored, more of their brain functioning remains active. Even in an under-stimulating classroom, girls are more likely to be able to concentrate and focus on the material at hand. They are more likely to listen carefully and be able to take notes. Researcher Ruben Gur at the University of Pennsylvania using magnetic resonance imaging (MRI) and other brain imaging technology (in Gurian & Henley, 2001) has shown that the female brain *at rest* is as active as the activated male brain. It would appear that there is more going on in the female brain. This does not suggest that the female brain is in some way better or more effective than the male brain. Ruben Gur is not saying the female brain "is necessarily superior, but he is showing that the female brain is using its resources, doing it quickly, and often, and in more places in the brain. The female brain...has a true learning advantage (p.29)."

Implications for the classroom

One of the pressing issues in gender differences in learning is the overwhelming proportion of boys as compared to girls who are diagnosed as Attention Deficit Disorder (ADD) or Attention Deficit Hyperactive Disorder (ADHD). In some boys there may be a biological basis for this. In others, however, we may be seeing poor attention and correspondingly disruptive behavior in classrooms because of a mismatch between the learning needs of boys and the learning organization of classrooms. This problem is brought to the forefront by the dramatic increase in the use of drugs such as Ritalin and Concerta. In our experience there is no question that some children benefit greatly from such medication. Without it, they would probably not be able to remain in school and could well be destined for incarceration in a juvenile detention center. However, we oppose the use of medication as an alternative for effective classroom management or for classrooms that are under-stimulating. Leonard Sax (2005) calls this "the medicalization of misbehavior." He writes "in a bizarre turn of events, it's become politically incorrect to spank your child, but it's okay to drug him (p.197)."

We also have a hunch that learning disabilities in girls may be under-diagnosed because girls are better able to mask them. Girls may be better at appearing to play the "school game". Because girls are better able to pay attention in class even when they are bored or completely uncomprehending of what is going on, it may be that teachers fail to recognize learning problems in girls as often as they do in boys.

Gender Differences in Competitiveness and Natural Aggression

The topic of competition in schools and in classrooms has been much debated both in educational journals and in faculty lounges around the world. We have witnessed the polar extremes. On the one hand, school X routinely posts student examination results together with student ranking on a public notice board. On the other hand, school Y has a teaching faculty so adamantly opposed to any form of competition that it voted to remove debate and forensics from the extra-curricular activities offerings.

The chemical oxytocin is present in the brains of both girls and boys, but in significantly greater quantities in girls' brains. Oxytocin has been called the "bonding" chemical and has been associated with the evolutionary instinct in girls and women under stress to "tend and befriend" (Taylor, 2002), as opposed to the male evolutionary instinct to "fight or flight". With less ocytocin in the male neural system, boys tend towards more risk taking behavior, greater impulsivity and more aggression.

We have all witnessed gender different reactions to high risk taking. The boys will often appear excited, energized and stimulated by the "thrill" of the experience. The girls, on the other hand, are often not only *not* excited but can be repulsed by the same situation that boys find so thrilling. Many studies over the last two decades have illustrated dramatic sex differences in bio-behavioral responses to stress. While the male in stressful situations is more influenced by the sympathetic nervous system which releases the thrill-producing chemical adrenaline, the female in stressful situations is more influenced by the parasympathetic nervous system which releases acetylcholine, which causes an unpleasant, nauseated feeling.

For a variety of neural and hormonal reasons, boys are generally more aggressive and competitive than girls. There are always exceptions, but on the whole the generalization remains true. This is not only the case in humans, but also in primates. Ironically, if young male primates are deprived of the opportunity to exhibit aggression in their play with other young males, they grow up *more* violent as adults, not less. They were deprived of the opportunity of learning how to bond with other males in a playful, aggressive way. There is evidence that this may also be true for human children (Sax, 2005). When we deprive boys of an opportunity to learn how to manage their aggressive drive constructively in childhood, there is a greater likelihood that the same aggressive drive will emerge in adulthood in unhealthy and anti-social forms.

Conclusion

While there is significant overlap in the learning of girls and boys, specific structural differences in their brains suggest implications for the classroom. Probably the most important one for the improved learning of girls and boys is simply an awareness on the part of teachers that there are very real physiological and hormonal differences in the brains of girls and boys that have significant effects on their learning in the classroom.

Putting aside our feelings about political correctness, we can allow for gender-specific student choice. In other words, we can allow a small group of girls to select a topic to write about or a project that appeals to them. Similarly, we can permit a group of boys to design a "boy friendly" project.

We can include in our flexible grouping strategies, gender groups. These can be short term work groups or longer term project teams. We would suggest that gender groups be *one* type of grouping among a variety that teachers employ. In the classroom setting, we believe it is important for students to get a clear message that they are expected to work with every student in the classroom. We believe that this can support respectful work relationships. In a coeducational setting, this expectation would obviously include students of a different gender.

We suspect that gender plays a significant role in how students come to perceive schools and the role of formal learning in their lives. Girls and boys do learn differently. They have different styles, learning needs, talents and gender-specific interests. When we are aware of these differences and incorporate them into our lesson planning, we optimize learning for all.

11 DIFFERENTIATING BY CHALLENGE: USING A TIERED PROGRAM OF INSTRUCTION IN MATHEMATICS

by David Suarez

Background

A respected colleague once said to me, "What sets great teachers apart is their ability to differentiate." This was a very humbling and somewhat disappointing statement to hear as I had previously thought of myself as a pretty good teacher while being perfectly comfortable to admit that I was not a differentiating teacher. This comfort was gone now. Many teachers can empathize with this feeling but would also agree that meeting individual student needs is one of the greatest challenges we face.

As I began my teaching career, I filtered much of what I learned during my coursework through the lenses of my daily struggle to meet my Oakland students' needs and of my own memories of being a bored middle school student. The concept that resonated most strongly from my coursework was Vygotsky's (1986) "zone of proximal development" (ZPD) – that "space" between what the child can do independently, and what he or she can do with teacher support. For me, the idea of ZPD represented an explanation of why I might be missing the mark with some of my students, and similarly, why my own teachers had missed the mark with me when I was a Middle School student.

My understanding of Vygotsky's theory linked well with Csikszentimihalyi's (1990) perspective that "enjoyment appears at the boundary between boredom and anxiety, when the challenges are just balanced with a person's capacity to act." This seemed like a reasonable explanation for why I didn't learn very much when I was in middle school. I had been bored due to a lack of challenge. Similarly, many of my students were either bored because of a lack of challenge or overly anxious as a result of having fallen behind in their learning. Either way, they were not learning at a level that was satisfying for them or acceptable to me.

During the spring of my fourth year, teaching Life Science classes at Roosevelt Middle School in Oakland, California, I received news that due to a change in policy, my five incoming classes would include a particularly diverse range of learners: native English speakers, students who had been living and learning in an English speaking environment for a year or less, and students with special needs. Roosevelt is an urban public school that serves a culturally and linguistically diverse student community, 86% of whom qualify for a free/reduced price lunch. This news arrived while I was already struggling to meet the needs of varied ability students in my relatively homogeneous classes.

In the fall of 2006, I was faced with a similar challenge while teaching integrated algebra-geometry classes to 8th graders at Jakarta International School (JIS). JIS is a very diverse school; my students ranged from those who had been recommended to take an alternative, remedial preparation course to others who had previously studied much of the curriculum about to be covered.

In both situations, one question weighed heavily on my mind: *How am I going to challenge all of my students so that each has the opportunity to experience significant academic growth?*

Striving to plan with the end in mind (Wiggins & McTighe, 1998), I struggled to select a learning destination that would be appropriate for everybody in a classroom where the starting points were so different.

Five years earlier, the only solution I could think of was to track students into different level classes. This time, I saw things differently, thanks in large part to Justin McNabney, an Oakland teacher who showed me a way to meet individual student needs while preserving the richness of learning opportunities available in a highly inclusive, heterogeneous class.

Since that moment, my colleagues and I have accepted the fact that there is no single learning target that is appropriate for all students. Accordingly, we have utilized a three-tiered instructional program that enables us to engage students in the study of essential course content at different levels of challenge. Given the opportunity to maximize their learning by challenging themselves at a level that suits them best, students select learning destinations that vary in terms of depth rather than distance. In other words, they wrestle with particular concepts and skills at deeper levels of challenge rather than moving on to additional skills that will be learned in future units or future math courses.

The results of our efforts have been very encouraging. Cathy Craig, a learning specialist at JIS commented: "I think the three-tiered system *is* the shift in education that differentiation calls for."

Getting Started in Mathematics

Anne-Pitt Kennedy and I worked together to implement the tiered math program at JIS. We first reviewed the learning outcomes expected of students at our grade level, distinguishing between foundational, intermediate, and advanced levels of understanding in each unit of Grade 8 mathematics. Beyond simply creating three levels of difficulty, we strived to ensure that all students would find one of the levels both accessible and challenging. It was critical that we establish a clear baseline expectation of what students should know and be able to do at their grade level, and then move deeply enough into content so that no student would be left unchallenged. We developed general descriptions for the different levels of mastery and designated a color for each (green, blue, and black). Challenge tends to increase as problems become less familiar, more applied, and more complex. We described the three levels as follows[30].

Green	The problem is foundational and looks familiar. Success requires that you recognize, recall, and demonstrate the appropriate skill. Green tasks meet the standard for Grade 8 mathematics at JIS and represent a level of mastery that every student must achieve in order to be considered proficient.
Blue	The problem is complex but still familiar. Success depends on your ability to recognize the subtleties that make the problem more complex and on having sharpened your skills enough to achieve success.
Black	The task is complex. Success will depend on creatively applying and extending your skills, based on understanding the problem and adjustments required to solve it. The problem may or may not be familiar.

With these guidelines, we began to set performance tasks within each level of challenge. The following table offers a glimpse of how we tiered some of our assessment tasks in different topic areas. Our intent was to ensure opportunities for students to deepen mastery of essential course content as

---

[30] To see how David explained the differences in assessments and for links to the actual assessments, please see
http://www.teachertube.com/view_video.php?viewkey=3c79e62f76cbf9fb277d

opposed to the most frequently advocated alternative, which would have advanced students move on to new content at similarly superficial levels of understanding. Deeper – *not farther* – is what we constantly reminded ourselves of while developing our tiered program of instruction.

Topic	Green	Blue	Black
Problem Solving with Linear Equations	The difference in the ages of two people is 8 years. The older person is 3 times the age of the younger. How old is each?	The length of a rectangle is 3 less than half the width. If the perimeter is 18, find the length and width.	When asked for the time, a problem posing professor said, "If from the present time, you subtract one-sixth of the time from now until noon tomorrow, you get exactly one-third of the time from noon until now." What time was it?
Understanding Slope	Find the slope of the line passing through the following pair of points: (-4, 6) and (-3, 2)	Find a so that the line connecting the points (-2, -3) and (2, 5) is parallel to the line connecting the points (6, a) and (0, -4)	If $a > 1$, what must be true about b so that the line passing through the points (a, b) and (1, -3) has a negative slope?

Set-up in Science

In Oakland, we had approached science differently, describing what the different levels of complexity would look like for each assessment *item*. Here is an example generated for the following 7th Grade California Science Content Standard:

> The anatomy and physiology of plants and animals illustrate the complementary nature of structure and function. As a basis for understanding this concept:
>
> a. Students know plants and animals have levels of organization for structure and function, including cells, tissues, organs, organ systems, and the whole organism.
>
> b. Students know organ systems function because of the contributions of individual organs, tissues, and cells. The failure of any part can affect the entire system.
>
> c. Students know how bones and muscles work together to provide a structural framework for movement.

We included the following assessment tasks for students to select from during a unit of study on human organ systems.

Item	Green	Blue	Black
Organ Systems Test	Student matches the names of organ systems to their functions and parts. From a metaphor, student matches parts of a metaphor to the appropriate level of organization in the human body.	Given the function and its parts, student names the intended organ system. Student identifies the metaphor and level of organization from a story.	Given a function, student names the intended organ system and lists its parts. Student makes up an original metaphor for the levels of organization in an organism.
Joint Model Project	Student crates a hinge joint that works.	Student creates a realistic hinge joint that works well.	Student creates a ball and socket or pivot joint model that works well.
Circulatory System Project	Student draws a simple cartoon and describes the life of a red blood cell, using green level vocabulary.	Student draws a detailed cartoon and describes the life of a red blood cell using blue level vocabulary.	Student draws a detailed cartoon and describes the life of a red blood cell, with characters, using black level vocabulary.

We explained each of these assessment tasks to students at the beginning of the unit with an emphasis on the skills that would be necessary for success. Writing and sharing the assessment summaries served as a helpful organizational tool for teachers and students as we progressed through the unit. It also enabled students to set appropriate long term goals for themselves based on the challenges described.

The skills necessary for success on the assessments varied. Memorization and writing skills were necessary for success on the organ systems assessments while more hands-on skills were critical for the joint model projects. An understanding of vocabulary was clearly required for the circulatory system projects. Within these options, students often found themselves selecting different levels of challenges depending on the skill required and their own strengths. Students explained the reasoning behind their decision as they selected each assessment item.

Susan Yee, my teaching partner at Roosevelt, reflected on the entire process. "I loved being able to offer options to students, and definitely think that it changed the way students viewed their learning. I also loved being forced to plan in such detail, so far ahead. The front end planning, and having to articulate the learning objectives in a way that students could understand, helped me rethink my teaching too."

James Narvaez, a graduate student at UC Berkeley who was student teaching with me at this time commented, "Highlighting for students what they needed to learn was one of the aspects that students decided really helped their learning."

Steps for Developing a Tiered Program of Study:

1. **Organize Units by Themes:** Look at your current assessment for a particular unit and identify themes (skill clusters) by asking yourself what links the knowledge and skills that students are supposed to

master. We strive to distinguish two broad themes that link all of the content within each of our units. An assessment will need to be developed for each theme. Consequently, you want enough themes that you're able to offer more than one choice within substantial units of study, but few enough themes that you're not caught up in writing and delivering an unrealistic or undesirable number of assessments.

2. **Collect examples of performance tasks at different levels of challenge** relating to each theme. Start with the green level - what all students must know and be able to do at the grade level you teach. Then, set your sights on finding the most challenging problems imaginable within the theme and problems at difficulty levels somewhere in between the foundational and super-advanced levels. The wider your spectrum of challenge, the more significant and authentic will be the choices you're offering to students. You'll be amazed at what your most advanced students are capable of doing.

3. **Develop assessments that will represent the learning targets** available for students on the instructional paths that you lay out for them. Designing assessments ahead of time will allow you to tier practice assignments as you uncover the essential understandings that all students need to learn.

4. **Use practice assessments (quizzes) to give students the opportunity to preview** what the level of difficulty will feel like. This will make students more comfortable when the time comes to select a color for their final summative assessment.

5. **Strive to assign practice assignments that have been tiered for challenge.** In this way, students are working towards their ultimate color choice destination as you move through the unit of study, rather than simply at the end when it's time to take an assessment.

6. **Sit back and watch your students rise to the occasion.** Avoid pushing students into particular color choices. Maintain a long term perspective. Students will gradually fine-tune their decision making skills as they experience success or failure with the choices they select.

7. **Allow students maximum flexibility to make choices and**

change their minds. For example, I allow students to look at different color assessments on the day of the final assessment if they'd like to preview each before making their final choice. Without this freedom, students will generally opt for the conservative route. By remaining flexible, I extend the window of time available for students to opt for the more challenging of the two options they're considering.

Student Responsibilities and Perspectives

At both Roosevelt and JIS, *students* selected the level of challenge most appropriate for their learning. My reasoning was that students generally know themselves better than their teachers do. Better decisions will be made if students are choosing for themselves, and there are three significant side benefits. First, choices are motivating, and in a middle school classroom where motivation is often the key determinant for student achievement, any instructional approach that increases student motivation is beneficial. Second, students benefit from having the opportunity to make decisions. The opportunity to reflect and adjust is a skill we want middle school students to develop. Lastly, by asking students to make their own choices, we eliminate the risk of offending students who may believe that a decision made for them by their teacher is unfair or inappropriate. All of this is consistent with Glasser's (1988) writings on Choice Theory.

Some colleagues have been surprised by my suggestion that students be allowed to select challenge levels for themselves. Counter opinions are generally that students lack the maturity required to select the appropriate levels of challenge for themselves. Even while conceding that students are usually fully aware of their abilities, some colleagues point to peer pressure and laziness as reasons why students would make inappropriate choices.

I, too, had similar concerns when I began this initiative, but my experience has convinced me that such a perspective is rarely valid. Within classroom environments that encourage effective decision making, middle school students within both the low and high income communities where I've taught have shown themselves to consistently select levels of challenge appropriate for their learning. I have disagreed with choices made by students in very few instances. Not only do students make appropriate choices, they are very enthusiastic about having the opportunity to do so. Here are some comments from my current 8th graders:

> "I feel that being asked to choose from three different levels of difficulty has given more choices and opportunities to challenge myself. I like the choices because I feel that I have more "say" in the level of math I am learning. I would be disappointed [if we didn't have choices] because I

think that I'm the only one who truly knows the appropriate level of learning math for myself. With the three choices available, I am able to select the one closest to my level of math in that particular area." Ruth

"I like having freedom of choice, and I like being able to choose a level I'm comfortable at." Robert

"What I like about this is that we have a variety of levels so we can pick the one that is most appropriate for us, without making it too easy or too challenging." Mina

Rajinder offers a thoughtful, dissenting voice that is worth considering. He explained,

"[selecting from three choices] gives us a sense of where we think we are. But sometimes, I feel like I need someone else to determine where I am. It's just a feeling of not being sure."

When asked how he would feel if he was not given a choice, Rajinder stated,

"Happy, because I trust in my teacher and how much they know my skill."

Sure, it's a healthy sign that Rajinder trusts me and the rest of his teachers, but knowing Rajinder makes me feel more concerned about this comment than satisfied. I'd like Rajinder to develop trust in himself so that it becomes possible for him to look inward during times of doubt; he is among those students who require the most frequent validation that what they are doing is correct.

When discussing the appropriate selection of challenge with students, I constantly refer to the following graph, adapted from Jensen's (1998) work on how stress affects learning.

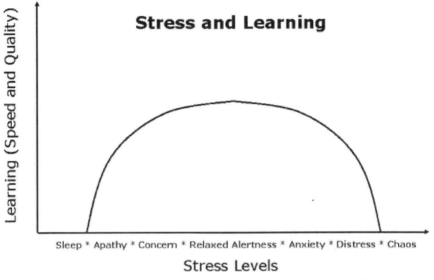

Chart from "Teaching with the Brain in Mind" by Eric Jensen

I encourage students to select the level of challenge that will maximize the speed and quality of their learning. I communicate the same idea to parents.

Grading Systems

While students, parents, and teachers are generous in their praise of our intent, they are also quick to raise concerns around issues of grading, especially in our very grade-conscious community at JIS. Creating a grading system that would complement a tiered instructional program was a high priority in both schools. In the absence of robust grading systems, efforts geared towards individualizing learning programs frequently lose momentum.

Approaches to grading were different in the two schools. In Oakland, the grade a student could earn was not directly tied to the challenge level selected. Equivalent grades on different color assessments were possible; however, we did conference with students to evaluate the appropriateness of the level of challenge selected. For example, two students of different abilities could both earn an "A" in the class while selecting assessments at different levels of challenge as long as each student was trying to maximize their learning. In Oakland, we were primarily concerned with promoting efficacy and evaluating personal growth.

My message to students was, "I'm giving you choices because it's the most effective way I can do my job, which is to make it possible for everyone to grow as much as they can. I expect each of you to learn as much as you can by taking advantage of this opportunity. Your grade will be a measure of how much you grow during your time in this class."

I had been teaching at Jakarta International School for a year when I decided to begin differentiating mathematics assessments. Based on my first year experience, it was clear that a grading approach emphasizing achievement more than growth would fit most naturally with our school community's values. In this system, grades would be weighted based on the challenge levels selected. I still encouraged students to select the learning maximizing level of difficulty for their own growth, but was completely forthright about the fact that different levels of challenge were linked to different grade possibilities. After marking assessments for accuracy, percentages were converted to a weighted four-point scale. These scaled scores were then used to determine a final grade at the end of the marking period. We are currently using the following conversion scales.

Individual Assessment Grades

Accuracy	Green	Blue	Black
90-100%	3.5	4	4.5
80-89%	2.5	3	3.5
70-79%	1.5	2	2.5
60-69%	.5	1	1.5
Less than 60%	0	0	0

Final Marking Period Grades

Weighted Average	Final Letter Grade
4.3	A+
4	A
3.7	A-
3.3	B+
3	B
2.7	B-
2.3	C+
2	C
1.7	C-
1.3	D+
1	D
.7	D-

Next year, JIS is undertaking our first attempt at "standards based reporting." Student performance will be linked to individual learning goals. I'm looking forward to reporting on individual learning goals rather than giving an overall grade. We will no longer need to use the weighted conversion system since an overall grade will not be calculated or reported. We plan to report both the level of difficulty selected by the student for each learning goal (as a color) along with the accuracy with which the student demonstrates mastery (as a letter grade).

Regardless of how a teacher or school approaches the issue of grading, the system must be compatible and complementary to the differentiation practices in place, the use of tiered assessments in our case.

Once tiered learning targets were identified and a grading system was in place, the next step was to plan instruction. Differentiating class and homework assignments became the primary means through which students could work with the same core sets of skills at different levels of challenge. This was the first time I had a clear vision of what differentiated instruction would look like in my classroom.

In the Classroom

If you were to walk into my classroom today, you'd see that lessons frequently begin with problems that are accessible to all students, designed to illuminate the essential understandings everyone should possess around the topic of study. Once these concepts are clear in students' minds, class work and homework assignments are differentiated by challenge level. Typically, green problems are found in our grade-level textbook, blue problems are taken from the textbook as well as supplemental resources, and black problems almost always taken from supplemental resources.

Students are encouraged to feel completely confident about a challenge level before moving on to the next level of challenge. Confidence may result from skimming the problems visually, practicing one or two in a set, or practicing more for a stronger sense of security. Students are given the freedom and responsibility to select the mix of problems that will both challenge them and offer sufficient practice with the day's primary understandings. It is conceivable that every student in the class will complete a different homework assignment, though most aim for the blue level of challenge. Black level problems are usually quite advanced, attempted by only a very small handful of students.

An example of this process is reflected in a recent lesson on triangles. The primary goals for the lesson were for students to know that the sum of a triangle's interior angles (180 degrees) and for them to apply equation solving skills to situations involving this understanding. Having already learned about special angle pairs formed by the intersection of a transversal with two parallel lines, all students were asked to grapple with the following warm-up problem:

What is the sum of the angle measures in any △ABC ? PROVE IT

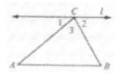

Students seated at heterogeneous table groups worked through the problem together. After a short period of time, the class came back together and listened to various solutions offered by different students. Through this dialogue, I became confident that students were ready to tackle problems involving the sum of a triangle's interior angles. A similar instructional approach was used during the same class session to help students learn that the measure of a triangle's exterior angle is equal to the sum of the measures of the two remote interior angles. Once the lesson's key understandings had been illuminated, the following assignments were given.

Green	Textbook Pages 157 – 159: Exercises 1-6, 13-18, 25-27.[32]
Blue	Textbook Pages 157 – 159: Written Exercises 28 – 30.
Black	JISNET Challenge Problems 1 – 4 (on my website)

An example problem from each practice assignment follows.

Green	Blue	Black
Find the value of x. 18.	In VABC, the measure of $\angle A$ is three times that of $\angle C$, and the measure of $\angle B$ is twice the sum of the measures of $\angle A$ and $\angle C$. Find the measure of each angle.	In any VABC, E and D are interior points of $\overline{AC}$ and $\overline{BC}$, respectively. $\overline{AF}$ bisects $\angle CAD$, and $\overline{BF}$ bisects $\angle CBE$. Prove $m\angle AEB + m\angle ADB = 2m\angle AFB$

Students completed an assignment of their choice, or a mixture of problems from different assignments, depending on their comfort level and personal approach to maximizing their learning. During class time, students generally work at mixed ability tables, occasionally seeking the help of another at a different table. All students seemed to be working in a manner indicative of high engagement.

The lesson on triangles was one in a group of lessons involving the theme of angle relationships. At the unit's conclusion, students selected a challenge level for a summative assessment designed to gauge their understanding of the learning objectives associated with this theme. Students usually selected challenge levels consistent with the practice assignments they had been completing during the course of the unit. Non-graded formative assessments also helped students understand the type of challenge that would be involved in the unit's eventual, graded summative assessments.

Separating our units into themes has been a helpful organizational tool in our approach to tiered instruction. Specific skill outcomes fall within a given theme. This has enabled us to tier assessments by theme rather than by individual skill, keeping the number of summative assessments at a manageable level of two per unit. The following table summarizes the units and themes studied during the first half of our course.

Linear Equations
Understand the meanings of operations and how they relate to one another, especially as a means to solve equations and evaluate expressions
Represent and analyze mathematical situations and structures using algebraic symbols while using problem solving processes to solve real world problems
Introduction to Graphing
Convert between graphical, numerical, and symbolic representations of data
Analyze functions and patterns
Geometry I
Apply visualization and algebraic reasoning skills to problem solving tasks in two and three dimensional space
Solve problems involving angle pair relationships

Results of Differentiating Assessments

We have been extremely pleased with the results so far. Students demonstrate greater motivation to learn and are performing successfully on more challenging tasks while assuming more responsibility for the process. Parents are grateful that their children's needs are being met. And as teachers, it feels pretty good to say and believe that we're delivering on our promise to facilitate the academic growth of *all* students!

A comparison of the before and after realities in our classrooms reveals a surprising discovery. Student achievement has increased across the board through the tiered program of instruction. Raising the bar of student achievement has been an unanticipated, though natural by-product beyond our broader goal of meeting individual student needs. The curriculum has not been dumbed down by differentiating assessments. To the contrary, learning appears to have become more rigorous.

While reflecting on this discovery, a comment made by Cheryl Carl, a veteran 8th grade science teacher at JIS, gave us insights on the use of rubrics and the unexpected decrease in quality produced by a few of her students.

> "While rubrics give beneficial structure to the majority of students who need it, I often feel like they end up capping the quality of work produced by our most motivated and able students. The rubric seems to be more of an indication for when the student can stop producing, rather than something that inspires them to do their best possible work."

This message makes sense when I consider the way advanced students did not have the opportunity to demonstrate their learning on common assessments geared for all students.

Cheryl's observations are also consistent with research summarized by Alfie Kohn (2004) in "The Costs of Overemphasizing Achievement." Kohn writes,

> "[in a typical experiment], kids are told they're going to be given a task. Some are informed that their performance will be evaluated, while others are encouraged to think of this as an opportunity to learn rather than do well. Then, each student is given a chance to choose how hard a version of the task he or she wants to try. The result is always the same: Those who had been told it's "an opportunity to learn" are more willing to challenge themselves than are those who had been led to think about how well they'll do (p. 32)."

Introducing a rubric that emphasized performance to a single, pre-defined standard, unwittingly discouraged students from stretching themselves. As Kohn (2004) says, "[the students] adapt to an environment where results, not intellectual exploration, are what count (p. 32).

The following table summarizes student choices on summative assessments taken during the first half of the school year in the two 8th grade classes:

Topic	Green	Blue	Black	# of Students
Understand the meanings of operations and how they relate to one another, especially as a means to solve equations and evaluate expressions	34%	57%	9%	152
Represent and analyze mathematical situations and structures using algebraic symbols while using problem solving processes to solve real world problems	32%	60%	8%	151
Convert between graphical, numerical, and symbolic representations of data	28%	63%	9%	153
Analyze functions and patterns	38%	56%	6%	154
Apply visualization and algebraic reasoning skills to problem solving tasks in two and three dimensional space	32%	60%	8%	137
Solve problems involving angle pair relationships	35%	57%	8%	136

People often ask if students pigeon-hole themselves into a color category. The answer is that some do, but most do not. Specifically, when completing the 6 assessments for the learning goals listed above, 57% of students selected more than one color choice while 43% always selected the same color.

It has been clear to Anne, my teaching partner, and me that the average level of challenge met by students has increased through the tiered program of instruction. Our green level assessments closely resemble the single common assessments we previously gave to all students. With the majority of students selecting blue or black level assessments, on average, students are now tackling greater challenges than in the past. One conclusion is that we had actually been assessing for a minimal level of understanding prior to implementing a tiered instructional program. This was a huge surprise to us, as we had always sincerely thought that we held the highest possible expectations for students.

At the same time as students are tackling greater challenges and increasing achievement levels, grades are holding steady as can be seen in the following graph.

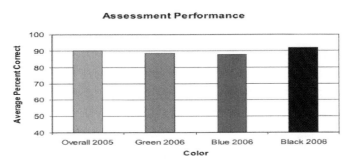

This graph reflects an interesting point: In 2005, students at the beginning end of the readiness spectrum tended to bring the average test score down; however, in 2006, they are performing at an accuracy level similar to students taking different color assessments. It is reasonable to conclude that students at a "green level" of readiness have improved their performance from 2005 to 2006.

Perhaps a simple psychological phenomenon has been at play. Students become increasingly motivated once they believe their teacher is developing performance tasks geared to maximize growth at their particular readiness level. Teachers know that students tend to perform at a level that matches their self-concept. If a group of students views themselves as consistently lagging behind the majority of the class, they'll generally perform below average as a way of realizing that self-fulfilling prophecy.

Implications for student achievement and teacher behaviors are significant. If a single common assessment is offered to all students, lower achieving students usually find themselves at the bottom of the class when grades are compared. Having designed an assessment that results in a relatively wide spread of student grades, the teacher is left to modestly tinker with an assessment's challenge level. The teacher is unlikely to significantly increase the challenge level since doing so might cause the students at the bottom of the class to drop into an unacceptable level of performance. Consequently, assessment tasks tend to hover around a challenge level commensurate with our *minimum* expectations for student achievement, however high we believe those expectations to be. Borderline performances of students at the bottom end of the class must be evaluated to determine whether or not they meet the grade level standard.

This process plays out differently with a tiered program of instruction. While we have students who are incredibly diverse in terms of their mathematical readiness, Anne and I have classes in which all students are in realistic shooting range of the minimum grade level target. As a result, we have been able to design our green level assessments so that they represent the standard for Grade 8 mathematics at JIS, a level of mastery that every student must achieve in order to be considered proficient.

Our language of instruction has naturally evolved so that students are made explicitly aware of our baseline expectations. Through the assignments we provide as practice, they are also aware of our expectations at the most challenging end of the spectrum.

The students for whom this increasingly transparent communication is most beneficial are those at the beginning of the readiness spectrum. These students, who usually performed at mediocre levels in the single assessment scenario, tend to have a very different outlook when thinking about their performance on a green level assessment in the tiered approach.

Now, these students know exactly what is expected in terms of meeting the baseline grade-level standard. *All* students are expected to be successful on the level of challenge they select. This expectation is shared between teachers and students, and serves as a positive self-fulfilling prophecy.

Sure, students who select the green assessment know they're still at the bottom of the class in terms of color choice, *but* they expect more of themselves relative to their choice, and raise their performance to match this raised self-concept. They're also happier to be highly successful on an assessment designed specifically for their level of readiness as compared to turning out a relatively mediocre performance on an assessment that was designed, as they would see it, for them to fill the bottom of the class bell curve.

Following the completion of each unit, students are asked to reflect on the learning they experienced relative to their stress level over the course of the unit.

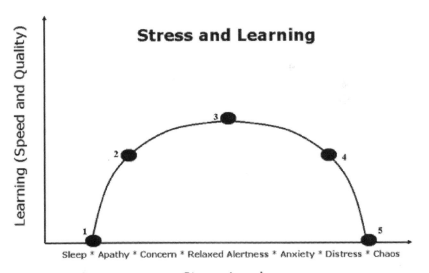

Students select the position on the above graph that best represents how they felt during the unit. The following graph summarizes their responses during the first half of the year.

Overall Stress and Learning
(183 student reflections)

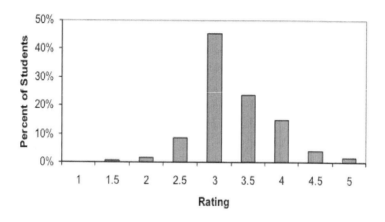

Two students who tend to take green level summative assessments after attempting a mix of green and blue level homework problems commented:

> "I like having choices because you can decide if you are ready for a harder challenge or not." Bonnie

> "I think it is useful because you can challenge yourself, but have some control of your math." Tobias

At the upper end of the readiness spectrum, students are tackling unprecedented levels of challenge with enthusiasm and pride. After taking a black level assessment, Wa-Lee, a student who would have been bored by the ease of the single common assessment offered the year before, enthusiastically exclaimed, "That was hard!" With a smile, Johannes softly responded, "I'm excited!" when asked how he was feeling about an upcoming black level assessment.

You can imagine the satisfaction of hearing these comments, especially knowing that students at the beginning end of the readiness spectrum were also growing through challenge. Wa-Lee offered a firm opinion on tiered instruction:

> "The JIS 8th grade math department must keep the 3 color choice system as it benefits many students by providing them with the levels of difficulty that suit their current math skills."

186

The following table summarizes student responses when asked about the appropriateness of the assessments they selected.

	...reported that the assessment was "_____" towards the goal of maximizing their learning.			
Students who selected:	"too Simple"	"Appropriate"	"too Challenging"	Total Reflections
Green	9%	90%	1%	152
Blue	6%	86%	8%	333
Black	4%	90%	6%	48

Results indicate that students generally feel appropriately challenged by the assessments they select. Offering choices also allows students to modify future decisions if they viewed the assessments they selected as either too simple or too challenging. In retrospect, the only students who couldn't have made better choices were those who selected black assessments and found the tasks too easy, or students who selected green assessments and believed the tasks were too difficult. Students finding themselves in one of these positions represent a very small number of occurrences. This differs significantly with numbers in previous years who would have reported the assessments as either too simple or too challenging.

In other words, one student's growth and success was not now coming at the price of another student's opportunity for challenge and achievement. Students at different ends of the ability spectrum can find success in a heterogeneous class! I'm so happy we didn't settle for my early conclusion that more tracking was the way.

Beyond growing academically, students are also learning a lot about themselves. They are constantly making choices and value judgments about their education when selecting challenge levels. Rather than having a teacher tell them what is best for them, students spend the year grappling with that very question. This provides for many opportunities for decision making and self-reflection. Rebecca reinforces the point of non-academic personal growth with the following comment,

> "I think the color system is a great idea because students have to make many decisions after they become independent members of society, and . . . the color system gives them a chance to practice their choice making skills. If they regret choosing a certain color, they learn from their mistake and try to do better."

I try to capitalize on opportunities for introspection by prompting students with reflection questions at the end of every unit. Below are student responses to the following prompt: *How did you select your challenge level? Are you satisfied with your choice?*

> Vishali: "It is what I am comfortable with. I know I am capable of blue. I am satisfied with my choice, because I learnt and understood many new things. My proof of that statement is the "A" I got on my test. I know that if I had chosen black, then I would have been stuck in chaos. I am still developing my skills. They have not been mastered enough for me to choose black."

> Madira: "I wanted to choose something easy for a change, just to see how it was. I was confident about green, so I just went for it. I am satisfied with my grade. I was confident with my work and I got a good grade for it. I think I could've done blue, though. I had gotten good grades for my quizzes and common assessments, which were all blue, so I think I could've gone for it."

> Le-Ta: "I chose black to see what the black level was in graphing. The test was not too hard and not too easy. I think it was a nice difficulty."

> Sarah, who opted for green, explained, "I was a little shaky with my knowledge of everything we had learned. I am *not* satisfied. I believe that the test was too easy. I think I could have taken blue."

The figures below show a common format used for reflection at the end of a unit.

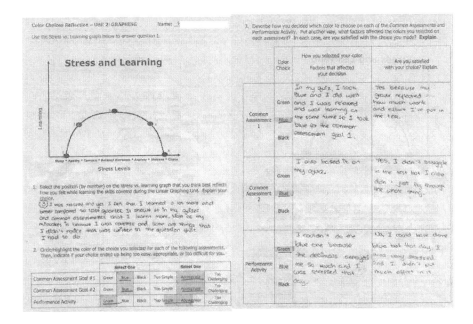

The students' comments speak for themselves on the subject of personal growth:

> "I really enjoy being able to select levels of difficulty. It means that, depending on my skill level for each goal, I can challenge myself every time. Sometimes, I can make the wrong choice, though." Tillie

> "I enjoy the challenges. However, some people might choose the wrong color and regret what they have chosen." Hugh

These comments begin to reveal one of the most satisfying aspects of what occurs through the implementation of this system. Students are constantly making choices, evaluating decisions, and moving forward with new information about themselves with which they can strive to make better choices in the future. The use of a tiered program of instruction has been one way to incorporate more decision making opportunities into the curriculum.

Just over half-way through the school year, students were asked, "Do you think the three color choices system is helping you to improve your decision making abilities?" Of the 132 student responses, an overwhelming 90% said "yes" and 10% said "no." Here are some of their thoughts from both sides of the spectrum.

"Yes, to know our ability and skill and also to choose the right level for ourselves is not an easy job. Choosing the level makes us consider and look back at our math skills, and it's very helpful to make decisions." So Hee

"It allows us to come to terms with our skills and admit certain weaknesses/strengths. Since we have our math grade on the line, it helps us carefully weigh the options and possibilities before plunging into one of the choices. All of this practice at making wise decisions could be extremely useful in the future." Rina

"I think it is helping me because I can adjust when I feel uncomfortable." Rickie

"Yes, because this year I know that I am responsible for what I do, and if I want to learn more and do well, I should choose what I think my level is and try to improve on that." Jenny

"It gives us a choice, making you consider the consequences if you choose that color, allowing you to take more risks if you want to." Brian

"I am very indecisive, so it takes time to choose, and sometimes I choose a wrong one and end up with a bad result. It makes me worry a lot." Amy

"No, I don't challenge myself enough with this system." Malcolm

On their own, I imagine that students are also dealing with many of the following questions as they navigate through the choices available to them: Am I learning as much as I can? Am I challenging myself the right amount, too much, or too little? Does it matter? How well do I understand this material? Am I confident enough in my abilities to take on a greater challenge at the risk of a lower grade, or should I take the more secure path? If I want to succeed at a more advanced level, how should I go about preparing in order to make sure I'm successful? How much practice is enough? If I achieve success at a more foundational level, am I satisfied that I've learned as much as I can? How does the answer to the previous question make me feel?

The list of questions goes on and on. In the midst of so many things to think about, you can imagine that moans and groans start to fade away. Who has time to dwell upon how difficult something is when so many choices for success are possible? In fact, an opposite effect on classroom culture seems to develop. Students increasingly take pride in taking on more challenge and start to adopt behaviors that are geared towards accelerating their learning so that they can meet challenge with success. Positive peer pressure seems to be at its height. Charlotte, a student who has gradually shifted from selecting green to blue levels of challenge, reflected, "I like the color choices. I think that when you choose the colors, you want to challenge yourself more."

With students making so many choices, there are also countless opportunities to reinforce the message that it's okay for everyone to be different with unique strengths and weaknesses. Students genuinely seem to support each other in reaching their goals while respecting everyone's right to make different choices without being put down.

Related to this topic, Charlotte also wrote the following comments.

> "I have never felt anxiety related to the color I choose. I don't consider what other people think, because it's what I want for myself. Sometimes, a friend can tell you to do 'Blue' because they say that you are up to it."

Sure enough, Charlotte usually selected green level assessments at the beginning of the year. As she has developed confidence, she has attempted blue level problems with greater frequency.

Viewpoints differ, but overall, students appear comfortable selecting the colors they want, and they are motivated to increase their challenge level when they see a window of opportunity that suits them.

Esther connects the color system with the opportunity for challenge. She commented, "Making a decision in colors helps me to be challenged with more tension in learning. It's also quite a proud thing to be in a high level."

Adding to students' perspectives, parents also offer comments worthy of reflection. With regard to the individual needs of their children, parents of students who take black level assessments have told me, "My child is finally being challenged in math class. Those problems are really hard." Speaking of a child at the other end of the readiness continuum, another parent said, "This is the first time my child is feeling successful in math."

When a parent expressed concern that students who tend to work at a green level of challenge *may* develop lowered self-esteem, another parent responded by explaining that her son, who has thrived as a result of having the opportunity to do black problems, never makes the soccer team when he tries out. She said that it's important that he be able to accept that disappointment, and just as the children who made the soccer team deserve the opportunity they've earned, her son deserves no less an opportunity to excel in math class.

Across the board, parents comment on the non-academic learning that is also taking place. One said, "My child has to make choices about which test to take. This is making her think about her learning and gives her a chance to practice decision-making. This is exactly what kids should be doing in middle school."

Sometimes, a child's choice will lead to a family debate. Parents will ask, "Don't you think my child could do the blue (or black) level assessment?" My honest response is usually, "Yes, I think so." If I think the child is better off remaining at his or her current level, I'll also be open about that. In either case, the decision is left to the student.

Over the course of time that I've tiered assessments, not a single parent has indicated that their child's needs are not being met in my class. This was not the case when I gave a single common assessment for all students. Similarly, parents seem to accept the shift in responsibility that has taken place. They solicit my opinion about their child's readiness for different challenge levels, but accept my refusal to force students into particular tracks.

While pleased with the results so far, we recognize that our efforts are a work in progress. Questions on our mind these days include: How does having choices now affect learning outcomes down the road? When (if ever) and how much should we guide students in the process of selecting their challenge levels? How do we improve our differentiation practices in the classroom so that students working at all levels of challenge have equal access to instructional support from the teacher? How would we handle a situation in which there are one or more students for whom even the foundational, green level of challenge represents a challenge that is outside their ZPD? What is the relationship between a tiered program of instruction and establishing a continuum of learning for mathematics across grade levels in a middle school? For what age range is this approach appropriate and desirable? Would this approach work well outside of mathematics and science?

Conclusion

Using a tiered program of instruction in mathematics has proven to be effective for everyone involved in this process. Students develop deeper understanding of content while growing as decision makers. Parents are happy as they feel that their children's needs are being met. Teachers feel more successful towards the goal of meeting all students' needs while feeling less pressure to design the perfect assessment that will be both a challenge and an opportunity for success for all students.

I get a lot of personal satisfaction from sharing the design and results of our work with other teachers because I appreciate the opportunity to hear their concerns. With regard to this particular system, I'm still looking for a concern that leaves me stumped. In this way, a tiered program of instruction has proven itself to be a very robust approach.

If you're interested in trying something like this yourself, here are a few final words of encouragement and support:

> ➤ **Realize that the process of developing a tiered program of instruction gets easier over time.** If you feel intimidated because you're not sure how you're going to do this, try not to worry so much that you're paralyzed into doing nothing. Believe me, when we embarked on this journey, we also felt that we were making a big leap of faith, and it was scary at first. Developing a set of tiered assessments is the first step. Figuring out how you'll enable students to reach the destinations comes second. Like any destination, you can't figure out how to get there until you know where you're going. Once the destinations are set, travel routes become clear.

> ➤ **If you're planning to implement tiered assessments in mathematics, keep your eyes open for challenging problems.** There are no shortage of foundational level skill-building problems available in traditional textbooks. We found there to be a shortage of assessment tasks and related practice problems that involve higher level problem solving that extends our study of core content at deeper, "black" levels of complexity.

> ➤ **Take advantage of opportunities to collaborate by splitting up the work of writing tiered assessments.** Working with a colleague (or colleagues) and agree together on what skills/concepts need to be taught and then separate the search for assessment tasks linked to those skills and concepts.

> ➤ **Figure out what your grading system will be and be completely open about it.** Develop a system that you can feel comfortable talking openly about with students, parents, and colleagues. Doing so will ultimately allow you to shift focus away from grading once all concerns are addressed. Also, don't be afraid to admit that you're embarking on something that is new to you and that you expect to make adjustments along the way. When you make adjustments, make students and parents aware of why you've modified the approach. The first year of implementation is a honey moon year, in which you should take advantage of being in the "experimental phase" by tinkering freely with your approach. My teaching partner, Anne, will tell you that we ended up getting far fewer parent concerns than she was worried about before we started the process. Students and parents are quite willing for their teachers to experiment if they believe that the experimentation is in the best interests of the learner.

> ➤ **Lastly, enjoy the ride!** I've enjoyed teaching so much more since I began using a tiered program of instruction. It never feels good to know that you're failing a student or group of students. My sense of success as

a teacher has risen dramatically since I began this effort. Offering different learning targets for different students in the middle school classroom is a critical way to ensure that all students are able to grow academically during this phase of their adolescence.

Acknowledgements

There are many individuals who deserve thanks for having helped make this work possible. In Oakland, I'd like to thank Justin McNabney for sharing his own tiered color system, which was the seed from which all of our work has grown, Susan Yee for jumping on board for the first attempt at this work, enthusiastically co-captaining a ship that was heading into uncharted waters, James Narvaez for allowing me to witness a formative period in his development as a teacher while he admirably implemented this nontraditional instructional approach during his first student teaching assignment, my Oakland students for demanding my best and for destroying all stereotypes held of urban youth by striving for their best and succeeding at academic levels exceeding all of our expectations, Theresa Clincy and Darcel Stockey for providing the leadership necessary for Susan and I to pilot our ideas at Roosevelt, and the rest of my Oakland colleagues for constantly inspiring me to improve as a teacher through their own determination to meet individual student needs under extremely challenging circumstances.

In Jakarta, Anne Pitt-Kennedy deserves accolades for willingly embarking on an exploration of these ideas in her own classroom. I'm very grateful to Geoff Smith and Steve Meade, my principals, for trusting me enough to fully support the implementation of our ideas, and to Mindy Weimer, Cathy Craig, Craig Money, David White, Stephen Kimber, and Cynthia Ruptic for generously assisting me in the writing process.

Thank you for constantly reminding me that there is no shortage of people who care enough about children to passionately work on their behalf.

* * * * *

Sources for Challenging Problems in Mathematics:

Sources for *all* the challenging problems we've used.

Balanced Assessment in Mathematics

http://balancedassessment.concord.org/

Posamentier, A. & Salkind, C. (1988). *Challenging Problems in Algebra*. New York: Dover Publications.

Posamentier, A. & Salkind, C. (1988).*Challenging Problems in Geometry*. New York: Dover Publications.

MathCounts School Handbooks. See the MathCounts Home Page at

http://www.mathcounts.org/

McDougal Littell Resource Book Problems. "Challenge" Supplementary Handouts.

12 DIFFERENTIATION & THE INTERNATIONAL BACCALAUREATE PROGRAM[31]

One evening over dinner in Bangkok, Laurie McLellan, a veteran international school administrator, told us the story of how he had presented the International Baccalaureate examination results to the Board of Directors at a European international school. The Board listened as Laurie presented an analysis of the exam results. He compared the school's scores with the world-wide averages and answered questions as to what the marks meant and how the scores were arrived at. At the conclusion of the presentation, a Board member asked Laurie to convey the Board's heartiest congratulations to two students whose total point count was more than forty points. Only a very small proportion of IB Diploma students world-wide score more than forty points. Laurie paused for a moment and then agreed to do so *on the condition* that the Board also extend its congratulations to Sophie (named changed) who had achieved a 24 point diploma, the minimum IB qualification. The Board Members appeared momentarily confused. Laurie explained that Sophie had a learning disability and had been receiving learning support since grade two. Her effort, persistence and commitment had been truly remarkable. In Laurie's mind, Sophie's achievement was equally worthy of recognition and congratulations.

We suspect that Sophie's achievement was also a result of sensitive and skillful teachers who were able to differentiate instruction in a meaningful way for her.

Advanced learner programs such as the International Baccalaureate Diploma Program are sometimes characterized as elitist. Unfortunately during such conversations, the term "elitist" is rarely defined. Elitism is a belief that certain persons or members of certain classes or groups deserve favored treatment. We would argue that there is nothing (except perhaps the cost) that is inherently elitist in the IB program. However, there are schools that

---

[31] Many of the observations, practices and principles addressed in this chapter can also be applied to other external examination systems such as the College Board Advanced Placement, British 'A' levels or the IGCSE.

have implemented it in an elitist fashion. The question, in our mind, comes down to equity of access.

Several years ago Bill was on an accreditation team visiting a large international school that included the IB Diploma Program in its high school. During an interview, the IB Coordinator proudly announced to the visiting team that for past five years, the school had a 100% IB pass rate and an average diploma score of 35 points. These results were annually published in the school's newsletter and were a considerable source of pride in the community. There is no question that an average diploma score of 35 points for a large school is a very good result.

In fact, it is *too good*.

Such a high average diploma score over five years suggests that student admission to the IB program was strictly controlled and highly selective. The only students who were admitted were those that the gatekeepers were confident would succeed and be a credit to their school. This particular school didn't take risks on students. This school would not have given Sophie the opportunity to earn her 24 point diploma.

Bill faced a similar situation when he first arrived at the International School of Kuala Lumpur and he informed his Board of Directors that it was his intention to increase the number and range of students admitted to the IB program. He went on to inform them that this would reduce the average IB diploma scores and possibly the pass rate. After some discussion, the Board accepted that the individual learning needs of students outweighed the school's need for glowing statistics.

We believe that an elitist approach to the implementation of advanced learner programs, such as the IB, have colored some teacher and administrator perceptions and made it difficult for individuals to see the important role that differentiation can and should play in these programs. In some respects this is a self-fulfilling perception. If schools only admit those students who are sure to achieve very good exam results, there is a very strong likelihood that the school will achieve outstanding results overall. When this happens, there is a strong temptation on the part of those responsible to interpret the glowing exam results as proof positive of a highly successful program. It is natural to want to celebrate success. However, this sometimes leads a school to wonder what possible role differentiation might play in a program that is already working so well. This is another way of saying: "If it isn't broken, don't fix it."

We would argue that highly selective admissions in a program such as the IB suggests that the system is fundamentally broken.

In our twenty five year experience with the IB program, we believe that most students in our international schools are intellectually capable of the challenge in one form or the other. In fact, we would suggest that the critical success predictor for students entering the IB program is not intelligence, but rather maturity of attitude and work habits. For example, for fifteen years in the 1980's and 1990's the International School of Tanganyika Ltd only offered the IB program in grades 11 and 12. There was very little selectivity in admissions and approximately 60 to 70% of the students completed the full IB diploma with a very creditable pass rate of between 90-95%. The remaining students did IB certificate courses. In those 15 years, only a very small handful of students were denied admission to the high school.

It would also appear from a review of the IB Assessment Handbook (2004) that students with learning disabilities and attention deficit disorder (ADD) are *expected* to be admitted and to take the examinations. In fact, the IB Assessment Handbook clearly outlines the procedures and modifications that may be allowed for these students (IBO, 2004, p. 11).

In our experience, very bright, highly motivated students will achieve outstanding exam results -- some times in spite of their teachers. Sophie, however, needed outstanding teachers and differentiated pedagogy to support her in her bid for the diploma.

Differentiated instruction in advanced learner programs such as the IB is the marriage of excellence and equity in education.

Five Frequently Asked Questions about Differentiation in the IB

When we conduct differentiation workshops in international schools around the world, we are often asked questions about how differentiation fits with external examination courses, such as the IB or AP. We have collected five such questions and will examine the assumptions upon which they may be based and their possible implications.

1. **"IB exams aren't differentiated – in fact, most college courses aren't differentiated – are we really doing kids a favor by making things easier for them?"** The question suggests a misunderstanding about what we should and should not differentiate. Success on an IB examination *is* the learning standard (in UbD terminology the 'desired outcome") and should NOT be differentiated. However, we can choose to differentiate how we help

students achieve this outcome. There are numerous pathways to understanding. As Mel Levine (2007) writes: "Students…benefit from discovering their preferred routes to comprehension. Some understand best verbally; others thrive on graphic representation; still others gravitate towards hands-on, experiential learning. In all instances, we should encourage them to represent information richly in their minds and, if possible, in multiple modalities (by thinking of examples, using mental imagery, rewording and elaborating, and so on (p.17)."

Teachers support student learning enormously when they make learning easier by capitalizing on student strengths or interests.

It is true that many university courses do not include differentiation. A college introductory biology course with three hundred students is unlikely to be differentiated. However, the absence of varied, student-centered pedagogy at university level is hardly an argument for its absence in relatively small, at least in comparison, high school classes.

In this context, we are wise to recall Arthur C. Clarke's (1986) observations in an article entitled *July 20th, 2019: Life in the 21st Century*. He calls for a paradigm shift in education's basic emphasis: "Our current educational system evolved to produce workers for the Industrial Revolution's factory-based economy, for work that requires patience and docility… Students learned to sit in orderly rows, to absorb facts by rote, and to move as a group through the material regardless of individual differences in learning speeds…" If you ever wondered why so many schools in the past were perceived to be boring, Clarke provides a possible answer. Life as an assembly line, factory drone was boring, and the ability to endure boredom was considered to be an essential life skill. Boring schools were excellent preparation for boring lives. But, as Clarke points out "no factory jobs will be left in 2019. Except for a few technicians to watch over control panels, tomorrow's factories will be automatic, with computers directing robot workers (Powell, 2000)."

Do we do students a favor by making learning *easier* for them? In a word, *yes*. There is no intrinsic value in difficulty for difficulty's sake. There is no value in complexity when the alternative is simplicity. The days are past when we believed that the stoic endurance of boredom or chronic anxiety produced admirable character traits. The question suggests that there may be confusion between what is "rigorous" and what may be "onerous" or "arduous". Alfie Kohn has commented: "A lot of horrible practices are justified in the name of 'rigor' or 'challenge'. People talk about 'rigorous' but often what they really mean is 'onerous', with schools turned into fact factories. This doesn't help kids become critical thinkers or lifelong learners (in O'Neill & Tell, 1999)."

'Making learning easier' means making it more stimulating, challenging and meaningful for students. It is one of the most fundamental obligations of every teacher.

2. **"Differentiation is fine in the elementary and middle schools, but is it really applicable for the IB in the high school?"** The question seems to suggest that as we grow older, we somehow become homogenized as learners; that our experience in schools wears smooth our unique rough learning edges; and that a "one size fits all" teaching in the high school will be as effective as differentiated instruction. The research, however, suggests that at least some of our intelligence preferences and learning styles are hard wired in our brains and will be with us for a lifetime. High school learners need a varied, student-centered approach to learning just as much as their younger colleagues do.

The question might also imply that the learning experience in the high school is significantly different from that of the elementary or middle school and might not lend itself to differentiation. While there is no question that learning in the high school involves greater complexity of concepts and increased content, we need to beware of falling into the false dichotomy that pits content coverage against teaching for understanding. The IB course of study will have a prescribed syllabus that the teacher will need to cover. That is non-negotiable. The students must be prepared for the examination. However, content coverage isn't, by itself, sufficient examination preparation. When content coverage becomes king and teaching for understanding the vassal, we end up with instruction becoming more important than learning. We would ask, not rhetorically, whether something can be taught that isn't in fact learned. More than fifty years ago Ralph Tyler (1949) argued that suggesting that "I taught them, they just didn't learn it" was as foolish as saying 'I sold it to them, they just didn't buy it."

The IB examinations reward students who show deep conceptual understanding of what they have studied. Students do this by demonstrating higher order thinking skills such as analysis, comparison, evaluation, prediction and by applying concepts in novel situations or new circumstances. Teachers need to teach for understanding as well as cover content. This isn't an either/or situation. One of the most effective ways of accomplishing this is to use varied instructional approaches that tap into student strengths, intelligence preferences, learning styles and interests.

3. "I have barely enough time to teach the IB syllabus, where does the time come from for differentiation?" There are two time-related issues when it comes to differentiated instruction. One is classroom time and the other is planning and preparation time. Let's look at them separately.

Classroom time is usually not something the teacher has much control over. The master schedule of classes usually dictates when classes will meet and for how long. So, teachers have little flexibility in terms of increasing instructional time. They do, however, have control over how classroom time is used. In other words, it is their responsibility to prioritize the use of classroom time with respect to the most important learning outcomes.

The idea that differentiated instruction takes more classroom time than "one size fits all" teaching is predicated on the misunderstanding that differentiation is something added – like an extra-curricular activity or an optional field trip. It is, in fact, a different way of doing the same thing – but, from the perspective of the learner, doing it more effectively and more efficiently.

Teachers do, however, have control over the amount of time they spend planning lessons and there can be no question that, at least initially, differentiated instruction takes more preparation time. This is why we counsel teachers who are embarking on the differentiation journey to "keep it simple and social." Teachers need to budget the planning time so that it is adequate but that they also preserve a life for themselves outside of school work.

While differentiation will require more planning time initially, over time teachers will come to build a repertoire of successful differentiation strategies and instructional activities. Once this repertoire is established, lesson planning time may actually decrease.

Marie-France Blais, a French teacher at the International School of Kuala Lumpur wrote to us about how differentiation had changed her teaching over the years. "Whereas it used to be a mammoth task to 'include' differentiation in my planning, it has now become a way of thinking / planning / teaching."

4. **"IB course selection and admission criteria result in pretty homogenous classes. Is there really a need for differentiation?"** It is a fallacy to think that IB students represent a homogeneous or monolithic set of high achieving students. Like their peers in non-examination classes, they too learn in unique ways and find specific subjects more difficult or easier than others. Many go through periods of self-doubt and wonder if they should have registered for the program in the first place. Nick Bowley, head of school at the International School of Tianjin, China, notes that one of the marks of a truly outstanding school is the number of borderline students who go on to earn the full IB diploma.

   Having said that, course selection does provide for a degree of differentiation, in the sense that students select courses that will be of interest to them and at an appropriate readiness levels (Standard vs. Higher level courses). However, course selection doesn't take into consider how individual students learn most efficiently.

   If a variety of instructional approaches represents a more effective learning environment than a single style (e.g. lecture or question and answer seminar), why wouldn't we want this for IB students?

5. **"Doesn't differentiation stigmatize kids?"** In this case, the question is a valid in the elementary or middle school as it is in an external examination program such as the IB. We suspect that the questioner may be confusing "streaming" or "tracking" with differentiation. In our experience, skillful differentiation does not stigmatize students. In fact, the opposite is the case.

   In any classroom (differentiated or not) students take no more than a few days to figure out which of their classmates are achieving rapidly and those who are not. Some well-meaning teachers assume that if they ignore such differences in readiness and achievement rates, the students will as well. We know that this does not happen. In classrooms where learning differences are not addressed explicitly, students often develop status hierarchies of their classmates. This ranking contributes to perceptions of high and low status (Cohen,

1998) which in turn can profoundly affect learning. Cohen observed that low status children participate less in class activities and discussions and therefore benefit less from them. The perception of low status on the part of classmates actually inhibits learning.

When learning differences are addressed directly with students, they come to understand that intelligence isn't monolithic – that while Imran may struggle in math, he plays the trumpet beautifully; while Sarah may write beautifully, the thought of acting on stage petrifies her. In addition, when teachers address learning differences explicitly, they have the opportunity to help their students develop respect for diversity. Students come to understand that there are many ways to learn something and that each of us brings to the classroom a different mix of talents, strengths and proclivities. For these reasons, stigmatization is less likely to occur in a differentiated classroom.

A former colleague of ours, Oscar Nilsson, now head of Bandung International School in Indonesia, gave all incoming IB Diploma students the Dunn & Dunn Learning Style Inventory so that they could be aware of their own learning style and become conscious of what conditions they needed in order to optimize their learning.

Differentiation in the International Baccalaureate Diploma Program

In 2000, we published an article in the journal *IB World* (originally entitled "The Pedagogy of the Pressured"-- the editor, failing to see allusion of Paulo Friere's work, changed it to "The Pedagogy of Pressure"). The article was critical of both the IBO's lack of attention to pedagogy (in the diploma program) and the generally "one size fits all" teaching we had witnessed in the IB program in a variety of schools – some with outstanding reputations.

The article focused on the pressure and stress that students often encounter in the IB program and we suggested that one source of stress might be from the absence of attention that many IB teachers and the IBO place upon pedagogical craftsmanship.

The combination of bright, highly motivated students and vast content landscapes to 'cover' has often proved a deadly combination for the actual craft of teaching. From our experience, most IB pedagogy is the proverbial "chalk and talk", seminars and small group discussions. Science courses will include hands-on activities and projects are used when the IB program requires them, but for the most part the teaching strategies are traditional and unimaginative and are oblivious, sometimes blithely so, to recent developments in the educational implications of brain research, learning styles, cognitive psychology, multiple intelligence theory and constructivism. In the absence of direct attention to instructional practice, most teachers teach as they themselves were taught.

(*Powell and Kusuma-Powell, IB World, Fall 2000.*)

However, the times are changing.

In 2006 the IBO published a critically important document entitled *The IB Learner Profile Booklet.* The learner profile in the IB is not a new concept. It was originally part of the Primary Years Program (PYP) and was called the "PYP Student Profile." What is significant now is that the IBO has extended the profile to all three of its programs, including the Diploma Program. "The IBO is introducing the learner profile into all three programs so that it becomes the common ground on which all IB World Schools stand, and contains the essence of what they, and the three programs, are about (IBO, 2006, p. 1). The profile describes a series of attributes to which IB students and their teachers should be striving. These include inquiry, critical and creative thought, open-mindedness, collaboration, effective communication, compassion and reflection. It is a comprehensive and impressive document and its applicability to the Diploma Program is most welcome.

Established in the late 1960's, the IB Diploma Program set out to develop in the last two years of secondary school a course of study for international schools which would be recognized as a university entry qualification by prestigious universities around the world. This was much needed at the time and a major development focus was understandably on developing the credibility of the diploma. While important innovations, such as CAS and Theory of Knowledge, were included, there was little focus during those early years on pedagogy or how the most efficient and effective learning took place. We wrote in 2000: "How many times have we heard from IB teachers that "constructivism" isn't applicable to the IB program or that IB teachers simply do not have the time to explore brain-based teaching?...If quality teaching is often sacrificed upon the altar of content coverage, the largest single group to suffer will be...the students. The unspoken assumption is that within the IB Diploma program there is so great a demand for content coverage that there is no time for examining or reflecting upon effective pedagogy. Not only is this untrue, but it actually undermines intellectual rigor, waters down otherwise stimulating syllabi and creates unnecessary stress and anxiety in both teacher and student (Powell & Kusuma-Powell, 2000)."

Over the years, the IB has stressed the importance of students "learning how to learn" and the publication of the *IB Learner Profile* is a significant milestone in that direction. From our perspective, it provides a most welcome emphasis on pedagogy, including differentiated instruction. "The curriculum can be defined as what is to be learned (the written curriculum), how it is to be learned (the taught curriculum) and how it is to be assessed (the learned curriculum). *This gives equal focus to content, teaching methodologies and assessment practices* (emphasis ours) (IB Learner Profile, 2006, p. 2).

The *IB Learner Profile* encourages teachers, IB coordinators and school administrators to ask questions such as:

- "Is it possible to create more experiences and opportunities in the classroom that allow students to be genuine inquirers?"
- "How much attention do we pay to how students interact with other students in group-work activities? Could we give more time to helping them work effectively as part of a team?"
- "Could we create more opportunities to discuss ethical issues that arise in the subject(s) we teach?"
- "How well do we model empathy, compassion and respect for others in our classrooms and around the school?" (IBO, 2006, p. 3)

These are the kind of questions that will cause schools and teachers to recognize the importance of differentiation within the Diploma Program. However, the IB itself recognizes the challenge that the Learner Profile may pose:

> *The IBO recognizes that the introduction of the IB learner profile may present a challenge for schools. It invites schools to evaluate critically their learning environment and make the changes necessary to enable all its students and teachers to work towards developing the values of the profile. Such changes should lead to a truly collaborative learning environment, the strengthening of professionalism among the teaching staff and a commitment by the school to invest in professional development. For most schools this will not mean starting from the beginning, but may involve a refocusing of attention, creative thought and resources. For some schools the introduction of the learner profile will necessitate a major shift in direction.*

> --*IB Learner Profile Booklet,* 2006

From 2006, schools offering the MYP and Diploma programs are expected to focus on monitoring student development (in light of the learner profile) by "engaging students and teachers in reflection, self-assessment and conferencing...The implementation of the IB learner profile is specified in these practices, and schools will be expected to address them as part of the self-study in the programme evaluation process (IBO, 2006, p. 3)."

If there were still a question about the place of differentiation within the IB Diploma Program, the *IB Assessment Handbook* would seem to put the matter squarely to rest. Over the years the IBO has recognized that some assessment procedures unfairly discriminated against students with learning disabilities. The *IB Assessment Handbook* includes the following paragraph which describes it policy in terms of assessment bias in special education.

> *A further aspect of bias that must be countered is the potential for an assessment task to discriminate unfairly against students with special educational needs such as dyslexia, attention deficit disorder or impaired vision. The conditions under which assessment tasks are taken should make appropriate allowances for such students, so that they can demonstrate their level of educational achievement on equal terms with other students.*

IB Assessment Handbook, 2004, p.11

Presumably, if the IB makes provision for students with learning disabilities in terms of assessment, we should also do so in terms of our differentiated instruction.

A Few Examples of IB Differentiation in Action

IB English Language A:

A number of years ago Janet Tan and Lynn Coleman, high school English teachers at the International School of Kuala Lumpur, devised an extremely effective differentiated learning activity for their study of Joseph Conrad's *Heart of Darkness*. Janet and Lynn had their IB student design and paint a mural along the corridor in front of their classroom depicting the novel's plot, characters, and important themes. The novel is a picaresque tale that follows the narrator's journey up the Congo River as such it lends itself beautifully to visual representation. The students were instructed to represent the key scenes in the novel and include important symbols, themes and quotations.

The first panel of the mural depicts Marlowe, sitting "Buddha-like" at twilight on the deck of a ship anchor in the Thames. Beneath Marlowe are the words: "We live as we dream – alone." In the background, we see the cityscape of

London against the words: "And this also has been one of the dark places on earth."

The Thames River merges almost surrealistically into a map of West Africa showing the Congo River. Within the map we see Africans chained to trees (presumably rubber trees). The next few panels depict the voyage up the river, replete with significant quotations from the book. The final panel depicts a prostrate Kurtz, pale and drawn with the words beneath: "The horror, the horror."

Following the IB English examination, Bill questioned the students on how it went. Without exception, all the students he spoke with commented that when they had been writing about *Heart of Darkness,* they had been able to "see" the mural in their mind and draw upon it. The process of having the students select important images, identify significant quotations and represent them visually was unquestionably a most powerful learning strategy for these students.

IB History and Economics

Michael O'Leary, Chairman of the Social Studies Department at ISKL also uses murals in his IB Economics classes. He writes: "Aside from the traditional pen and paper tasks, I really like using murals. I ask students to pick 10 to 15 concepts from the unit and create a mural showing the audience how they fit together and why they are significant… There is a writing component that goes with the mural to assist the viewer to know what he or she is looking at…The visual approach allows students to show me what they understand…I find this the most effective and fun way to get to understanding."

Michael and his colleagues also look to differentiate when it comes to the selection of reading material. In addition of the standard text, they try to identify supplementary readings (e.g. from *The armchair economist, The world is flat,* and *The undercover economist*) from popular mainstream books that have as their target audiences, readers who don't have a background in economics.

The social sciences lend themselves to high interest simulations and Michael and his colleagues orchestrate simulated trials on the subject of war guilt for World War One and Two and in IB Economics they do a large scale pit market where students are able to see for themselves how pricing structure works.

On a more individual note, if Michael knows that a student is going to have difficulty with a particular type of question, he will often provide a prompt of some kind. For example, he will include in the margin of the student's test paper a partially worked out example. Michael recognizes that this is a "touchy" issue, because if students plan on taking the IB exam, they will have to learn to work without this support. However, he see this classroom support in building student confidence so that students are more relaxed and therefore better able to access their memory. For Michael, fair is not equal; fair is getting what you need.

IB Biology

In this instance, the IB biology students at International School of Tanganyika in Dar es Salaam seemed to know intuitively that a kinesthetic activity would support their learning. During the last six weeks before the examination, the teacher assigned small groups of student the responsibility for reviewing with the entire class important aspects of their study of biology. The trio that had responsibility for how human vision works drew a diagram on the whiteboard labeling important parts of the eye and brain including the optic nerve, the optic chiasma and the visual cortex of the brain.

They then distributed to the rest of the class different colored ribbon and had the students form a physical tableau illustrating how visual images cross from the left side of the eye to the right side of the visual cortex. Each student in the class was then provided with an opportunity to stand on a desk and have a "bird's eye view" of how visual images travel from the left and right eyes to the visual cortex of the brain. It was a simple and brief and effective learning activity.

IB Psychology

IB Psychology teacher, Elaine Scroggins, created a series of activities and reporting alternatives for a unit of how attitude may correlate with human behavior. The alternatives allowed students choice in terms of learning styles and production preferences.

IB SL PSYCHOLOGY	
Objective: To assess the extent to which attitudes and behaviors correlate	
Activity Alternatives	**Reporting Alternatives**
Choice #1: With at least 3 other students, plan a debate which reflects various theoretical findings regarding the correlation between attitudes and behaviors. Incorporate examples from everyday life which support and challenge these findings.	**Choice #1:** Orchestrate and participate in the 10-15 minute debate. Have members of the class who are not participating judge the debate, according to the criteria you and the 3 other students have created.
Choice #2: Write a news story reflecting the latest information regarding the correlation between attitudes and behaviors. Design a series of at least 5 questions which highlight aspects of the attitude-behavior relationship reflected in the news story.	**Choice #2:** Invite 4 – 5 classmates to read your news story and to answer the accompanying questions in writing for you to correct.
Choice #3: Create a series of skits (mini-play with at least 3 scenes) reflecting the various relationships social psychologists believe exist between attitudes and behavior and which you believe are present in everyday life. Generate at least 2 questions to prompt discussion at the close of each scene.	**Choice # 3:** Perform skits for 4/5 classmates. Between each scene facilitate discussion about what has been illustrated.
Choice #4: Design a visual representation (e.g. poster, collage) reflecting your understanding of the correlation between attitudes and behaviors and how you believe this relationship is reflected in society. Create a worksheet which asks questions about information reflected in your representation.	**Choice #4:** Provide a 5-minute presentation explaining your visual representation to at least 4 of your peers. Have students complete the worksheet and return it to you for correction.

IB Geography

Our friend and colleague, Nick Bowley has taught IB Geography at a number of international schools. Nick developed the following kinesthetic learning activity at the International School of Tanganyika, but has subsequently used it with international school students in Syria and China. The learning activity is a massive board game that takes place on two enormous shower curtains.

In Nick's words: "The game is a kinesthetic review (or pre-test) of population policies, family planning and economic development. The players throw a giant die to move around a board, spread over the floor, on which there are questions and hazards. The winning team is the first to reach 'home' which in this game means a mummy, daddy, and two children with full tummies...I used the game last year with a group of 11th graders, and they loved it. The scale of the thing, and the movement it required, was quite a hook for them and for the passers by (because we had to play it in the lobby)."

IB Physics

Oscar Nilsson, physics teacher and head of school at Bandung International School, developed a differentiated astronomy unit based on the concept of a learning contract. Each student was called upon to read through the "Contract Package" and determine how he or she would fulfill the various obligations. Some examples from the "Contract Package" include:

Objective #1: Recall the stages in the evolution of a star.

Choose at least two.

Activity Alternative	Reporting Alternative
Make a map or chart representing the information you have gathered	Display the map or chart and answer questions about it.
Put together a power point presentation on the topic.	Present the program to your classmates.
Imagine that you are a Universal Travel Guide and are taking tourists on a tour of the galaxy. Prepare a voice/video commentary to be played on the Universal Space Transport Shuttle as it tours the hot and cold spots of the universe	Play the commentary/video to your classmates.
Produce a booklet by searching the web for more information on the topic.	Share this booklet with your colleagues

Objective #2: Describe the main processes involved in the formation of young stars, red giants, white dwarfs, supernovae, neutron stars and black holes.

Choose two activities.

Activity Alternative	Reporting Alternative
Develop a game using the ideas from the topic.	Play the game with several other fun loving astrophysicists.
Put together a presentation/lecture on the topic with overhead transparencies and posters to illustrate your points.	Present the lecture to your classmates.
Make models of the stellar objects to display in the classroom.	Display the models and answer questions from your classmates.
Produce a booklet by searching the web for more information on the topic.	Share this booklet with your colleagues

Objective #3: Classify stars using a Hertzsprung Russell diagram.

Choose two activities.

Activity Alternative	Reporting Alternative
Write and perform a play inspired by the topic.	Present the play to your classmates
Produce a different type of diagram that classifies stars.	Explain the diagram to your classmates.
Write a poem/song about the topic	Share your work with one or two classmates.
Produce a booklet by searching the web for more information on the topic.	Share this booklet to your colleagues

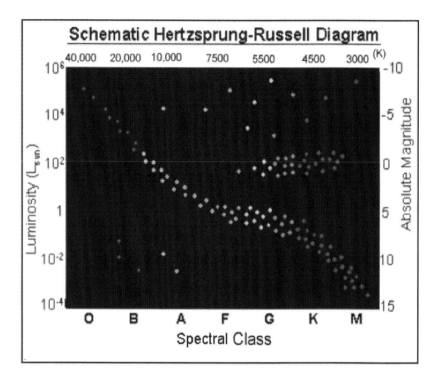

Objective #4: Evaluate astronomical observations as evidence for the existence of neutron stars and black holes.

Choose two activities.

Activity Alternative	Reporting Alternative
Construct a crossword puzzle based on the topic.	Let other students try to complete it. Check and return their answers to them.
Write and perform a (detective?) story inspired by the topic.	Present the play to your classmates
Produce a 2D flowchart of the process.	Display the chart and answer questions from your classmates.
Search the web for more information on the topic and produce a booklet.	Share this booklet with your colleagues.

IB Math

Colette Belzil, an IB math teacher from the International School of Brussels has developed a brief (5-10 minute) interactive review activity that is particularly effective with complex concepts with numerous details. In this example, Colette uses logarithms.

Review Activity: Instructions to students

"Take out a piece of paper. Put your name on it.

Put #1

Next to #1, write down one thing you remember about logarithms.

When you are done put your pencil down.

(Once all the students are finished writing something...)

Pass your paper to another student.

Put #2 on this person's list. Write down one thing you remember about logarithms that is not already written on this sheet.

When you are done put your pencil down.

Pass this paper to another student. (you cannot take a student's paper if you have already written on it)

Put # 3 on this person's list .Write down one thing you remember about logarithms that is not already written on this sheet. When you are done put your pencil down.

Pass this paper to another student.

....and so on..."

Continue to circulate the papers for several rounds. The idea is to not repeat any item on any piece of paper.

On the last round, ask students to return the paper in front of them to the original owner.

They can rewrite a rule (eg. $\log\dfrac{a}{b} = \log a - \log b$, or $\log_a b = \dfrac{\log b}{\log a}$ or draw a sketch of what a log graph looks like....) as often as they want so long as it has NOT already been written on the list.

This is a GREAT way of reviewing, writes Colette:

> The number of times I have students circulate the papers depends on the number of elements involved in the lessons I am reviewing. I have used this with log graphs and log rules, exponential graphs and exponent rules, with the different asymptotes and graphing rational functions... I have used it with vector vocabulary as well.
>
> It is a great way of revisiting a previous lesson or lessons that were done before a school break or a long weekend and before going on to the next step, because even if they only remember ONE thing that was covered in the previous 1-2 lessons, by having to see what others have written, it refreshes their minds. They sometimes also see something they had written earlier and realize they had made a mistake ☺ or else find a mistake on the paper they have been handed (and their new entry is the correction).

Alternate method: Sometimes Colette adds the extra step of asking students to look at the list that is returned to them at the end and see if there is anything that may be missing. She may let them take out their notes or book for verification and then ask students to volunteer what may have been missed. If she notices that a key element has been overlooked, it gives her the opportunity to bring it up and review it as needed.

Modern Languages: French

Although Marie-France Blais, a Middle School French teacher at the International School of Kuala Lumpur, is not currently teaching in the IB Diploma Program, many of the differentiation strategies that she has developed could easily be adapted for IB classes. She classifies them in terms of Speaking, Listening, Writing and Reading.

Speaking

"Most students easily master key phrases as well as memorize scripted conversations that can be delivered in the target language. Yet promoting spontaneous exchanges has always been a challenge for me. This year, I have devised tasks that bridge the gap between memorized dialogues and pure unscripted speech.

After Malaysia Week (a week-long experiential learning program) the students re-created their Malaysia Week itinerary on an A3 paper labeling the items on their maps with nouns. They then framed their work by writing a selection of infinitive verbs / un-agreed adjectives / link words and adverbs. Armed with this thematic vocabulary and the illustrated map, students were able to share their Malaysia Week (MW) experiences with the whole class or in a small groups, constructing their sentences as they described their surroundings and activities. While the sophistication of the phrases varied, each student was able to communicate his/her message. Some students folded the frame underneath their map as they were able to talk about their MW without the visual help of the words.

Some students challenged themselves further and exchanged their maps and described another person's MW experience, which of course implied the use of different pronouns and possessives."

Listening /Understanding

"I believe most language students often understand far more than what they can express in the target language. In the past, I have had students respond to questions in English about a French story that I would read out loud. This practice allowed me to truly assess whether the students understood the story. If I had made them answer in French, I might have unwittingly assessed their ability to respond *in* the target language rather than their understanding *of* the target language. Last year I was introduced to TPRS (Teaching Proficiency through Reading and Storytelling). While I have not been able to embrace all the tenets of this method, I have come to see its questioning method as an invaluable tool in class. It allows me to differentiate the complexity of the questions as well as personalize the issue at hand.

I read the story in French and students are also expected to respond in the target language. Scaffolding the questions gives options to students (see Levels I and II below) and they do not remain tongue tied with nothing to say. The comprehension questions of Level 3 ask students to form a hypothesis and even if it is wrong, they are still using the target language. The elaboration questions of Level IV are seemingly more difficult, but some students do surprisingly well on them.

Here is the sketch of a story and samples of possible 'scaffolded' questions:

Simon Leblanc told his wife that he would bake a birthday cake for her 30th birthday on the 5th of May. Mr. Leblanc is a very busy attorney and he forgot about his promise. On the day of his wife's birthday, he went to a different part of town and bought a scrumptious cake. His wife loved the cake and asked him for the recipe. The next day, Simon hurried back to the bakery to ask the baker for the recipe. The baker saw Mr. Leblanc rushing back looking tense. The baker thought that Mr. Leblanc was unhappy with his cake so he hid behind the counter of his store.

I. "Either /Or" questions

* Students can either answer with a complete sentence or short answer.

1. Is Mr Leblanc married or single?
2. Did his wife like or hate the cake?
3. Do you prefer chocolate or vanilla cake?
4. Is Mr. Leblanc busy or lazy?
5. Is the baker a brave or cowardly man?

II. "Yes / No / 1 word" questions

* Students can answer either with yes/no or with a complete sentence.

1. Is Mr. Leblanc a baker?
2. What is the profession of your dad / mom?
3. Is the date of Mr. Leblanc's wife May 5th?
4. When is your birthday?
5. Where did the baker hide?

III. Comprehension questions

1. Why did the baker hide?
2. Why did Mr. Leblanc choose to buy the cake in a different neighborhood?
3. Why did Mr. Leblanc have to buy a cake?
4. Why was Mr. Leblanc looking tense?
5. What assumption did the baker make?
6. How can you assume that Mr. Leblanc's wife loved her cake?

IV. Elaboration

* There are no wrong answers in this section. Debates can spontaneously occur if the students feel particularly drawn to a subject.

1. Do you think that Mr. Leblanc's wife was fooled by her husband? Why?
2. What are some of the ways to ensure that you remember an important date?
3. Relate a time when you or someone you know felt tense or stressed.
4. What might have happened if Mr. Leblanc told his wife the truth?
5. Is 'total honesty' preferable to the telling of 'white lies'? Explain.
6. List the top 3 qualities that you look for in a friend.
7. Re-tell the story from the angle of Mr. Leblanc's wife / the baker.
8. Who do you identify with most in the story? Why?

Writing

Students have a small writing book that they begin in Basic French which they will keep through Intermediate French until the end of Advanced French. It shows the writing progress made by the students and it becomes a (small or big) source of pride for all. Twice a month (minimum), the students write a story / dialogue in this book. The themes of the writing vary but the students are asked to showcase the structures/vocabulary that they know in French.

For students who suffer from 'writers' block', I provide a file of wordless illustrated stories / postcards / advertising pictures to choose from. Once they have an idea, those students can write up a storm.

For creative students who are hesitant to use newly learnt structures, I provide a 'must-have' list of grammatical structures that I expect to see in their writing. The students glue the list next to the story and tick the items as they use them.

Ex.: 10 passé composé avec avoir and 3 with être; 3 demonstrative pronouns; 3 temporal adverbs; 2 partitive articles…

For students who are petrified in front of a blank page, I give a list of various stems / nouns / verbs / adjectives that the students weave together in order to create story.

Ex.: (stems) On the first day / Then he fell heavily / In my humble opinion

(nouns) the lawnmower / some loose change / a multicoloured wig

(adjectives) wrinkled / stubborn / dry

Some students have great difficulty "to think in French" and insist on "writing in English first" - their writing thus reflects a direct translation from English to French. I teach these students how to modify their English text in order to achieve a French sounding text.

Some students challenge themselves by taking the text of a well-known French author and imitating its style. It is quite difficult to do but some kids have been quite successful at it.

Daru est instituteur d'une petite école française qui se situe dans une région rude, sèche et solitaire, sur les hauts plateaux d'Algérie. Il regarde deux hommes qui montent lentement la pente à sa rencontre. L'un est à pied, l'autre à cheval. (Albert Camus)

Reading

Again as a result of becoming acquainted with TPRS, I have instilled a 15 minutes individual free reading period once a week in class. Students pick a book from the various genres/themes on the bookshelves, pick a comfortable spot / cushion / corner and read! Not having questions to answer after the reading helps students relax about looking up every word they encounter. I have also found some stories on-line which have proven popular with the 'techie crowd'

Another form of reading that we do is "peer reading". Every 2 weeks, I select a piece from one of our students, type it and give it to the whole class. The readers not only enjoy the stories but they are very keen to discover its writers. The writers themselves bask in a small patch of glory! This practice also subtly allows everyone to gauge their own level of writing as it provides a type of anchor paper (an exemplar of the desired outcome).

I recall enjoying in-class oral reading from my own school days . . . So my classes are also getting to read stories out loud by taking turn (most of the time they are volunteers but at times I "call" on specific students). I make sure that we stop at a crucial point in the story and I love it when they yell for one more page!

Texts (authentic and made for target language learners of varied genres and themes) are regularly used in class. For each of these texts, I provide an optional glossary for the students.

I find summarizing a very powerful way to cut to the chase and find out whether the students have understood the fundamental premises of a particularly difficult text. I quite often have the students working in groups where each provide "one thing" from the text to their group. It often turns into a game as to who has the last morsel to contribute after the others have exhausted their offerings.

Conclusion

Instruction in the elementary, middle and high school takes different forms and differentiated instruction is no exception to this. It will look different in the different divisions of a school. Advanced learner programs, such as the IB, are challenging, rigorous and, to some degree, stressful for both the student and the teacher. Our experience and the experience of many of our colleagues around the world has shown that differentiation in the IB can make the challenge and rigor more manageable for all learners, but particularly for diverse learners. Differentiation can also decrease the stress and anxiety that is commonly associated with this challenging program.

As Marie-France Blais puts it, differentiation is "like a scaffold used to scale a wall. Some students start below others and some will reach far beyond the top of the wall. The speed and energy expended will differ from student to student and so will the route that individuals choose to take -- but all students will end up higher than where they started."

13 ASSESSMENT & GRADING IN THE DIFFERENTIATED CLASSROOM

Assessment as We Used to Know and Loathe

In the 10th grade, Bill faced a major test in American History. The teacher had stressed how important the test was and how it was modeled on the kind of tests that the students would encounter in university. Bill spent hours studying in preparation for the test as it represented a very significant portion of his grade in the course. As he entered the classroom on the day of the test he felt fairly self-confident. He had thoroughly reviewed the chapters in the text book and his class notes. He felt he was well-prepared for the test. However, as he began to read through the question paper, he realized that the test focused on content that he hadn't studied at all. It was as though the test had come out of a different course altogether. Panic and self-doubt swept through him.

Bill scored poorly on the test and the teacher wrote on his script: *You must learn to study harder. This test does not represent what you are capable of.*

Thirty years later, Bill reflects that the test taught him several lessons about life in schools that had nothing to do with American History. First, despite all the platitudes espoused by parents and teachers to the contrary, there wasn't necessarily any relationship between effort and achievement. Hard work didn't necessarily pay dividends. In some classrooms, it still doesn't. Bill is confident that he could have achieved the same dismal score without the hours of studying. There is *only* a correlation between hard work and accomplishment when the assessment is reasonably predictable.

When teachers, however unwittingly, cause students to disassociate effort and achievement, they do the learner a major disservice. Madeline Hunter's classic work with Attribution Theory in schools (Hunter & Barker,1985) suggests that there are aspects of causality that are perceived to be controllable (e.g. effort) and aspects that are not controllable (e.g. ability, task difficulty and luck). When the controllable aspects of causality are perceived to be connected to achievement, individual potency and efficacy are enhanced and the likelihood of future success is increased. The opposite is also, unfortunately, the case.

The second lesson Bill learned from the experience was that some teachers couldn't be trusted. The test did not represent a fair assessment of the major ideas and concepts of the Great Depression and Roosevelt's response to it. Instead, it was an idiosyncratic collection of questions – some of which were tangential, some of which were merely trivial. The test was clearly a "gotcha assessment" in which the teacher attempted, with considerable success, to uncover what the students didn't know -- as opposed to what they had actually learned.

Bill learned from this experience that school success was not so much about learning or achievement as it was about being able to out-guess the teacher as to what was going to be included on the test. He learned to play the "guess what I'm thinking game".

This is not only bad assessment practice; it is malpractice.

Fortunately, standards-based curricula and common assessments have made these practices rarer today.

In this chapter, we will attempt to do three things. First, we will look at some principles that international schools are using in the assessment of student learning. Secondly, we will examine a relatively new paradigm in assessment (Assessment *for* Learning) that appears to complement differentiation remarkably well. Finally, we will look at the knotty issues surrounding grading student work. Grading and assessment often become confused in teachers' minds. We perceive them as separate and different functions. Assessment has to do with the analysis of student work and the formulation of useful feedback; whereas grading has to do with communicating student achievement and progress to valued stakeholders (parents, university admissions officers, etc.). We will examine why so many teachers feel conflicted about grading and suggest some principles that can be used for grading student achievement in the differentiated classroom.

Assessment *of* Learning

The world of educational assessment is undergoing tectonic shifts that are literally moving the ground beneath the feet of the educational establishment. We are not just looking at assessment practices and classroom strategies, but we are reflecting on and re-examining the very purposes of assessment.

Consider that the traditional purpose of assessment in schools was to sort and rank students. Given the class hierarchies and the stratified job market of the

20th century, it was imperative to have a means of funneling young people into productive employment. When Bill grew up in Britain in the 1950's, the Eleven Plus Examination was still in effect. Taken at the age of eleven, the results of this exam determined whether a child would enter further academic study or be shunted into vocational training. The old British "O" Level Examinations further sorted and ranked students at age 16. The top 10% of candidates, irrespective of their actual performance on the examination, received "A"s and the next 20% "B"s and so on. These so-called norm referenced tests compared student performance against other students sitting the same examination.

The SAT fulfills a similar sorting function in terms of university admission in the United States. The ranking and sorting of students continues to be a primary purpose of educational assessment in highly competitive educational systems (e.g. India, South Korea, etc.) around the world.

Teachers who grew up in norm-referenced systems often find it very difficult to think about assessment without comparing students against each other even within a relatively small classroom. This comparison inevitably works to the detriment of *all* students. Students at the bottom of the teacher's achievement hierarchy experience lower expectations and achieve less. Even those students "fortunate" enough to be sorted and ranked at the top of the heap are not compared against their own potential and are often under-challenged. They become the victims of benign neglect since "they will learn it anyway".

Another traditional purpose of educational assessment was to dole out punishments and rewards. Students who did well received accolades, were placed on the Honor Roll and received awards and prizes. Students who didn't do well were also recognized, sometimes publicly, with scorn and ridicule. We can see the Skinnerian hand of operant conditioning at work. In the traditional perception of assessment, fear was seen as a powerful motivator of student achievement. And so one of the strategies used by teachers was to build within the students an urgent sense of assessment anxiety. Stiggins (2002) writes: "We all grew up in classrooms in which our teachers believed that the way to maximize learning was to maximize anxiety and assessment has always been the great intimidator (p. 761)." We still see the legacy of this connection between assessment and anxiety when we assign students a task and their first question is: "Will it be graded? Will it count?"

About thirty years ago, a few educational systems began to focus attention on so-called criterion-referenced assessment. This represented a revolution in thinking about the purpose of assessment and schools. The ranking and sorting of norm-referenced testing perpetuated antiquated class structures and privilege and flew in the face of the democratization of society that was inherent in the movement in Britain and the United States toward compulsory, universal education.

In criterion-referenced assessment, a student's achievement is not compared against other students, but rather the student's work is evaluated against pre-determined achievement criteria. For example, does the child use a variety of sentence structures? How well organized is the child's paragraph? Is there a topic sentence? How accurate is the child's spelling? Is punctuation used appropriately? The purpose of criterion-referenced assessment is to chart student growth in regard to valued skills and knowledge. The bell curve is jettisoned and in theory all students who meet the pre-determined criteria for success can get "A"s. The advent of criterion referenced assessment truly stands as a milestone in our educational journey to balance and marry *excellence* and *equity*.

Another critical advantage of criterion-referenced assessment was that it allowed individual teachers and schools to use data gathered through the assessment process to help in planning the most appropriate learning experiences for given individuals and groups of students. And so enters the idea that the results of assessment can and should inform future instruction. Teachers can analyze data and learn from the assessment results. In the sidebar below, Tom Guskey (2002) suggests a simple but powerful way in which teachers can analyze assessment results.

Analyzing Assessment Results

An easy but effective way to gain evidence from tests and assessments for improving teaching is to conduct a simple analysis of each test item or each criterion used in evaluating a paper, performance, or demonstration. This can be done by just tallying how many students missed each item or failed to meet a particular criterion. Special attention should be paid to those items or criteria missed by half or more of the students in the class. These identify the trouble spots.

The first thing to consider in such cases is the quality of the item or criterion itself. In other words, the teacher must determine if the problem rests with the test or assessment. Perhaps the question is ambiguously worded. Perhaps the criterion is unclear. Perhaps students misinterpreted what the teacher wanted. Whatever the case, teachers must look carefully at those items or criteria to see if they adequately address the knowledge, understanding, or skill they intended to measure.

If no obvious problems are found with the item or criterion, then teachers must be willing to turn to their teaching. If half the students in a class miss a clear and concise question on a concept that was taught, then apparently the concept wasn't taught very well. Whatever

---

> *strategy was used, whatever examples were employed, or whatever explanation was offered, it simply didn't work. When half the students in the class answer a question incorrectly or fail a particular criterion, it's not a student learning problem, it's a teaching problem.*
>
> --Tom Guskey, (2002) "Twenty Questions? Twenty Tools for Better Teaching", *Principal Leadership, (1)3,* Winter, 2002

Criterion-referenced assessment of learning has come to play a central role in the movement towards developing standards-based curriculum. In other words, we determine what we want the students to learn -- what we want them to know, understand and to be able to do (school-wide standards). We set benchmarks of grade level quality and then we design assessments that allow us to determine the degree to which our students have achieved these standards. International schools around the world are wrestling with this process and are developing principles of assessment that are both linked to school-wide learning standards and offer students a variety of ways in which they can demonstrate their achievement.

An Example of Essential Agreements for Assessment

Preamble:

Student progress towards achieving curriculum standards is assessed in a variety of ways. A combination of class work, common assessment tasks and unit projects are routinely used to monitor learning. Teachers use student work to make adjustments to the pace of instruction, to differentiate learning activities and to modify teaching methods in order to promote greater student achievement. One of the most important purposes of assessment is to support the student on their journey toward realistic and healthy internal (self) assessment. Our assessment essential agreements and practices are guided by the following research based principles:

1. Assessment must be aligned with circular standards and benchmarks and shall reflect separate academic and non-academic evaluations.
2. Assessment tools (tests, portfolios etc.) and criteria (e.g. rubrics) will be matched to learning tasks and used to improve learning by both teachers *and* students.
3. Major assessment tools should be determined before a unit of study begins and should follow... the Understanding by Design (UbD) process.
4. A balance of assessments should be used such as: common assessments, contextual performance assessments, mastery/proficiency, baseline, student self-assessment and teacher

observation, etc.

5. Students should receive major assessment criteria and models of work at the start of a unit of study to improve performance and ensure assessment transparency.

6. Assessment should be collected and analyzed regularly to inform instruction and refine curriculum and performance expectations.

7. Results from assessments should be communicated to students in a timely manner.

-- *Essential Agreements on Assessment*,
International School of Kuala Lumpur. Revised October 2005

The sidebar above includes an example of how one school (International School of Kuala Lumpur) collaboratively reached some essential agreements about assessment.

Assessment in a standards-based curriculum framework is deceptively simple —at least to those who have never tried to make it work. Again, the process includes determining what the students will learn in terms of school-wide standards; setting benchmarks of grade level quality; and designing assessments that will allow us to determine the degree to which our students have achieved these standards. This process sounds straight-forward enough, but is actually a difficult and complex task.

Herein resides its Achilles Heel.

Some of our most important standards are difficult, perhaps even impossible, to assess objectively. For example, we believe that an important learning standard for schools should be the enthusiasm and joy that children are developing for the learning process. This is virtually impossible to measure on a so-called objective assessment. So we are faced with a choice. We can simply *not* measure it, in which case, it will probably be relegated to the column of desirable but optional standards that may happen by spontaneous combustion; however, in most classrooms it won't be part of the planned curriculum. There is truth to the old adage that what is measured is taught.

Alternatively, teachers and administrators can accept the challenge that some assessment must include a degree of subjectivity. For the most part, this is a challenge that international school teachers have been ready to embrace. While subjectivity is often associated with a lack of reliability resulting from either bias or caprice, it doesn't need to be so. When teachers use informal assessment, when they gather data and evidence, and engage in clinical observation of students, this subjectivity can be transformed into sound *professional judgment*. We would argue that such professional judgment is a critical and indispensable component to assessment. Without it, some of our most meaningful learning standards are lost, resulting in shallow and mono-dimensional assessment of student achievement.

Teacher-proof assessments strip the curriculum of some of its most important and meaningful objectives.

Having said that, there are many aspects of student achievement that *can* be meaningfully evaluated through criterion-referenced assessments. Certainly one of the most challenging aspects of such any assessment is the construction of a performance rubric. The rubric contains the key criteria that are being assessed and descriptions of various levels of student achievement. For some procedural knowledge, rubric construction can be fairly straight forward. For example, some excellent rubrics exist for the assessment of expository writing. However, when we get into areas of declarative knowledge and critical/creative thinking, rubrics can be more problematic. For instance, the descriptors of quality in the rubric need to be clearly understood by the student and reasonably easy to measure. For this reason, teachers will often *quantify* the description of quality rather than attempt to *qualify* it. For example, the highest level of achievement on a social studies rubric might demand that student include in their essay at least three reasons for the Chinese Cultural Revolution, but the rubric may make no mention of the appropriateness or meaningfulness of the reasons. Again we can be faced with the tendency towards measuring only that which is easily measurable.

Our colleague Ron Ritchart, a researcher from Harvard University, is skeptical about the use of rubrics. He sees shallow rubrics being used by students as a "paint by number" approach to classroom "success". Such rubrics actually limit student critical and creative thought. The value of a rubric will always be measured by how well it promotes student growth in learning.

Another way of looking at Assessment: Assessment *for* Learning

"You don't fatten a cow by weighing it."

--Anonymous

When we look at assessment in the differentiated classroom we need to look at it through different lenses. We need to start by asking some very basic questions about what we do in classrooms and why. If the purpose of differentiation is to maximize the learning of all students – to take a high quality curriculum and to provide the maximum access to it for *all* learners, then we would suggest that any assessment that takes place in the differentiated classroom needs to be aligned to this. To this end, we see two purposes for assessment in the differentiated classroom:

1. to analyze student progress and to determine the status of learning, and
2. to serve as an essential component of the learning process in order to promote and enhance further learning.

We distinguish between these functions by talking about assessment *of* learning and assessment *for* learning. However, it is important to understand that assessment *of* and assessment *for* learning are not mutually exclusive. One does not need to choose between them.

We would suggest that while assessment *of* learning is almost certainly going to be a feature of the educational landscape for the foreseeable future, the principles and practices of assessment *for* learning are remarkably well aligned to the values and practices of differentiated instruction. Both differentiation and assessment *for* learning strive to make student learning success their central purpose. Both initiatives strive for seamless integration of instruction and assessment, for the well-being of the learner. Differentiation and assessment *for* learning are centrally concerned with how students learn most efficiently; this reflects recognition that emotions and self-confidence are inseparable from cognition, and that motivation plays a critical role in furthering learner success. Perhaps the most striking commonality is the emphasis that both differentiation and assessment *for* learning places on recognizing and building on student strengths in order to further develop learner self-directedness and self-management.

Two groups are spearheading the assessment *for* learning initiative: in the United Kingdom, the Assessment Reform Group (ARG)[32] and the in United States, The Assessment Training Institute[33] in Portland, Oregon.

Assessment *for* learning has a great deal in common with what teachers often refer to as "formative assessment" – assessment strategies that are not included in a students grade, but rather serve as a means for teachers to check on student progress and modify instruction if need be. However, there is a crucial difference between what we have customarily thought of as "formative assessment" and assessment *for* learning.

Assessment *for* learning seeks to promote and enhance learning, not merely to check on it. Assessment *for* learning places the learner at the heart of the

[32] http://www.assessment-reform-group.org/
[33] http://www.assessmentinst.com/

assessment process. The purpose is to enhance and further learning, and therefore assessment is not something that happens to the learner but rather something that the learner is an active participant in. It is really the role that the student plays in the assessment process that distinguishes assessment *for* learning and makes it so compatible with differentiated instruction.

The Assessment Reform Group in the United Kingdom has played a key role in bringing the research evidence about assessment *for* learning to the attention of the educational community through the commissioned work of Black and William (1998) *Inside the black box,* and the follow-up work *Assessment for learning: Beyond the black box* (1999). It has identified ten research-based assessment *for* learning (AFL) principles to guide classroom practice:

Principle #1: AFL is part of effective instructional planning. Assessment is not an after-thought to see how much of what has been taught has been caught. Like Understanding by Design (UbD) (Wiggins & McTighe, 1998) assessment for learning is not something that simply happens at the end of the unit or semester. It is integrated into the instructional process. The planning includes strategies to insure that students understand the learning objectives they are pursuing and the criteria that will be applied in assessing their work. The planning should also provide opportunities for *both* students and teacher to obtain and use information about progress towards learning goals. Critical features of this are: how learners will receive feedback, how they will take part in assessing their work, and how they will be helped to make further progress.

Principle # 2: AFL focuses on how students learn (not just "what" they learn). Teacher planning must take into consideration the process of learning. The on-going assessments need to provide students with opportunities to reflect on the learning process. This is the meta-cognitive piece in which learners actually think about thinking. Teachers need to plan classroom strategies that will help students to come to know themselves better as learners.

Principle # 3: AFL is central to classroom practice. We need to think about assessment as something which occurs daily in the classroom, not just something that happens at the end of a chapter, a unit or a semester. We need to be aware that assessment is taking place every time a teacher asks a question or sets a task that requires students to demonstrate their knowledge, understanding or skills. Assessment is both a formal and informal process that involves teachers and learners in reflection, dialogue and decision making. Assessment and instruction should be the seamless process in which the teacher and learners gather and use information about progress towards learning goals. Stephen Chappuis (2004) from the Assessment Training

Institute writes that "assessment begins to look like instruction when we deeply involve students in the process." In other words, students need to be inside the assessment process. Chappuis and others identify seven classroom strategies that engage the learner in assessment (see sidebar below).

Principle #4: AFL is a key professional skill. Assessment is a complex and demanding task. Teachers need to plan for assessment, observe learning, analyze and interpret evidence of learning, give feedback and support learners in self-assessment. Teachers need to think like designers and assessors. Accordingly, teachers need to be supported in developing these skills through specifically focused professional development.

Principle # 5: AFL is sensitive and constructive. Any form of assessment has an emotional impact on the learner and therefore should be sensitive and constructive. Teachers need to be aware of the impact that a grade or mark can have on learner confidence and enthusiasm and should be as constructive as possible in the feedback they give. Feedback should comment on the work under analysis, NOT the person. Please see further comments later in the chapter on the distinction between *evaluative feedback* and *descriptive feedback*. Stiggins (2002) suggests two questions that we might ask ourselves about the feedback we give students and its emotional impact on the learner's motivation and confidence: "How can we use assessment to help all our students *want* to learn? And, how can we help them feel *able* to learn? (p. 758)"

Principle #6: AFL fosters motivation. Assessment needs to encourage learners. By encourage, we are not simply referring to praise. Encouragement comes through recognition of personal progress and accomplishment. Therefore the focus of the assessment needs to be on what the learner *has achieved*, not on what he or she still cannot do. A focus on student learning deficits is unlikely to motivate students. By emphasizing individual achievement and process, learners develop greater confidence as they watch themselves succeeding. Students actually come to understand what it means to be in charge of their own learning. "Motivation can be preserved and enhanced by assessment methods which protect the learner's autonomy, provide some choice and constructive feedback, and create opportunities for self-direction (ARG, 2002, p. 2)."

Principle #7: AFL promotes understanding of goals and criteria. In order to maximize achievement for all students (the goal of both differentiation and assessment *for* learning) students need to *understand* and be able to articulate what they are trying to achieve and, equally important, they need to *want* to achieve it. Student commitment to learning goals is enhanced when assessments are discussed in class, when students are provided with specific examples of how criteria can be met and when learners are engaged in peer and self-assessment.

Principle #8: AFL helps learners know how to improve. The primary purpose of assessment is to support the learner in improving his or her performance -- whether it be in writing an essay, analyzing a poem, solving a complex math problem or writing a lab report. Students need guidance on what they need to do next in order to improve. Teacher feedback needs to identify the learner's strengths and advise on how to further develop them. Teachers need to be clear and concise regarding deficits or weaknesses in student work and how these might be addressed. Learners must be provided with opportunities to improve their work. The use of constructive feedback is one of the most important and powerful life skills that we can help students to develop.

Principle #9: AFL develops the capacity for self-assessment. Teachers have many different reactions to and perceptions of student self-assessment. A few very traditional teachers look upon it with overt suspicion. They see it as a massive conflict of interest – analogous to putting the foxes in charge of the henhouse. Fortunately, this perspective is increasingly rare. However, many teachers treat self-assessment as a nice, but optional add-on, like one of those extras that isn't included in the standard model, but can be added if time permits. Our view is radically different. We would argue that the *only* significant enduring purpose behind assessment is to help students to internalize healthy, accurate and reasonably challenging self-assessment. Self-assessment supports the learner in becoming reflective and self-managing. These are vital skills and habits of mind that students will need for the rest of their lives. Self-assessment is a learning objective that can truly stand the twenty year test. Black and William (1998) write: "Self-Assessment by pupils, far from being a luxury, is in fact *an essential component of formative assessment* (p. 143)"

Principle #10: AFL recognizes all educational achievement. Specialist teachers often see students through the perceptual filter of their academic discipline. This can enhance learning if the perception is positive. It can be crippling when the perception is negative. For example, when we think that Sabrina doesn't have an aptitude for math or foreign language acquisition or higher level science courses, we convey that message to Sabrina in hundreds of verbal and non-verbal ways. Many, many students who are failing classes in schools are doing so because they have learned from their teachers that they are no good at the subject. These students are not learning disabled, they are *teacher disabled*. Assessment *for* learning should enhance learners' opportunities to learn in all areas of educational activity. "It should enable all learners to achieve their best and have their efforts recognized (ARG, 2002, p. 2)."

In an outstanding article entitled "Helping Students to Understand Assessment", Jan Chappuis (2005) writes that students need to be able to answer three basic questions about their learning:

- Where am I going? (What specifically is the learning target?)
- Where am I now? (What can and can't I do?)
- How can I close the gap?

In this same context, she summarizes seven relatively simple strategies that teachers can use to help to systematically involve students in the formative assessment process:

Seven Strategies for Engaging Students in the Assessment Process

- **Strategy One: Provide a clear and understandable vision of the learning outcome.** Provide learning coherence by keeping students focused on the large learning objectives and connected to a vision of quality as the learning takes place, continually defining and redefining for students the learning expectations.

- **Strategy Two: Use anonymous examples of strong and weak student work.** Ask students to evaluate the work samples and to discuss the criteria they used. Have them use the language of the rubric or scoring guide. Such an activity will assist students in understanding what high quality work looks like and will support them in self-assessment.

- **Strategy Three: Offer regular descriptive feedback.** Providing students with regular descriptive feedback enhances their learning. We would, however, make a distinction between evaluative feedback which consists of marks or letter grades. Such evaluative feedback often signals to students that the learning associated with a piece of work is finished. Descriptive feedback gives them insight about current strengths (success) and how to do better next time (corrective action). We also know that quality in feedback is vastly more important than quantity.

- **Strategy Four: Teach students to self-assess and set goals.** Insist that students engage in activities that teach the skills of self-assessment, help them to regularly collect evidence of their own progress.

- **Strategy Five: Design lessons that focus on one aspect of quality at a time.** This strategy breaks learning into manageable pieces for students. Many of us have received a piece of work back from a teacher with so much red ink on it that it was overwhelming. Focusing on one aspect of quality at a time fosters enhanced learning.

- **Strategy Six: Teach students focused revision.** Insist that students

---

revise their work. Teach them how to use feedback in the revision process. Focus on a single aspect of quality. Don't allow them to bite off more than they can chew. Providing students practice with an anonymous poor quality piece of work is a very useful activity.

- **Strategy Seven: Engage students in self-reflection and let them document and share their learning.** Use daily strategies in the classroom that require students to articulate specifically what they are learning and the progress they are making. Use a variety of strategies to have students communicate their own understanding of what they have learned and develop goals to close the gap between where they are now relative to the desired learning outcome and where they need to be in order to meet learning standards.

--Adapted from the work of Stiggins, Arter, Chappuis & Chappuis, 2004

The goal of both differentiation and assessment *for* learning is to engage the student in the assessment process for the process of enhanced learning. By coming onto the inside of the assessment process, the student comes to know him or herself better as a learner. The student, not the teacher, becomes the most important end-user of assessment data.

Grading in the Differentiated Classroom: A Process at War With Itself

The figure below includes thirty five common purposes behind grading. We stopped at thirty five not because we had exhausted the subject, but because the page was full and we thought we had made our point -- which is that there are many, many different purposes behind grading, *some of which are totally contradictory to each other*. Take for example, the teacher who wants to use grading as means to encourage a struggling student. She perceives that a positive grade will bolster the young person's self-confidence and serve as a boost to his motivation. However, the grade will go on a high school transcript that will be used by universities to make selective admissions decisions.

The fact that we are trying to use grading for so many different purposes, some of which are mutually exclusive, accounts for some of the reason that so many teachers feel conflicted about the subject of grading. However, there is another aspect to this as well.

Tomlinson & McTighe (2006) write that the process of grading often leaves "student-centered educators feeling uncomfortable and compromised…Their classroom practice honors and attends to variance in student readiness, interest, and learning profile. In their classrooms, student variability is viewed not as a problem but as a natural and positive aspect of working with human beings. Seemingly in contrast, the report card and its surrounding mythology looms as a reminder that at the end of the day, students must be described through a standardized and quantitative procedure that seems insensitive to human difference (p.128)."

Some elementary schools don't use grades at all, preferring to use a continuum of achievement from: *Not Yet Apparent* to *Emerging* to *Consistently Applied*. This approach is much less common in middle schools and high schools. For a wide variety of reasons, grading in the secondary school appears to be a process that will be with us for some time to come. The emphasis then is to minimize its pernicious outcomes and to make the process as compatible as possible with differentiation. We are wise to take Mel Levine's advice (2003) about testing: "*do no harm*" and apply it to grading.

The traditional or customary purpose behind grading was to assign symbolic letters or numbers at the end of a specified time to indicate student achievement and to report these evaluations to students and parents. In the differentiated classroom, we believe that the primary goal of grading and reporting is *to communicate to important audiences (students and parents) high quality feedback that will support and enhance the learning process and encourage learner success.*

We also believe that grading and reporting will always (and should always) involve a degree of subjectivity. Subjectivity only gets a bad name when it is arbitrary and/or capricious. When it is anchored in informal assessment data such as teacher observation, subjectivity is sound professional judgment.

At the 2003 EARCOS Administrators conference, Tom Guskey began his keynote address by pointing out that grading is <u>not</u> an essential part of the learning process. Teacher checking on student work is, but placing a grade or mark on a piece of work is tangential to the learning process. An important decision that teachers need to make is what student work will be graded and which will not be. Sometimes, an un-graded piece of work can provide for a much deeper and more meaningful learning experience.

Some Common Purposes for Grading

To communicate student achievement status to parents	To identify students for gifted and talented programs	To punish a student for lack of effort	To determine GPA	To provide specific evidence for student improvement
To document student progress in order to evaluate the curriculum	To inform parents as to how they can support their child in learning	To identify students for specific scholarship aid	To create a class ranking	To compare individual teachers' grades to school-wide patterns
To provide incentives for students to learn	To correlate grading patterns to standardized test results	To maintain high academic standards	To identify honor roll students	To provide evidence of a student's negative attitude
To communicate achievement and progress to the student	To compare student achievement to grade-level benchmarks	To provide information for student self-assessment	To select students for competitive educational programs	To benchmark the school against other schools
To use grading to inform future instruction	To inform universities of individual student achievement	To gather data on the effectiveness of the educational program	To praise and recognize student excellence	To identify the valedictorian
To determine whether the student can enter the IB program	To qualify to educational grants or government loans	To enable students To transfer to other schools	To determine who will win the end-of-year academic awards	To reward a student for hard work
To encourage and reward a student	To describe inappropriate behavior	To qualify for a high school diploma	To criticize parents for a failure to support their child	To demonstrate to the administration how difficult the class really is

Drawing on the work of Tomlinson & McTighe (2006), Guskey & Bailey (2001), and O'Connor (2002), we have adapted six principles which we believe makes the process of grading more compatible with the differentiated classroom.

Principle One: Grades should be based on clearly defined learning goals and pre-determined performance standards. Being crystal clear about the learning objectives that we have for students is the foundation of quality assessment and meaningful grading. Performance standards allow us to address the question: "How good is good enough?" and "What criteria of quality constitute an 'A'? Just as a high quality rubric will have descriptions of the performance standard for each level of attainment, so a meaningful grading scale will have descriptions for each level of achievement (e.g. 'A', 'B', 'C' and so on).

Principle Two: The evidence and data that the teacher draws upon to grade a student should be valid. By validity we mean that the data should reflect a measurement of what we have set out to measure. In other words, we need to be able to eliminate, as much as possible, extraneous factors that will cloud and confuse validity. For example, if we are measuring a student's ability to apply mathematical concepts such as percentage and ratio, we will not want to confuse the process by evaluating at the same time the student's fluency in English or ability to read the directions. If we are looking for evidence that a student can organize a five paragraph essay, we simply obfuscate our results if we take points off if the student forgot to put his or her name on the paper or didn't provide for a three quarter inch margin.

Principle Three: Grading should be based on pre-determined, meaningful criteria, not on arbitrary norms. As we have stated earlier in this chapter, norm-based assessment and grading suffers from three problems: it doesn't provide the student with any useful information about his or her strengths and deficits; it doesn't provide the student with ideas or advice on how to improve; and it promotes unhealthy competition which can undermine efforts at cooperative learning, student-to-student collaboration and the development of a constructive classroom community. For this reason, we discourage teachers from grading "on a curve." Communicating assessment criteria that will be used in grading involves discussing them with learners, using language that is age-appropriate and student-friendly and providing students with examples of how the criteria can be met.

Principle Four: Not everything needs to be *or should* be included in a grade. As we have noted earlier, assessment and grading are not the same things. Assessment is the on-going gathering of evidence of student learning which can then be used to inform instruction. Grading, on the other hand, is a summative judgment of student achievement at the end of a specific time period. There are certain assessments that should not be included in the grading process. These include diagnostic assessment, pre-assessments and most formative assessments. The latter provide students with an opportunity to practice and learn from mistakes. Teachers facilitate intellectual risk-taking in students when they don't have to fear making mistakes. For the most part, grades should be derived from a variety of carefully designed summative assessments that take into account student learning styles and intelligence preferences and allow students to demonstrate their achievement related to the specific learning outcomes.

Principle Five: Avoid arriving at grades based on averaging. We agree with Tomlinson & McTighe (2006) when they write: "We join with other grading experts in challenging the widespread practice of averaging all of the marks and scores during an entire marking period to arrive at a numerically based final grade (p. 132)." The problem with averaging scores is that can lead to misleading results. Again, the goal of differentiation and assessment is to maximize learning. Grading should reflect this outcome. If learning is the goal and the student masters the desired outcome in the fifth or sixth week of the marking period, why would we penalize the same student for not having mastered it in the second or third week? Learning is not a race to the finish. When we average all the scores of a marking period, we turn learning progress in the classroom into a race. Those who learn fastest win. Ken O'Connor (2002) supports the use of teacher professional judgment when it comes to assigned grades. He suggests that grades should be determined from a variety of sources, rather than calculated in a strictly quantitative manner. He goes on to suggest that if a school policy requires averaging, it makes more sense to use the median or mode than the mean as a basis for grading.

In terms on some alternatives to averaging, we would suggest that teachers consider giving priority to:

- the most recent evidence
- the most comprehensive evidence; and
- Evidence related to the most important learning goals or standards.

Principle Six: The Grade should reflect the student's achievement. Other factors should be reported separately. Teachers have a tendency to want to include everything in the grading process. We see teachers including factors such as effort, timely completion of work, class participation, attitude, attendance, behavior, etc. in the student's grade. When we include factors such as these in our grades, the problems of interpretation become enormous and self-evident. Accordingly, we also suggest that teachers do not assign a zero for work that is not turned in. When the zero is calculated into a student's grade, this skews the data and makes meaningful communication of student achievement next to impossible. There are other ways to respond to assignments that are not handed in. One way is to assign an "incomplete" and to communicate to the student and his or her parents that there is "insufficient evidence" to assign this student a grade.

This is not to say that teachers shouldn't report on student work habits. Actually, we consider this to be some of the most important information that teachers can share with students and parents because these work habits are a much more accurate predictor of the young person's success in the real world of work than student academic achievement.

We strongly recommend that schools report on three separate aspects of a students work in school:

- Grades that accurately reflect the student's achievement of the learning goals.
- Progress towards those learning goals (personal achievement.) A student may still not be reading at grade level, but may have made huge progress towards it. This needs to be recorded and celebrated.

- Work habits. (These might include effort, persistence, the use of feedback, revision etc.)

Conclusion

When the purpose of assessment is to maximize learning for all students, the principles and practices of such assessment correspond to those of the differentiated classroom. The principles embedded in assessment *for* learning strive to personalize and differentiate learning, to capitalize on student strengths, to utilize descriptive feedback in order to promote student learning and ultimately to make the student a partner in the assessment process. The combination of differentiation and assessment *for* learning offers teachers a powerful means to balance excellence and equity in the classroom and maximize learning for all students.

14 THE SCHOOL LIBRARY AND MEDIA CENTER & TECHNOLOGY: PROFESSIONALS & RESOURCES TO SUPPORT DIFFERENTIATION

by Patsy Richardson

Many teachers do not think of the school library as a place to turn to when seeking support for differentiated instruction. The school library or media center is often overlooked when teachers are developing curriculum, writing unit plans and performance assessments or generally looking for ways to differentiate. However, it might be one of the most promising places to start.

Some might question: "Sure, there are more books in the library than teachers have in their classrooms, but how does that relate to differentiation?" The answer to that question is, like differentiation, multi-dimensional and multi-leveled. It involves a combination of the resources available in a library media center, including print, audio-visual and online materials, as well as the teaching and collaborative expertise of the professionals who work there. These professionals go by many names: school librarian, school media specialist, teacher-librarian, etc. Irrespective of what title they go by, these individuals can offer invaluable support to teachers who have embarked on the differentiation journey.

Unfortunately there are numerous misconceptions and misunderstandings about the role that the library and librarian can play in student learning.

What exactly do school librarians do? Ask most people and their first response is likely to be something related to shelving books. Then they get a puzzled look as they try to figure out what else a librarian might do. Keep students quiet? Check out books? Read? Some may think of these as the primary tasks of librarians. A few others cling onto an even worse idea of librarians -- the stereotypical image of the shushing, stern, horn-rimmed-glasses-wearing librarian whose job it is to protect the books from students who might want to read them!

A degree of confusion is understandable, and it is also not entirely surprising that teachers and administrators would be unsure of what their librarian does all day. First of all, many teachers and administrators (and librarians too, for

238

that matter) do not have positive memories, or any memories at all, of school librarians from their own childhoods. It's hard to imagine what a good school librarian or library program can be when there is little or no prior experience to base that on (Lindsay, 2005).

Teacher preparatory programs rarely address the potential uses of the library or the idea of collaboration with the librarian in planning or developing units of study (Lindsay, 2005). When there has been no such explicit expectation or modeling, it is no wonder that only a few teachers consider incorporating library resources or working with their school librarian. To make the situation even more confusing, school library media training programs *do* emphasize the need for librarians to work closely with teachers, and encourage school librarians to foster collaborative relationships with their colleagues. This responsibility puts the librarian in the unenviable and awkward situation of seeking collaborative partnerships with teachers who for the most part do not expect to have such relationships and may not perceive the value of them. Some teachers must think it is awfully strange that librarians keep offering to work with them. But our training also emphasizes persistence.

Finally, librarianship is a unique job and there is usually only one person in that position in a school. The solitary nature of the position can create a sense of distance and isolation from others, making it difficult for teachers to understand and relate to the work that librarians do. All these factors conspire to leave teachers with an incomplete and not entirely accurate idea about the overall purpose and role of the library and librarian in a school, and specifically how they might support differentiation.

So what do librarians really do, then? And if the library can support differentiation, how?

The following proposal for a school library classroom begins to an answer to these questions. Perhaps surprisingly, it was written in 1915 by Mary E. Hall, the second appointed school librarian in the United States. While Mrs. Hall's audio-visual equipment is charmingly out-of-date, her vision of the library as an attractive and welcoming "home for learning" is as relevant today was it was when she wrote it.

> The *library classroom adjoins the library reading room and should be fitted up to have as little of the regular classroom atmosphere as possible. It should be made quite as attractive as the reading room and have its interesting pictures on the walls, its growing plants and its library furniture. Chairs with tablet arms on which pupils can take notes, one or more tables around which a small class can gather with their teacher*

> *and look over beautiful illustrated editions or pass mounted pictures and postcards from one to another, should surely form a feature of this classroom...There should be cases for large mounted lithographs...for maps and charts, lantern slides, mounted pictures, and clippings. A radiopticon or lantern with the projectoscope in which a teacher can use not only lantern slides but postcards, pictures in books or magazines, etc... For the English work and, indeed for German and French, a Victrola with records which make it possible for students to hear the English and other songs by famous singers, will help them to realize what a lyric poem is...The room will be used by the librarian for all her classes in the use of reference books and library tools, it will constantly service teachers of history, Latin, German, French, and be a boon to the departments of physical and commercial geography* (Hall, as cited in Woolls, 1999, p. 13).

Not only does this challenge my own stereotype of school librarians from the past, it also demonstrates that at least some school librarians have always been passionate about working with students and teachers, and have always sought ways to help students connect with subject matter in meaningful ways. With her radiopticon, projectoscope, and Victrola, Mrs. Hall was ready to help teachers give students a multi-faceted experience of people, places, and poems. In essence, she was addressing *differentiation*.

Mrs. Hall's description is strikingly similar to this one, from Judith Anne Sykes' book, *Brain Friendly Libraries*, written in 2006:

> *Think of this "learning laboratory" as a warm, inviting, welcoming place with stimulating work areas as well as reflective sites. Instead of a harsh, "hushed" environment, hear soft music, laughter, projects being worked on, students reading silently, orally, being read to, dialoguing. View multiple displays of student cognitive work such as poetry, art, sculpture, and Web pages that are altered every four to six weeks, as brains thrive on novelty. Have comfortable, functional furniture for working, reading, studying, and collaborating. Facilitate learning with warm, caring, qualified personnel so that students feel supported, challenged, and trusted (p. 39).*

In both descriptions, nearly 100 years apart, the school library is not portrayed as a static, text filled room where only the strong readers or the academically gifted (in the traditional sense) will feel welcome. It is a space that should be designed to be welcoming, stimulating, and inspiring to all, providing a wide array of resources and encouragement for a variety of individual student strengths, interests, and needs.

The goal of school librarians is much more than simply managing a warehouse of materials, checking them in and out, and maintaining a studious atmosphere. June Gross and Susan Kientz (1999), media specialists from the United States, articulated it quite clearly in an article about collaboration between media specialists and teachers:

How school library media specialists can help teachers:

- gathering resources (print, audio-visual, online) from the library collection for classes to use in their units
- cooperating with the technology specialists, in order to help teachers stay current with developments in educational uses of new technology and new information resources
- creating a variety of "pathfinders," research guides, and webquests to address student and teacher needs
- helping students and teachers to wade through the mass of information available to them on the Internet by pre-selecting sources for units of study
- guiding classes through the research process
- teaching students and classes how to evaluate sources
- teaching students and classes about reliable resources on the Internet and in subscription magazine and newspaper databases
- helping students and teachers to locate and use a variety of primary and secondary sources
- providing professional resources to address teacher requests and needs
- working with individual students and teachers who come with questions about how to find or use information
- teaching students and classes about citation methods and how to avoid plagiarism
- teaching "mini-lessons" to classes on aspects of using library resources (print and online) or conducting research
- teaching more in-depth lessons on aspects of the research process
- team-teaching with teachers
- planning, implementing and assessing lessons or units with teachers

"Student learning is the reason school libraries exist." Librarians seek to create spaces, to collect materials, and to work with students and teachers for the main purpose of helping students to grow and learn, and we want to do all we can to help and support teachers in this endeavor. We can do this in a variety of ways, from simply providing useful resources to teachers and students to assisting in the development of units of study.

School libraries do not have to be antiquated rooms full of dusty books, nor do librarians have to be antiquated book-shufflers, either. Instead libraries can be, and in many schools are, vibrant and dynamic resource centers where teachers and librarians work together to design, deliver, and assess effective, student-centered, resource and inquiry based learning experiences.

Sounds nice, but what does all that have to do with differentiation? How can the library help teachers with that? We already know that there are three main areas that can be differentiated: content, process, and product, and that these can be differentiated in terms of student readiness, learning preference, and interest. How better to differentiate content than by looking to see what range of resources the library has on a particular subject so that students who need easier materials, or students who are ready for more challenging materials can have access to information about similar topics or concepts? The librarian may know of excellent alternative sources and can save teachers the time and work of having to locate the sources themselves. In terms of process, why not consider brainstorming ideas for a new unit with the library media specialist, who might be able to bring a new perspective or new resources to the planning? Media specialists might also know new product ideas that can tap the various strengths of students.

The remainder of this chapter will focus specifically on how librarians (or media/technology specialists as I will refer them) can support differentiated learning.

How We Can Help: Differentiating for Content

This may seem like the most obvious place for media and technology to support differentiation. Indeed, the general philosophy of libraries has always supported the basic idea of differentiation. It is a place that welcomes, accepts, and serves all. People of all strengths, needs, and learning styles should feel welcome (teachers included!) and should be able to find materials and assistance to meet their individual needs. In an international school setting, this means that media specialists make sure that the materials (print, audio-visual, and online) address all of the curricular areas as well as professional needs. The resources should be of high quality, and be appropriate and accessible for the varied needs of all the students. These resources also represent the multiple cultures, countries, and perspectives present in the school community. In other words, library materials can help address the readiness, interest, and learning preference needs of students. Achieving this does not happen without frequent and open communication with teachers and students. Media specialists pay close attention to what is taught in their school, and at what level, in order to make sure that library materials support those subjects by offering materials for the basic and advanced needs of students.

We also pay close attention to student interests. We listen to the questions that students ask, and pay attention to the activities that students participate in at school, and in general try to glean a clear idea of who the students are and what matters to them. This helps us to better understand their personal interests so that we can make sure we are addressing those needs as well. There are no value judgments made about the interests and needs of the students; one subject is as important as another, as is any information need that a student has. The student interested in information about how to take care of their new pet turtle is given the same level of attention and care as the student who wants to study the fractal patterns present in nature. Students who feel welcome and accepted are more likely to feel comfortable asking for help when they need it.

The variety of student learning styles can also be supported with library resources, which can provide multiple access points to the content. The needs of the student who wants to study fractal patterns in nature but who struggles with more challenging text because he or she is learning English can be assisted to locate resources written with simpler language. A verbal learner can be directed to audio-visual materials or educational podcasts (online audio programs) related to the subject they are studying. Another student who struggles with reading might benefit from an audio version of a book that they can listen to while they read along with the print version. And a visual learner who is studying history can have access to video materials on specific subjects, giving them a visual access point to the material. Encyclopedias, print or online, are excellent sources for "global" learners who do better when they understand the big picture first. Encyclopedia entries can help them to see that big picture so that they can organize the more detailed information in their mind. The very organization of information in a library is also an example of how information can be categorized and broken down into subsets of information. This can be used as a model to help students create their own mental categorization schemes for what they are learning. The table below suggests resources from a school library and/or technology department that can support students with specific learning needs and styles. It contains suggestions for a variety of content related resources with specific regard to student readiness, learning preference, and interest.

Support for Differentiation for Learning Preference

Aspect of Differentiation	Library or Technology Resource
Readiness	Library can provide a range of resources, from basic to advanced, on curricular subjects. These can include: • Print, such as non-fiction books or encyclopedias of varying levels, or • Online resources such as easy to advanced databases or online encyclopedias. Materials can be pre-selected by the teacher or media specialist and identified for specific students. The easy and more advanced materials can also be gathered together so that students can look through them and select for themselves the ones that best meet their needs.

Learning Preference/Multiple Intelligences	
Verbal - Linguistic	• Text-based materials – The library is full of these, as is the Internet. • Audio books (both fiction and non-fiction): These can be on CD-ROM or downloadable. • Educational Podcasts, which can be played on computers or downloaded onto handheld devices.
Logical - Mathematic	• Statistical or numeric information available in print and online sources on various subjects. Students can use this kind of information as an entry point to many topics. • Timelines, chronologies *Examples:* • Elementary School: Students could begin a unit on life cycles by comparing the similarities and differences between the numbers of days that certain life cycles take to complete. • Middle School: Students studying ancient civilizations could plot all of the known major events of a civilization on a timeline. • High School: In a unit on war, students with strong logical or mathematic understanding could research and analyze the economic effects of a specific conflict.
Musical - Rhythmic	• Music collections: Some libraries include music collections, which can be useful to students in the arts. • Students might be asked to select music that represents a particular theme or concept in a novel, poem, or other subject area. • Several online databases offer historical music clips, which can be a good entry point to historical subjects for musically-minded students. *Examples:* • Elementary School: Students can create a sound-scape for a story including any sounds, music or songs that "go with" the story, explaining their choices.

	• Middle School: Students can listen to the music of a particular time period and compare similarities and differences with time periods before and after.
	• High School: Students can research the development of music in the Harlem Renaissance in order to develop a deeper understanding of the time period.
Visual - Spatial	• Videos and DVDs • Online video sources such as Youtube.com (free) or Discovery Channel/United Streaming (subscription). • Posters on different subjects can serve to present information visually. Libraries often have posters in their collections. • Check library books for their visuals. Many, especially at the elementary and middle school level, will be full of graphics and illustrations related to concepts and subjects. • Many online databases now have image collections, which can also help provide accurate and reliable visuals for students. • Free online video and image sources on the Internet grow daily. Check these for accuracy and appropriateness before use.
Bodily - Kinesthetic	• Important scenes in stories or novels can acted out • Technology support: Online simulations can sometimes be found that can assist students.
Interpersonal / Intrapersonal	• Personal narrative accounts, from most any subject area, and either fictional or non-fictional may be helpful entry points to subjects. • Oral histories or interviews ***Examples:*** • Fiction: Historical fiction is available about many subjects, from many different cultural perspectives, and for all grade levels from elementary to high school. These can be great jumping-off points for students who understand subjects better if they can see them through personal experiences. This can also allow for cross-disciplinary explorations between literature and social studies, math, science, art, etc. • Non-fiction: Personal narratives, diaries, oral histories, and memoirs are also available for most all subjects and grade levels. Like fiction, they can create interest in subjects by illuminating the real people and relationships involved.

Whole-to-part (global) learners	• Encyclopedia entries (print or online) can be excellent sources for students who do better when they understand the big picture first. Encyclopedias come in many forms, from general to subject-specific. • Table of contents: encourage students to look at the table of contents of a book. This can sometimes give them the overview they need.
Part-to-whole (sequential) learners	• Resources that contain detailed examinations of subject will be most helpful for these students. These are available for all levels with the difference being the level of detail and the complexity of the language.
Interest	• "Branch-off" materials -- Materials on a range of topics related to curricular subjects. For research projects, these allow for students to select topics of interest to them that are still related to the unit of study. • Materials of general interest to students for their own personal exploration, to encourage individual curiosity. • Materials written about students' countries and culture. Some students prefer materials written by an author from their own country.

Of course all of these resources can be used with all students to encourage them to explore and develop multiple aspects of their own intelligence.

How to Find These Materials:

Working With the Media/Technology Specialist

In any school, the most important asset is the teaching faculty. The school library is no exception. A strong media/technology specialist can make an invaluable contribution to student learning. While the list of potential materials above is meant to encourage teachers, it can be overwhelming, especially when we are attempting to identify appropriate resources for very diverse groups of learners. This is where the media/technology specialists can enormously helpful, assisting teachers to identify and find these kinds of resources.

Information about the subjects taught in schools has evolved greatly since the days when textbooks were first developed as the primary, and sometimes *only* tool to be used by students and teachers (Linsday, 2005). There is little concern now that teachers or students will struggle to find *something* related to _que hagan un collage de revistas Animals_

the subject being taught. However, finding _quality_ and _reliable_ information that is accessible to students can be more challenging. Identifying resources specific to the readiness, learning preference and interest needs of diverse students can also be challenging. The expansion of online sources such as magazine and newspaper databases and online versions of encyclopedias and books (or ebooks), many of which incorporate multimedia features, is a great "antidote" to the increased usage of the Internet (and oftentimes lower quality sources) by students. Learning which source to use, when, and how, takes time, however, not to mention learning the details of how to search these sources effectively. The media and technology specialists are there to help and support teachers by locating relevant resources and by teaching students and teachers how to use the resources effectively.

How We Can Help: Process and Product

This leads us directly into differentiation in the process of learning. Providing a wide range of materials that meet the needs of diverse learners is just the beginning of how technology and library media centers can help teachers to differentiate instruction. Another effective way to make use of these materials, a way that encompasses content, process, and product, is to do so by teachers collaborating with the library media/technology specialist in the planning of units and lessons. Research conducted by Keith Curry Lance (2001; 2002) investigating the factors that affect student achievement found that in addition to having a strong school library media center, student achievement is also positively impacted when teachers and media specialists plan together.

When two or more professionals are working together, they can draw upon a wider range of resources and ideas. Charlene Leaderhouse (2005) described her personal experience of the benefits of collaboration between media specialist and teacher. She found that the new perspective, resources, and ideas that the media specialist had to offer complemented the teacher's knowledge of what had worked (and not worked) in the past, as well as the teacher's in-depth knowledge of the students. The media/technology specialist can provide the sounding board to bounce ideas off in order to design effective and creative learning activities. The media/technology specialist also brings into the planning process knowledge of new resources that may address specific readiness, learning and interest needs. When teachers and media or technology specialists plan together, they may be more able to design lessons and units that can be modified based on the needs of the students. For example, a research project might allow for some students to use more complex resources while others use resources that contain basic information. Alternatively, lessons or units can be designed that ask students to rotate through a series of resources on the topic. These can be chosen based on the strengths and needs of the students, exposing all to a variety of learning styles. The media/technology specialist can help identify these resources and can work directly with students, either as guides or instructors, as they work with each source. Sharing planning and assessing tasks allows for each teacher to bring his and her particular strengths and expertise to the team (Hylen, 2004). Students can benefit from the sharing of instruction as well. Not only does this create more opportunity for individual attention, it also exposes students to different *teaching* styles, which can in turn help students with different learning styles (Hylen, 2004). Many articles and books exist that describe this kind of collaboration. Violet Harada and Joan Yoshina's (2004; 2005)[34] works are recommended as excellent resources for teachers and librarians who would like to explore in more detail the collaboration between teacher and media specialist.

An additional way that the media/technology specialist can support differentiation is by providing an alternative learning environment – particularly for students who learn differently. We know that students have specific preferences when it comes to how and where the can concentrate most effectively and efficiently. The library can provide an alternative space to the classroom for group or individual work, and while many school libraries are no longer the silent places they used to be, they can offer space for quieter, individual work. Online databases that can be accessed from home can also offer an alternative to having to use the library or classroom for research. Similarly, technology resources are no longer limited to computer labs. Schools with access to laptops and a wireless network can allow students the flexibility to find the places to work that are best for them.

The media/technology specialist can be of particular assistance when it comes to teaching students how to create a variety of technology products. In recent years it has become quite common for students, even at the elementary level, to design electronic presentations using software such as painting programs, Hyperstudio, and PowerPoint. Using these tools, students can synthesize their information with text, images, and sound. New technology tools make it possible for students to create websites, webquests, podcasts, desktop published documents, spreadsheets with visual

---

[34] Harada, V. & Yoshina, J. (2004), *Inquiry learning through librarian-teacher partnerships*. Worthington, OH: Linworth Publishing; and (2005). *Assessing learning: Librarians and teachers as partners*. Westport, CT: Libraries Unlimited.

representations of data in charts and graphs, as well as simple or complex databases.

Collaborative planning between the teacher and the media/technology specialist underscore the fact that information research and technology skills are important cross-disciplinary skills that are critical for students to acquire. These skills (locating and accessing information, analyzing, summarizing, paraphrasing, synthesizing information, presenting information, evaluating the research process and product) need to be taught in the context of a content-based unit of study. As such, it stands to reason that a collaborative partnership between the teacher and media/technology specialist will be particularly powerful. Students need a combination of direct instruction in how to use certain sources followed up with relevant and meaningful practice. Collaboration between media/technology specialists and teachers can integrate the teaching of information and technology skills into units of study.

This is not meant to suggest that teachers should completely change their practices and work with the media/technology specialist on everything that they do. That would be impossible, impractical, and unnecessary.

There are also times when all is needed is a short, mini-lesson from the media/technology specialist on the use of a particular kind of resource, software, or an introduction to a particular kind of literature. What will make these mini-lessons most effective is when the teacher and media/technology specialist communicate clearly about the overall project before any specific planning is undertaken. Even the timing of when students receive instruction about a new resource can impact how effectively they will use it. If the process of using a journal and magazine database is taught before the students have chosen a research topic, they will not get to practice searching the database with a real need in mind. Accordingly the chances are small that they will remember this skill when it comes time to actually begin their research.

What It Looks Like: Examples of Differentiation With the Support of the Media Specialist

Elementary School: Collaboration between 3rd grade class, Art, and Library Media

A third grade class is studying fairy tales from different cultures as a part of the social studies curriculum. Knowing that this is a part of the regular curriculum, the library maintains a large collection of fairy tales from around the world. The teacher and librarian meet to plan this year's exploration with the goal of helping students to see the similarities and differences between stories across different cultures. The class consists of children from about ten different countries. Several of the students have just arrived at the school, and some are also learning English for the first time. In their discussion the teacher notes that several students in this year's class are fond of art. As they begin to brainstorm the teacher and librarian develop a series of activities designed to meet their goal of students reading and understanding several fairy tales, comparing and contrasting them, and learning about the countries and cultures that the stories come from.

Elements of differentiation include:

- Fairy tales available in the library range from easy to more challenging reading levels for the students. Students who are just beginning to learn English or who are struggling with reading will be able to read stories written in simpler English while stories written with more challenging vocabulary and language will be available to students who are ready for more complex text.

- Some of the fairy tales are available in audio format as well so that the story can be listened to and read at the same time.

- Students can choose fairy tales from any country, including their own. This can be helpful for students who might be new to the school looking for ways to connect to home.

- As stories are read, they can be plotted on a map of the world so that students can see where the stories come from.

- Another part of the unit is to do basic research about the countries that the stories come from. Students can work in small groups to gather information.

- Taking into consideration the love of art of several of the students, the teacher and librarian decide to ask the art teacher, who also works with these students, if there is a way to incorporate some aspect of this unit into the work they are doing in their art classes. The art teacher is excited by the idea and after discussion with the teacher comes up with

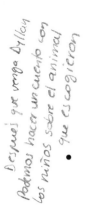

a project that involves the students creating abstract "landscapes" for the stories. They will use the information that they learn about the country to inform what their landscape will look like.

- As a culminating activity, a gallery display is set up in the library including the stories, the student created landscapes, their research about the countries, and their comparisons of the similarities and differences found. Students are dressed up as characters from their stories and explain the stories to the "gallery" visitors.

Middle School: Social Studies and Library Media

6th grade studies the origin of humans as a way of addressing the question, "Where do we come from?" One year there is a larger than usual number of beginning level ESL students who enter 6th grade. Teachers are concerned that the materials they have used in previous years will not be accessible for their ESL students. They believe that the students will be able to understand the concepts, but will need different kinds of resources. They ask the librarian for assistance. The librarian asks questions about the overall unit plan so that she understands what important learning outcomes the teachers have identified. With these in mind, she is able to find alternate resources for students to use. She presents these to the teachers and together they develop activities that the students learning English will be able to learn from. Elements of differentiation include:

- Images that depict different brain and body sizes of early man to help students visualize the physical changes that occurred over time.

- A timeline completed by students allows them to follow the progression of early man. This is also helpful for the students with strong logical / mathematical skills.

- Print and online resources with simple content are found that explain other developments in prehistoric man such as development of tools and changes in eating. Student plot these on their timelines as well, and begin to make connections between physical changes in early man and the changes in their way of living.

- The final product is identified as their completed timeline with captions for each entry. Students are allowed to create this in using paper or using a computer. Often times students who are learning English will still have strong computer skills. This gives them a chance to demonstrate their strengths.

High School: 10th grade Social Studies and Library

A culminating research paper asks students to explore an issue related to any topic studied during the course of the year. Throughout the year students have engaged in "mini" research projects that have focused on certain aspects of the research process. The librarian has worked with the classes on each mini-project to teach a new resource, a new skill such as advanced search techniques, evaluation of sources, or correct citation of sources. A benefit of this ongoing work is that the librarian has gotten to know the students and has gained a better understanding of individual needs, preferences and interests. When the final project begins, the librarian, in collaboration with the teachers, is able to help guide students through this final project. The teachers allow students to choose their own topic to encourage students to choose something they are interested in, which also allows them to reflect back on all of the subjects they have studied and explore one in more depth. Elements of differentiation include:

- The librarian deliberately collects a wide range of materials related to the subjects taught in World Studies so that students will be able to locate quality materials, in a variety of levels, on the topic of their choice.

- Students must develop a focused research question. This allows for students with different learning preferences to explore an aspect of their topic that they feel strongly about. For example, a student with a strong musical intelligence might choose to examine the songs that developed as a result of oppression in different settings. In this way, they are able to focus on their own area of strength and interest while still exploring important curricular subject matter.

- The librarian works as individual consultant for students in need of assistance. Rather than find the materials for the students, the librarian, drawing upon the lessons of the year, can help guide the students as they conduct their search.

The school library and library media and technology specialists can be valuable resources for teachers as they develop curriculum, write unit plans and performance assessments, and look for ways to differentiate. Media specialists seek to develop collections of materials that are as diverse as the communities they serve, meeting the needs of a variety of learners, and helping students connect with subject matter in ways that help them to grow and learn. This means providing a range of print, audio-visual, and high quality online resources that represent the students' readiness, learning preferences, and interests. Media specialists seek to support teachers as they explore options for differentiation. We can provide assistance in ways as simple as identifying a range of resources that meet the variety of needs in their classrooms, but also through more in-depth cooperation and collaboration with teachers, always with the goal of helping to improve *all* students' learning.

15 HOW ADMINISTRATORS CAN SUPPORT DIFFERENTIATION

Using Observation to Improve Instruction[35]

By William Powell and Susan Napoliello

Many teachers and administrators in East Asia and Africa are wrestling with fundamental questions regarding differentiated instruction: Does differentiated instruction mean preparing 23 different lesson plans? Where do teachers find the time? How can teachers assess students fairly? What does differentiation actually look like in the classroom? (Kusuma-Powell, 2003).

To address such questions, the International School of Kuala Lumpur (ISKL) in Malaysia, which serves international students in preschool through high school, has focused a great deal of professional attention on differentiation. Like many schools around the world, ISKL has witnessed a significant demographic shift in student population during the last two decades. Because of economic patterns in South East Asia, more students from non-English speaking countries – particularly Japan and Korea – are attending our school. And the many students who still come from school experiences in the United States arrive expecting individualized support for any learning disabilities they may have, comparable to those mandated by legislation in their home countries.

As a result, we believed that our school needed to do more to support differentiation than send teachers to conferences and bring in helpful reources. As two of the school's key administrators, we developed a classroom visitation strategy we call a "protocol for the rounds." This strategy encourages and supports differentiated instruction by giving teachers constructive feedback focused on differentiated teaching and by establishing a process for teacher collaboration. The initial results and teacher responses have been extremely promising.

---

[35] Reprinted with permission. This article first appeared in *Educational Leadership,* February, 2005.

The protocol confirms an instructional norm that classroom teachers at ISKL will take into account the needs of students who learn differently as they plan units of study. Although teachers and learning specialists share in planning and arranging instruction for students with learning disabilities, the responsibility for seeing that these students learn belongs to their teachers.

The protocol also reinforces the use of effective pedagogical strategies and actively connects practice to learning theory. Often, what master teachers do effectively in the classroom is based on intuitive knowledge. The protocol shines a light on what may be happening unconsciously and connects these strategies to recent research, helping teachers to validate their practices.

Another benefit of the protocol is that it stimulates intellectually challenging professional dialogue among teaching colleagues – one of the most important barometers of school improvement (Barth, 1990). Our thinking and planning for the walk-through protocol were influenced by the work of the administrators at the International School of Bangkok and guidelines from Curriculum Management Service (2001).

Four Keys to Differentiated Instruction

We first set out to identify from the research literature the foundations underlying differentiated instruction (Kusuma-Powell & Powell, 2004; Tomlinson, 2001). Our investigation suggested four keys to differentiated instruction, which became simultaneously the benchmarks and the goals of the protocol (Kusuma-Powell & Powell, 2004). The four keys are:

- Deep knowledge of the student as a learner;
- Deep knowledge of the content of the curriculum;
- A broad repertoire of effective instructional strategies; and
- A willingness to engage in collaborative planning, assessment, and reflection.

The Observation Protocol

To move from theory to practice, we compiled various indicators of differentiated instruction that we might expect to see and hear when visiting classrooms, such as flexible grouping, student choice, the use of wait time, and other attributes of a classroom environment that promotes equal access to the curriculum. These teacher and student behaviors served as an initial dipstick of effective differentiation within the school. We then scheduled ourselves to conduct brief walk-through observations (about five minutes long) of every elementary class in the school on a grade-by-grade basis. We hoped to observe each elementary class twice a semester. Our purpose in these walk-throughs was to engage in focused observations and gain a snapshot perspective of the state of differentiated instruction in the school.

We announced the initial walk-throughs in advance, specifying when we would be visiting the grade level teams, and explained the purpose of the observations at an elementary faculty meeting. Although we tried to make clear that the walk-through observations were *not* evaluations of specific teachers, some teachers still feared that the walk-throughs might include an element of appraisal.

To avoid causing teachers anxiety, we decided against showing them the list we had complied of indicators of differentiation. We did not want teachers assuming that every strategy had to be present in every lesson or, worse still, coming to believe that differentiation was a simplistic pedagogical recipe – that if the "right" collection of activities is present, differentiation is happening (Kusuma Powell & Powell, in press).

Providing Feedback

After each walk-through, we sat together for about 10 minutes and analyzed what we had just seen in terms of the indicators of differentiated instruction. One strength of the protocol was the power of joint observation of classroom instruction. Not only did the two of us pay attention to different features of the classroom, but we also actually saw different things. Our individual interpretations of what we witnessed led to intellectually stimulating conversations, probing questions, and, on occasion, powerful insights.

In several of the kindergarten classes, we observed the skillful use of student choice (Glasser, 1988), with students allowed some degree of discretion in planning their own learning activities for the day. Students' possible choices – such as focusing on math work, art, games, writing, or the class library – were color coded, and teachers ensured that the students didn't end up with a steady monochromatic diet. Most important, teachers held students accountable for following their individual work center plans. When a youngster strayed from his or her choices, we heard teachers asking, "Are you changing your plan?" This strategy kept the focus of responsibility internal to the student (Deci & Ryan, 1985).

Following our walk-through observation for each grade level and our analysis of the data, we drafted a brief e-mail to the grade-level team of teachers giving feedback on what we had observed. The e-mails went out on the same day we did our walk-throughs because research shows that timeliness is essential for feedback to be effective (McCauley, Moxley, & Van Velsor, 1998). Feedback simply described effective differentiation strategies we observed, without giving criticism, advice, or recommendations. Although we discussed teacher and student behavior that we witnessed in a specific class, we kept the feedback collectively focused without referencing individual teachers. We saw this feedback as a significant strategy toward reaching our goal of making differentiated instruction a norm at the school. Feedback had three important purposes: to recognize the skillful work of most of the teachers, to reinforce the use of effective instructional strategies, and to establish schoolwide pedagogical norms for differentiated instruction.

As we had hoped, our feedback helped teachers connect strategies that they used intuitively to research and theory that might broaden their use of those strategies. For example, in one grade level, we observed teachers skillfully paraphrasing student responses to teacher questions. In our feedback, we discussed three different types of paraphrase and the meditative effect they have on student thinking (Lipton & Wellman, 1998). Teachers had in fact been using the paraphrasing strategy intuitively, and they were excited to learn there was a solid research base to support it.

Posing Reflective Questions

In addition to providing positive feedback, we posed to each grade-level team of teachers a specific reflective question related to situations we had observed. We requested that the teachers discuss the question at their next team meeting. Both of us actively participated in the team discussion at the meeting.

Drawing on the work of Costa and Garmston (2002) and Ben Hur (2002) on meditative questioning, we created questions that

- *Started with positive assumptions.* For example, the question "What strategies do you employ to include student choice in your lessons?" assumes that teachers do employ such strategies and that their lessons include an element of student choice.
- *Used plural forms.* In the previous example, the teachers are asked to identify multiple strategies, not just one.
- *Were open-ended rather than yes/no.*
- *Called for intellectual effort.* In many cases, we were also challenged by the questions.

Reflective questions posed to the various grade-level teams included the following:

- *Preschool/Kindergarten team:* What are some things you look for as evidence that a student is in his or her zone of proximal development while that student is engaged in student-directed play?
- *Grade One team:* What strategies do you use to sustain the cognitive engagement of all students while providing wait time for a specific student?
- *Grade Two team:* When developing higher-order questions for your students, how do you consider the needs of diverse learners?
- *Grade Four team:* What strategies help student grasp the objective of a lesson, and how is knowing the objective linked to constructing enduring understandings?

The teaching teams' initial reaction to reflective questions varied from enthusiastic engagement to suspicious detachment. At first, a few teachers misunderstood and thought that they were facing some sort of oral examination or were expected to research the question before the meeting and then make a presentation. One teacher actually appeared at a team meeting with a stack of reference books. As the teams became more accustomed to engaging in professional dialogue, however, teachers came to realize that this was not a test and that there was no prescribed outcome other than a stimulating discussion of teaching and learning.

We hoped teachers would realize that differentiation is a joint venture; no one needs to go it alone (Kusuma-Powell & Powell, 2004; Showers & Joyce, 1996). Fortunately, these professional discussions fostered learning partnerships and a climate of shared accountability, which led to reduced individual stress.

Discussing the reflective questions led the teaching teams and the administrators in many curious, unpredictable, but professionally rewarding directions. One team asked for a demonstration lesson showing how different levels of paraphrasing could be used to mediate student thinking. Teachers decided they would film this demonstration lesson and then critique the video. A particularly rich discussion of instructional strategies emerged from this venture. In other teams, teachers have begun to collaborate in providing differentiated instruction, sharing professional articles and books and planning follow-up activities to improve classroom instruction individually and in teams. Some teachers are collaboratively using the strategies of

Cognitive Coaching[sm] (Costa & Garmston, 2002) to plan and reflect on differentiated instruction.

A Store of Familiar Strategies

The International School of Kuala Lumpur is now in year two of the protocol for the rounds, and plans are afoot to extend it to our middle school. Teachers have positively embraced the process. Several teachers have expressed a desire to join us in the walk-through observations and subsequent data analysis. When we surveyed teachers for their perceptions of the walk-through observations and follow-up reflective questions, their feedback was more positive than either one of us would have predicted. One teacher wrote, "Having the administration team visit our classroom validates the work that is going on there."

The administration and teaching teams are currently developing what we refer to as threshold teaching strategies for differentiation, a collection of research-based classroom instruction techniques that have emerged from the walk-through observations and subsequent discussions and that are linked explicitly to learning theory. These teaching strategies are particularly powerful because they have emerged in large part from the practice of the teachers themselves, so teachers feel ownership of them. The strategies and the research behind them are becoming a common knowledge base for our teachers.

The protocol for the rounds is still a work in progress at the International School of Kuala Lumpur, but it has initially shown itself to be a powerful tool for school improvement.

REFERENCES

Altschuler, E., Pineda, J., & Ramachandran, V. S. (2000). Abstracts of the Annual Meeting of the Society for Neuroscience.

Amabile, T. (1983). *The social psychology of creativity.* New York: Sringer-Verlag.

Aristotle. (2000). *Nichomachean ethics, Book II,* translated by W.D. Ross, Internet Classic Archives Web Site. Retrieved August 15, 2004.

Aronson, E. (1999). *The social animal, 8th Edition.* New York: Worth Publishers.

Assessment Reform Group. (2002). *Assessment for learning: Research-based principles to guide classroom practice.* Retrieved April 27, 2007, from: http://k1.ioe.ac.uk/tlrp/arg/index.html

Bailey, J. M. & Guskey, T. R. (2001). *Implementing student-led conferences.* Thousand Oaks, CA: Corwin.

Baksh, I.J., & Martin, W.B.W. (1984). Teacher expectation and the student perspective. *The Clearing House,* 57, 341-343.

Barth, R. (1990). *Improving schools from within.* San Francisco: Jossey-Bass.

Barth, R. (March, 2006). Improving relationships within the schoolhouse, *Educational Leadership, 63(6),* 8 – 13.

Birdwhistell, R. (1970). *Kinesics in Context.* Philadelphia, Pa.: University of Pennsylvania Press.

Black, P. & William, D. (1998). Inside the black box: Raising standards through classroom assessment. *Phi Delta Kappan, 80(2),* 139 – 148.

Bloom, B. S. & Krathwohl, D. R. (1956). *Taxonomy of Educational Objectives: The Classification of Educational Goals. Handbook I: Cognitive Domain.* New York: Longmans.

Blum, D. (1997) *Sex on the Brain: The Biological differences between men and women.* Viking: New York.

Boydston, J.A., Ed. (1991) *The Collected Works of John Dewey*. Carbondale: Southern Illinois University Press, 1967-1991. Online Resource.

Brooks, J. G. & Brooks, M.G. (1993) *In search of understanding: The case for constructivist classroom*. Alexandria, VA.: Association for Supervision and Curriculum Development.

Brooks, R. & Goldstein, S. (2001). *Raising resilient children*. New York: McGraw Hill.

Brophy, J., & Good, T. (1986). Teacher behavior and student achievement. In M. Wittrock (Ed.) *Handbook of research on teaching* (pp. 328-375). New York: MacMillan.

Brophy, J.E. (1983). Research on the self-fulfilling prophecy and teacher expectations. *Journal of Educational Psychology*, 75, 631-661.

Brown, T. E. (February, 2007). A new approach to attention deficit disorder. *Educational Leadership(64)5*, 22 – 27.

Brunner, J. (1996). *The culture of education*. Cambridge, MA.: Harvard University Press.

Bryk, M. & Schneider, B. (2002). *Trust in Schools: A Core Resource for Improvement*. New York: The Russell Sage Foundation.

Caine, R. & Caine, G. (1991). *Making connections: Teaching and the human brain*. Alexandria, VA.: Association for Supervision and Curriculum Development.

Caine, R. & Caine, G. (1997). *Education on the edge of possibility*. Alexandria, VA.: Association for Supervision and Curriculum Development.

Campbell, A. (2000). Sex-Typed Preferences in Three Domains: Do Two Year Olds Need Cognitive Variables? *British Journal of Psychology*,18, 479-98.

Campbell, L. & Campbell, B. (1999). *Multiple intelligences and student achievement: Success stories from six schools*. Alexandria, VA.: Association for Supervision and Curriculum Development.

Chappuis, J. & Chappuis, S. (2002). *Understanding school assessment: A parent and community guide to helping students learn*. Portland, OR: Assessment Training Institute.

Chappuis, J. (November, 2005). Helping students understand assessment. *Educational Leadership, 63(3)*, 39 – 43.

Chappuis, S. (2004). Leading assessment *for* learning: Using classroom assessment in school improvement [Electronic Version]. *Texas Association of School Administrators Professional Journal-INSIGHT*. Winter *18*(3), 18-22.

Chappuis, S., Stiggins, R., Arter, J. & Chappuis, J. (2003). *Assessment for learning: An action guide for school leaders.* Portland, OR: Assessment Training Institute.

Clarke, A. C. (1986). *July 20th, 2019: Life in the 21st Century.* London: MacMillan Publishers.

Cohen, E. (March, 1998). Making Cooperative Learning Equitable. *Educational Leadership,56(1),* 18 – 21.

Cohen, E. G., Lotan, R., Scarloss, B., Schultz, S. E. & Abram, P. (2002). Can Groups Learn? [Electronic Version]. *Teachers College Record, (104) 6,* 1045-1068.

Coleman, J.S., Campbell, E., Hobson, C., McPartland, J. Mood, A, Weinfeld, F & York, R. (1966). *Equality of educational opportunity.* Washington, DC: US Government Printing Office.

Collins, M. & Amabile, T. (1999). Motivation and creativity. In R. J. Sternberg (Ed.). *handbook of creativity* (pp. 297 – 312). New York: Cambridge University Press.

Conlin, M. (2003). The New Gender Gap. *Business Week Magazine,* May 26, 2003.

Cooper,H. M., & Tom, D.Y.H. (1984). Teacher expectation research: A review with implications for classroom instruction. *The Elementary School Journal 85,* 77-89

Costa, A. & Garmston, R. (2002). *Cognitive coaching: A foundation for renaissance schools, 2nd Edition.* Norwood, Mass.: Christopher-Gordon Publishers.

Costa, A. & Kallick, B. (2000). *Discovering and exploring habits of mind.* Alexandria, VA.: Association for Supervision and Curriculum Development.

Costa, A.L., (Ed.). (2001). A new taxonomy of educational objectives. *Developing minds: A resource book for teaching thinking.* Alexandria, VA.: Association for Supervision and Curriculum Development.

Covey, S. (1989). *The 7 habits of highly effective people.* New York: Fireside Edition, Simon & Schuster.

Covington, M.(1989). Self-Esteem and Failure in School. *The Social Importance of Self-Esteem.* Berkeley, CA.: U.C. Press.

Csikszentmihalyi, M. (1991). *Flow: The psychology of optimal experience.* New York: Harper & Row.

Csikszentmihalyi, M., Rathunde, K.R., & Whalen, S. (1993). *Talented teenagers: The roots of success and failure.* New York: Cambridge University Press.

Curriculum Management Service. (2001). *Conducting walk throughs with reflective feedback to maximize student achievement.* Huxley, I.A.: author.

Damasio, A. (1994). *Descartes' error: Emotion, reason, and the human brain.* London: Pengiun Books.

Darwin, C. (1965). *The expression of emotions in man and animals.* Chicago, Il.: University of Chicago Press.

Deci, E.L. & Ryan, R.M. (1985). *Intrinsic motivation and self-determination in human behavior.* New York: Putnam.

Department for Education and Skills. (2006). *2020 Vision: The report of the teaching and learning in 2020 Review Group.* Nottingham, U.K.: DfES.

Dodge, J. (2005). *Differentiation in action.* New York: Scholastic.

Dubb A, Gur R, Avants B, Gee J. (September 2003). Characterization of sexual dimorphism in the human corpus callosum. *Neuroimage, 20(1).* 512-9.

Dunn, R.S. & Dunn, K. (1993). *Teaching secondary students through their individual learning styles: Practical approaches for grades 7-12.* Needham Heights, MA.: Allyn & Bacon.

Eide, B., & Eide, F. (2006). *The mislabeled child: How understanding your child's unique learning style can open the door to success.* New York: Hyperion.

Eisner, E. (1998). *The kind of schools we need: Personal essays.* Portsmouth, N.H. Heinemann.

Ekman, P. & Friesen, W. V. (1975). *Unmasking the face: A guide to recognizing emotions from facial clues.* New Jersey: Prentice Hall.

Elliot, C. (1971). Noise Tolerance and Extraversion in Children. *British Journal of Psychology, 62(3),* 375-80.

Feuerstein, R., Rand, Y., Hoffman, M., and Miller, R. (1980). *Instrumental Enrichment.* Baltimore, MD: University Park Press.

Fisher, C., Berliner, D., Filby, N., Marliave, R., Cahen, L., & Dishaw, M. (1980). Teaching behaviors, academic learning time, and student achievement: An overview. In C. Denham & A Lieberman (Eds.), *Time to learn* (pp. 7-32). Washington, DC.: National Institutes of Education.

Fiske, S. T., & Taylor, S. E. (1984). *Social cognition* (1st Ed.). Reading, MA: Addison-Wesley.

Friend, M. & Cook, L. (1992). *Interactions: Collaboration skills for school professionals.* White Plains, N.Y.: Longmans.

Fullan, M. (2000). Address at Summer Seminar for the Academy of International School Heads (AISH).

Gardner, H. (1993). *Multiple intelligences: The theory into practice.* New York: Basic Books.

Garmston, R. & Wellman, B. (1999). *The adaptive school: A sourcebook for developing collaborative groups.* Norwood, MA.: Christopher-Gordon Publishers, Inc.

Garmston, R. (2005). *The presenter's fieldbook: A practical guide, 2nd Edition.* Norwood, MA.: Christopher-Gordon Publisher.

Gladwell, M. (2005). *Blink: The power of thinking without thinking.* Boston: Back Bay Books.

Glasser, W. (1988). *Choice theory in the classroom,* (Rev. Ed.). New York: Harper Perennial.

Goleman, D. (1995). *Emotional intelligence: Why it can matter more than IQ.,* New York: Bantam Books.

Goleman, D., Boyatzis, R.E., & McKee, A. (2002). *Primal leadership: Learning to lead with emotional intelligence.* Cambridge MA.: Harvard Business School Publishing.

Good, T.L. (1987). Two decades of research on teacher expectations: Findings and future directions. *Journal of Teacher Education, 38,* 32-47.

Grandin, T. (2007). Autism from the Inside. *Educational Leadership, 64(5),* 29 – 32.

Grinder, M. (1991). *Righting the educational conveyor belt.* Portland, OR.: Metamorphous Press.

Grinder, M. (1997). *The science of non-verbal communication.* Battle Ground, Wa.: Michael Grinder & Associates.

Gross, J. & Kientz, S. (1999). Collaborating for authentic learning. *Teacher Librarian, 27* (1), 21-26. Retrieved March 15, 2007, from EBSCO database.

Gurian, M. & Henley, P, (2001). *Boys and girls learn differently.* San Francisco: Jossey-Bass.

Gurian, M. & Stevens. K, (2005). *The minds of boys: Saving our sons from falling behind in school and life.* San Francisco: Jossey-Bass.

Guskey, T. R. (, 2000). Twenty questions? Twenty tools for better teaching. *Principal Leadership, 1(3),* 5 - 7.

Guskey, T. R. (March, 1994). What you assess *may not* be what you get. *Educational Leadership, 51(6),* 51 – 54.

Guskey, T.R. & Bailey, J.M. (2001). *Developing grading and reporting systems for student learning.* Thousand Oaks, CA.: Corwin Press, Inc.

Hall, J. (1985). *Nonverbal Sex Difference.* Baltimore: Johns Hopkins Press.

Hallowell, E. M. & Ratey, J. J. (1994). *Driven to distraction: Recognizing and coping with attention deficit disorder from childhood to adulthood.* New York: Simon & Schuster.

Hammond, L.D., & Ball, D.L. (1997). *Teaching for high standards: What policymakers need to know and be able to do.* Prepared for the National Educational Goals Panel, June, 1997.

Harada, V. & Yoshina, J. (2004). *Inquiry learning through librarian-teacher partnerships.* Worthington, OH: Linworth Publishing.

Harada, V. & Yoshina, J. (2005). *Assessing learning: Librarians and teachers as partners.* Westport, CT: Libraries Unlimited.

Hargreaves, A. Ed. (1997). *Rethinking educational change with heart and mind: ASCD Yearbook.* Alexandria, VA.: Association for Supervision and Curriculum Development.

Hatfield, E., Cacioppo, J., & Rapson, R.L. (1994). *Emotional Contagion.* New York: Cambridge University Press.

Hunt, D.E. (1971). *Matching models in education. (Monograph No. 10).* Ontario, Canada: Institute for Studies in Education.

Hunter, M. & Barker, G. (October, 1987). 'If at first . . .": Attribution theory in the classroom. *Educational Leadership, 45(2).*

Hylen, J. (2004). The top ten reasons a library media specialist is a teacher's best friend. *Library Media Specialist, 77* (5), 219-221. Retrieved March 15, 2007, from EBSCO database.

International Baccalaureate Organization (2004). *IB Assessment Handbook.* Geneva: IBO.

International Baccalaureate Organization (2006). *IB Learner Profile Booklet.* Geneva, IBO.

Jencks, C., Smith, M.S., Ackland, H., Bane, J.J., Cohen, D., Grintlis, H., Heynes, B., & Michelson, S. (1972). *Inequality: A reassessment of the effects of family and schools in America.* New York: Basic Books.

Jensen, A. (1998). The g factor and the design of education. In R.S. Sternberg & W.M. Williams (Eds.) *Intelligence, instruction, and assessment: Theory into practice* (pp. 111-132). Mahwah, NJ: Lawrence Erlbaum.

Jensen, E. (1998). *Teaching with the brain in mind.* Alexandria, VA.: Association for Supervision and Curriculum Development.

John, P. (2006). Lesson planning and the student-teacher: Re-thinking the dominant model. *Journal of Curriculum Studies, 38(4),* 483-498.

Jones, A. & Moreland, J. (2005). The importance of pedagogical content knowledge in assessment for learning practices: A case study of a whole school approach. *The Curriculum Journal (16),* 193-206.

Joyce, B. & Showers, B. (1980). Improving inservice training: The messages of research. *Educational Leadership, 37*(5), 379-385.

Kaplan, S., Kaplan, J., Madsen, S., & Gould, B. (1980). *Change for children: Ideas and activities for individualizing learning.* Glenview, IL: Scott Foresman.

Kawecki, I. (1994). Gender Differences in Young Children's Artwork. *British Educational Research Journal, 20,* 485-90.

Kelley, H. H. (1967). Attribution theory in social psychology. Pp. 192 – 238 in D. Levine (Ed.) *Nebraska Symposium on Motivation.* Lincoln, University of Nebraska Press.

Keogh, B.K. (1998). Classrooms as well as schools deserve study. *Remedial and special education, 19,* 313-314, 349.

King, K. & Gurian, M. (September, 2006). With Boys and Girls in Mind: Teaching to the Minds of Boys. *Educational Leadership, 64(1),* 56 – 61.

Kohn, A. (1999). *Punished by rewards: The trouble with gold stars, incentive plans, A's, praise and other bribes.* New York: Houghton Mifflin.

Kohn, Alfie (2004). *What Does it Mean to be Well Educated.* Boston, MA: Beacon Press.

Krashen, Stephen D. (1988). *Second Language Acquisition and Second Language Learning.* Indiannapolis: Prentice-Hall International.

Kusuma-Powell, O. & Powell, W. (2000). *Count me in! Developing inclusive international schools.* Washington, DC: Overseas Schools Advisory Council, US Department of State.

Kusuma-Powell, O. & Powell, W. (2004, Jan 17-18). *Differentiation: Operationalizing inclusion.* Paper presented at EARCOS Weekend Workshop, International School of Kuala Lumpur, Kuala Lumpur, Malaysia.

Kusuma-Powell, O. (2003). *Report on the status of differentiated instruction in American overseas and international schools in Africa and East Asia.* Washington, DC: Overseas Schools Advisory Council, US Department of State.

Kusuma-Powell, O., Al-Daqqa, E., & Drummond, O. (April, 2004). Developing partnerships for differentiation. *International Schools Journal, XXIII(2)*, 28 – 35.

Kusuma-Powell,O. (November, 2002). A voice from the trenches: The importance of administrator attitudes on special-needs children and programme effectiveness. *International Schools Journal, XXII(1)*, 9 – 16.

Lance, K. C. (2001). Proof of the power: Quality library media programs affect academic achievement. *MulitMedia Schools, 8* (4), 14-19. Retrieved March 10, 2007, from EBSCO database.

Lance, K. C. (2002). Impact of school library media programs on academic achievement. *Teacher Librarian, 29* (3), 29-35. Retrieved March 10, 2007, from EBSCO database.

Langer, G.M. & Colton, A.B. (2005). Collaborative analysis of student learning drives improvement of instructional practice. *Educational Leadership, 62(5)*, 22 – 26.

Lavoie, R. & Rosen, P. (1989). *The F.A.T. city workshop: How difficult can this be?* United States: PBS Video.

Leaderhouse, C. (2005). Collaborative teaching and multiple intelligences: A rational fit. *School Libraries in Canada, 25* (2), 47-50. Retrieved March 15, 2007, from EBSCO database.

LeDoux, J. (1996). *The emotional brain: The mysterious underpinnings of emotional life.* New York: Simon & Schuster.

Levine, M. (2002). *A Mind at a time.* New York: Simon & Schuster.

Levine, M. (april, 2007). The essential cognitive backpack. *Educational Leadership, 64(7)*, 16 – 22.

Levine, M. (October, 2003). Celebrating Diverse Minds. *Educational Leadership, 61(2)*, 12 – 18.

Lindsay, K. (2005). Teacher/teacher librarian collaboration – A review of the literature. *School Libraries in Canada, 25* (2), 3-17. Retrieved March 15, 2007, from EBSCO database.

Lipton, L.E. & Wellman, B. (1998). *Pathways to understanding: Patterns and practices in learning focused classrooms* (3rd ed.). Sherman, CT. MiraVia.

Lipton, L.E. & Wellman, B. (2004). *Data-Driven Dialogue: A Facilitator's Guide to Collaborative Inquiry.* Sherman, CT: Mira Via, LLC

Lord, B.B. (1981). *Spring moon.* New York: HarperTorch Book.

Louis, K.S., Marks, H.M., & Kruse, S. (1996). Teachers' professional community in restructuring schools. *American educational research journal, 33 (4),* 757-798.

Lytton, H. & Romney, D. (1991). Parents' Differential Socialization of Boys and Girls: A Meta-Analysis. *Psychology Bulletin, 109,* 267-96.

MacLean, P., (1978). A mind of three brains: Educating the triune brain. *The 77th Yearbook of the National Society for the Study of Education,* 308-342. Chicago, Il.: University of Chicago Press.

Marzano, R. J., Pickering, D. J. & Pollock, J. E. (2001). *Classroom instruction that works: Research-based strategies for increasing student achievement.* Alexandria, Va.: Association for Supervision and Curriculum Development.

McCauley, C. Moxley, R.S. & Van Velsor, E. (Eds.). (1998). *The center for creative leadership handbook of leadership development.* San Francisco: Jossey-Bass.

McClelland, D. C. (1961). *The achieving society.* Princeton: Van Nostrand.

McClelland, D. C. (1975). *Power: the inner experience.* New York: Halstead.

McClure, E. (2000). A Meta-Analytic Review of Sex Differences in Facial Expression Processing and their Development in Infants, Children and Adolescents. *Psychology Bulletin, 126,* 424-53.

McTighe, J. & Wiggins, G. (2004). *Understanding by design: Professional Development Workbook,* Alexandria, VA.: Association for Supervision and Curriculum Development.

Mehrabian, A. (1971). *Silent messages.* Belmont, Ca.: Wadsworth.

Millet, C.T., Johnson, S.J., Cooper, C.L., Donald, I.J., Cartwright, S. & Taylor, P.J. (2005). Britain's most stressful occupations and the role of emotional labour. Conference Paper: BPS Occupation Psychology Conference, Warwick, January, 2005.

National Education Association. (2006). *The puzzle of autism.* Washington DC: National Education Association. Available online from http://www.nea.org/specialed/images/autismpuzzle.pdf

National Institute of Mental Health. (2006). *Attention deficit hyperactivity disorder.* Bethesda, Md.: National Institute of Mental Health, National Institutes of Health, US Department of Health and Human Services; updated 10.26/2006. (NIH Publication Number 3572). 49 pages. Available from http://www.nimh.nih.gov/publicat/adhd.cfm#symptoms

Neill, A.S. (1992). *Summerhill school: A new view of childhood.* New York: St. Martin's Press.

Newkirk, T. (2003). The Quiet Crisis in Boys' Literacy. *Education Week,* September 10, 2003.

Nisbett, R. (2003). *The Geography of thought: How Asians and westerners think differently and why.* London: Nicholas Brealey Publishing.

Nordemeyer, J. (in preparation). Balancing Language and Content: Teaching English Language Learners in the 21st Century.

O'Connor, K. (2002). *How to grade for learning.* Thousand Oaks, CA: Corwin.

Perkins, D. (Fall, 1993). Teaching for Understanding. *American Educator: The Professional Journal of the American Federation of Teachers, 17(3),* 8,28-35.

Pert, C. (1997). Molecules of emotion: Why you feel the way you feel. London: Simon & Schuster.

Powell, W. (April, 2001). Conversations that matter: The use and abuse of communication in our school. *International Schools Journal*

Powell, W. & Kusuma-Powell, O. (2007) Coaching students to new heights in writing. *Educational Leadership,* on-line article, Summer 2007.

Powell, W. & Kusuma-Powell, O. (April, 2000). Pedagogy and the pressured. *IB World, 23,* 32-33.

Powell, W. & Kusuma-Powell, O. (May, 2007). Differentiating for Girls and Boys, *International Schools Journal, XX(2).*

Powell, W. & Kusuma-Powell, O. (November, 2005). Seeing ourselves: The student perspective, *International School Journal, XX(X).*

Powell, W. & Napoliello, S. (February, 2005). Using observation to improve instruction. *Educational Leadership, 62(5),* 52 – 55.

Ramachandran, V.S. & Blakeslee, S. (1998). *Phantoms in the brain: Probing the mysteries of the human mind.* New York: William Morrow.

Renzulli, J. (1997). *The interest-a-lyzer.* Mansfield Center, Conn.: Creative Learning Press.

Renzulli, J. (1998). The Three-Ring Conception of Giftedness. In Baum, S. M., Reis, S. M., & Maxfield, L. R. (Eds.). (1998). *Nurturing the gifts and talents of primary grade students.* Mansfield Center, CT: Creative Learning Press.

Ritchart, R. (2002). *Intellectual character: Why it is, why it matters, and how to get it.* San Francisco: Jossey-Bass.

Robinson & Robinson, N.M., & Robinson, H.B. (1982). The optimal match: Devising the best compromises for the highly gifted student. In D. Feldman (Ed.), *New directions for child development: Developmental approaches to giftedness and creativity*. San Francisco: Jossey-Bass.

Rosenthal, R. & Jacobson, L. (1968). *Pygmalion in the classroom*. New York: Holt, Rinehart & Winston.

Rowe, M.B. (1986). Wait time: Slowing down may be a way of speeding up! *Journal of Teacher Education, 37,* 43-50.

Rudduck, J., Day, J. & Wallace, G. (1996). The significance for school improvement of pupils' experiences of within-school transitions. *Curriculum,17(3),* 144-153.

Sadker, M. &   Sadker, D. (1994). *Failing at fairness: How are schools cheat girls*. New York: Simon & Schuster.

Sandford, C. (1995). *Myths of organizational effectiveness at work*. Battle Ground, MA.: Springhill.

Sapolsky, R. (1999). *Why zebras don't get ulcers: An updated guide to stress, stress-related diseases, and coping*. New York: W.H. Freeman & Co.

Sax, L., (2005). *Why gender matters: What parents and teachers need to know about the emerging science of sex differences*. New York: Doubleday.

Scarcella, R. (1990). *Teaching language minority students in the multicultural classroom*. Englewood Cliffs, NJ: Prentice-Hall.

Seidel, T., Rimmele, R. & Prenzel, M. (2005). Clarity and coherence of lesson goals as a scaffold for student learning. *Learning and Instruction, (15),* 539-556.

Shaywitz, S. (2003). *Overcoming dyslexia: A new and complete science-based program for reading problems at any level*. New York: Vintage Books.

Shin YW, Kim DJ, Ha TH, Park HJ, Moon WJ, Chung EC, Lee JM, Kim IY, Kim SI, Kwon JS. (May 31, 3005). Sex differences in the human corpus callosum: Diffusion tensor imaging study. *Neuroreport, 16(8),* 795-8.

Shoda, Y., Mischel, W., & Peake, P. K. (1990). Predicting adolescent cognitive and social competence from preschool delay of gratification: Identifying diagnostic conditions. *Developmental Psychology, 26*, 978-986.

Showers, B. & Joyce, B. (1996). The evolution of peer coaching. *Educational Leadership,* 53(6), 12-16.

Showers, B. (1985). Teachers coaching teachers. *Educational Leadership, 42*(7), 42-48.

Skinner, B. F. (1976). *Walden Two*. New York: MacMillan.

Sommers, C. (2000). *The War against boys. New York:* Simon & Schuster.

Sousa, D.A. (2001). *How the Brain Learns.* Thousand Oaks, CA: Corwin Press.

Sternberg, R. (1985). *Beyond IQ: A triarchic theory of human intelligence.* New York. Cambridge University Press.

Stevens, S.H. (1997). *Classroom success for the LD and ADHD child.* Winston-Salem, NC.: John Blair Publisher.

Stiggins, R. J. (December, 2005). From formative assessment to assessment *for* learning: A path to success in standards-based schools. [Electronic Version]. *Phi Delta Kappan 87(4),* 324 - 328.

Stiggins, R. J. (June, 2002). Assessment crisis: The absence of assessment *for* learning [Electronic Version]. *Phi Delta Kappan 83(10),* 758 – 765.

Stiggins, R. J. (September, 2004). New assessment beliefs for a new school mission. [Electronic Version]. *Phi Delta Kappan 86(1),* 22 – 27.

Stiggins, R. J., Arter, J., Chappuis, S. & Chappuis, J. (2004) *classroom assessment for student learning: Doing it right – using it well.* Portland, OR: Assessment Training Institute.

Sykes, J. (2006). *Brain friendly school libraries.* Westport, CT: Libraries Unlimited.

Tannen, D. (2005) Sex, Lies, and Conversation: Why is it so hard for men and women to talk to each other? *Literature Across Cultures.* Upper Saddle River, NJ: Pearson Educational Inc.

Taylor, S. (2002). *The tending instinct: How nurturing is essential to who we are and how we live.* New York: Henry Holt & Co.

Tishman, S., & Perkins, D. (1997). The language of thinking. *Kappan, 78*(5), 368-374.

Tishman, S., Perkins, D. & Jay, E. (1995). *The Thinking Classroom.* Boston, Ma.: Allyn & Bacon.

Tomlinson, C. A. & Allan, S.D. (2000). *Leadership for differentiating schools & classrooms.* Alexandria, VA.: Association for Supervision and Curriculum Development.

Tomlinson, C. A. (2001). *How to differentiate instruction in mixed-ability classrooms* (2nd ed.) Alexandria, VA.: Association for Supervision and Curriculum Development.

Tomlinson, C.A. & Eidson, C.C. (2003). *Differentiation in practice: A resource guide for differentiating curriculum, grades 5-9.* Alexandria, VA.: Association for Supervision and Curriculum Development.

Tomlinson, C.A. & McTighe, J. (2006). *Integrating differentiated instruction and understanding by design*. Alexandria, VA.: Association for Supervision and Curriculum Development.

Tomlinson, C.A. (1999). *The differentiated classroom: Responding to the needs of all learners*. Alexandria, VA.: Association for Supervision and Curriculum Development.

Tomlinson, C.A. (October, 2003). Deciding to teach them all. *Educational Leadership. 61(2),* 6 – 11.

Torrance, E. (1995). Insights about creativity: Questioned, rejected, ridiculed, ignored. *Educational Psychology Review, 7,* 313-322.

Truss, L. (2003). *Eats, shoots and leaves: The zero tolerance approach to punctuation.* New York: Gotham Books.

Tyler, R. (1949). *Basic principles of curriculum and instruction.* Chicago: University of Chicago Press.

U.S. Department of Education. (2001). National Center for Educational Statistics, *Projection of Educational Statistics to 2011.* Washington DC: U.S. Government Printing Office.

U.S. Department of Education. (2006). *Children with Disabilities (IDEA) School Age XML Specifications.* Washington, D.C.: Office of Planning, Evaluation and Policy Development, Strategic Accountability Service, *X002.*

Vygotsky, L. (1978). *Mind in society: The development of higher mental processes.* M. Cole, V. John-Steiner, S. Scribner, & E, Souberman, (Eds.) Cambridge, MA: Harvard University.

Vygotsky, L. (1986). *Thought and language, Revised, A. Kozulin, Ed.* Cambridge MA.: The MIT Press.

Wiggins, G. & McTighe, J. (1998). *Understanding by design.* Alexandria, Va.: Association for Supervision and Curriculum Development.

Wiggins, G. (1993). *Assessing student performances: Exploring the purpose and limits of testing.* San Francisco: Jossey-Bass.

Winebrenner, S. (1996). *Teaching kids with learning difficulties in the regular classroom.* Minneapolis: Free Spirit Press.

Wolfe, P. (2001). *Brain matters.* Alexandria, VA.: Association for Supervision and Curriculum Development.

Woolls, B. (1999). *The school library media manager, 2nd ed.* Englewood, CO: Libraries Unlimited.

ABOUT THE AUTHORS

William (Bill) Powell and Ochan Kusuma-Powell have been international educators for over thirty years. They have worked in the United States, Saudi Arabia, Tanzania, Indonesia and Malaysia. They are the authors of *Count Me In! Developing Inclusive International Schools* (US State Dept. 2000), *Becoming an Emotionally Intelligent Teacher* (Corwin 2010), and *How to Teach Now: Five Keys to Personalized Learning in the Global Classroom* (ASCD 2011). They serve as consultants for Education Across Frontiers (powell@eduxfrontiers.org) and have presented workshops in over forty countries worldwide. Most recently, they are coordinating The Next Frontier: Inclusion initiative, which provides support to international schools that are attempting to become more inclusive of children with special learning needs.

Made in the USA
Lexington, KY
29 March 2014